Advance Praise for *Transformed by*
The Making of an Ir...

Jane Booth transformed her life by her willingness to take the risk—and try a
tri. She shares private and personal moments, wins and losses, and gives you
essential information to make your life experience more rewarding—triathlon or not.

—Sally Edwards,
Former Masters World Record Holder, Ironman Triathlon

It's not often that a book takes you on such a wondrous journey. *Transformed
by Triathlon: The Making of an Improbable Athlete* puts the reader in the water,
on the bike and in the sneakers with Jane Booth as she seeks not only the
finish line but answers.

—Michael Connelly,
author of *26 Miles to Boston*

After twenty years of racing triathlons at pro level, I found plenty in
Jane Booth's humorous, refreshing and honest account of her first steps
in the sport to re-inspire me. *Transformed by Triathlon: The Making of an
Improbable Athlete* reminds us that there is an athlete in all of us.
Time to get off that couch and get reading.

—Wendy Ingraham,
eight-time Ironman Triathlon champion

Compelling and entertaining, Jane Booth brings alive the journey of
a novice triathlete: the dreams, the fears, the garrulous obsession, the
humorous trials and errors, the victories. A must-read for the novice
endurance athlete, and a great story for anyone seeking to reconnect
with the joy and achievement of sport.

—Jayne Williams,
author of *Slow Fat Triathlete*

TRANSFORMED by TRIATHLON
The Making of an Improbable Athlete

Jane Booth

Fast Foot Forward Press

Copyright © 2007 Jane Booth
All rights reserved. No part of this publication may be reproduced or distributed in any form or by any means, or stored in a database or retrieval system, without the prior written permission of the publisher.

Published by Fast Foot Forward Press
fastfootforwardpress.com

Fast Foot Forward Press books are available at special quantity discounts for bulk purchase for fund-raising, sales promotions, educational programs and online and mail-order catalogs. Special books or book excerpts can be created to fit specific needs. For details, email info@fastfootforwardpress.com or contact Fast Foot Forward Press, 7 West 41st Ave, #302, San Mateo, CA 94403.

Cover and Interior Design:
Victoria Pohlmann
vpohlmanndesign.com

Printed in the United States of America.
10 9 8 7 6 5 4 3 2 1

Publisher's Cataloging-in-Publication Data

Booth, Jane.

    Transformed by triathlon : the making of an improbable athlete / Jane Booth. -- 1st ed. -- San Mateo, CA : Fast Foot Forward Press, 2007.
      p. ; cm.
      ISBN-13: 978-0-9987007-6-8
      ISBN-10: 0-9787007-6-7
      Includes bibliographical references.

      1. Booth, Jane. 2. Triathlon--Training. 3. Physical fitness. 4. Triathlon--Psychological aspects. I. Title.

GV1060.73 .B66 2007   2006905809
796.42/57--dc22   0701

Printed on acid-free paper containing at least 30% post-consumer content

For David, forever my rock,
and for Mum, forever proud of me.

Contents

Foreword
by Brandi Chastain

Fitness is something we owe to ourselves. Keeping fit physically provides mental balance and well-being. That's something we can overlook when we're busy, overwhelmed and faced with too much on the To Do List of life. At times like that, we need to look within. By taking care of ourselves, by maintaining that mental balance and well-being that comes from being physically fit, we find inner strength that allows us to provide a well of support to those around us.

Right now, I'm sitting on the sofa, two weeks away from giving birth to my first child. I've done exercises to keep fit throughout my pregnancy. But now that I'm this big, I've had to sit back and let nature take its course. I just can't run around and kick a ball with my stepson with the intensity I'd like.

Reading Jane Booth's book reminded me that no matter what fitness level we all start at, each one of us goes through a time when we have a mountain to climb. I laughed with her as she describes with such graceful humor her road to fitness. I willed her on through the tough times. And I celebrated her wonderful achievement. Once my baby is born, I'll start on the road to regaining my fitness. We start at different points on that road, but we all travel the same road.

Whether you are an elite competitor or a first timer, being inspired to get up, get out and find your inner strength is something we HAVE to do. Read this book to be inspired to start moving—and move like you have never moved before. To connect with your body and your inner strength in ways you've never felt before. And to become your own source of inspiration as you unlock your true potential, and perhaps inspire others to find theirs as well.

Athletics has been at my core my whole life. Sport has given me a sense of confidence, trusting that I can push myself to reach goals I sometimes thought beyond my reach. That confidence has sustained me through serious injuries and larger life setbacks. This same sense of achievement is available to anyone who puts in the effort. Jane's story joyfully illustrates that this power is not reserved for elite athletes but is available to all—no matter where you start out on the road.

—Brandi Chastain
Women's US National Soccer Team, 1988-2004
World Cup Squad, 1991, 1999, 2003, Winners 1999, 2003
Olympic Silver Medalist, 2000, Gold Medalist, 1996, 2004
Scored winning penalty kick, World Cup Final, 1999

Foreword
by Sally Edwards

The heart of being successful at triathlon, in fact at anything that we do, is to listen to what others have to say. Experience is such a fine teacher. Here in this book—*Transformed by Triathlon*—you have the words of a woman, Jane Booth, whose life has been transformed by her willingness to take the risk—and try a tri.

Jane shares private and personal moments, wins and losses, and gives you essential information that you can apply to make your experience more rewarding—triathlon or not. But it wasn't the mechanics of training that kept me turning the pages. Would a woman with little to no background in sports, with a supportive husband and coach, with a desire to change and explore her inner self, really touch what is inside each and every man and woman? Would she get to meet her inner athlete?

She did.

And if Jane can do it, so can you. You can. Endurance sport isn't easy. It takes time. It forces you to face your fears. But it's an experience that you will never regret nor never forget. When you hear that finish line announcer call out your name, you see the finish banner with the one word on it that you have trained for—FINISH—and you touch the medal around your neck, when at that moment you're overcome with joy, fatigue, pride and happiness, you too will know that it was worth it.

Start by reading this book.

Triathlon can transform you into a stronger person. It can provide you with a pathway to a different and more powerful life. It positively changes everything. And find out what it is like to get into shape. Fitness is not an option any longer. It is the key to our health and well-being.

I know.

I have been there for more than 190,000 women over the last seventeen years as they have crossed the finish line of their first triathlon, the Danskin Women's Triathlon. I have finished 106 consecutive races. Since I volunteer to finish last because I don't want any other woman to do so, I know as a professional triathlete what happens in the front and the back of the pack. Jane Booth is a middle-of-the-packer. She isn't a champion. She isn't a world record holder. She isn't an Ironwoman. She's just like the rest of us. And she has a story that has to be told.

Like Jane, I can't wait for the day when you hold up your first finisher's medal for all to see. That is a day that you will be transformed by triathlon. Guaranteed.

See you at the starting line.

—Sally Edwards
Former Master's World Record Holder, Ironman Triathlon
World Record Holder, Iditashoe 100-mile snowshoe race
Winner, Western States 100-mile endurance run
Triathlon Hall of Famer
CEO, www.heartzones.com

To Tri or Not to Tri

Number of adult years spent as a couch potato: 21

Number of life-changing events waiting for me round the corner: 1

My journey started with a visit to the dentist. We were having one of those listening and nodding exercises that passes for conversation when you have half a dozen instruments wedged in your mouth. Dr. Hofmann was describing his preparations for his first triathlon, his monologue punctuated by occasional drilling noises and the background music of KKSF jazz radio. He was about to do a one-mile lake swim, then jump dripping wet onto his bike and ride for twenty-five miles. To finish it all off, if he wasn't finished off already, he would leap into action and run for six miles. I listened, nodded, and multi-tasked by counting the patterned dots in the acoustic ceiling tiles above me. I needed something more to transport me away from the dentist's chair than talk of an assault course for the deranged.

Then he ambushed me with The Question.

"Hey, why don't you try a triathlon?" he said. "Don't you swim already?"

I arched my eyebrows in that "are you kidding me?" way and rolled my eyes. I did everything I could to indicate that his question was beyond ridiculous, short of removing the mouth hardware to declare an emphatic "no." Dr. Hofmann continued describing his training. I continued counting the dots. The Question was washed away along with the mouth rinse.

That should have been the end of it. After all, why would a fortysomething woman with no competitive sports history whatsoever suddenly decide to become an endurance athlete? Especially a not-particularly-overweight-but-could-lose-a-few-pounds sort of person, one who shuns the drudgery of exercise in favor of sharing fine wine and gourmet food with friends.

But over the next two weeks, the triathlon kept tapping me on the shoulder and demanding that I listen. You're going to try it. Yes, you are. No discussion. Get ready.

I tried to ignore it. I would hit a command like "plan next year's vacation," and this rogue code would issue an error message like "don't bother with June because you're doing a triathlon." It was as though an especially virulent virus had infected my decision-making function and reprogrammed me without my consent.

I dismissed it. I argued back. I shook my head in disbelief, trying to dislodge the virus as though I were shaking water out of my ears. I wasn't about to endure months of physical discomfort, train in three sports up to a competitive level, learn the ins and outs of getting from lake to bike to running trail and spend a fortune on a bike. Why should I? Just because the Rogue Code said so?

What's more, why go looking for trouble? Even if I did follow through with this bizarre triathlon nonsense, who knows what might lie on the other side? Would tackling something so far outside my everyday experience change the way I looked at life? A wet weekend in an off-season seaside resort doesn't hold the same allure after a vacation in Bermuda. What if life after triathlon were like that? I didn't want this unwelcome intruder introducing any elements of dissatisfaction into my pleasant, comfortable, thoroughly satisfying life. I liked things just the way they were, thank you.

Even worse, what would life be like if I tackled the triathlon and failed? Coping with repercussions of failure would be a hundred times more painful than any unknown effects of success. Why risk introducing the permanent, unfixable stain of failure into my life? I knew how I would react. I'd hate it and I'd hate myself for failing.

But the Rogue Code refused to let go. I was taken aback at the astonishing speed with which this intruder had entwined itself round my inner core and planned to make a permanent home there. Every argument I threw at it met with a plain, simple rebuttal: quit fighting, it's a done deal.

I was beginning to feel uneasy. My peaceful existence was being totally disrupted by these insistent, relentless commands. Maybe if I could nail the reason I was being driven to do the triathlon, I would have a chance of deleting the Rogue Code and returning to a normal life. I went for a swim to calm down and try to make sense of it all.

Before we go any further, let me clear up any misunderstandings you may have about my swimming ability. Yes, I swam. In fact, I swam one mile a couple of times a week. But don't think I've lured you into reading my story under false pretences, that I was a brilliant swimmer and omitted to tell you to make my story work. Not so. I swam while having nothing better to do before lunch.

If you're bored with housework and shopping and you have two hours to kill before your friend the swim instructor finishes teaching, you may as well swim to the end of the pool and back. That happens to be fifty yards. Then you chat with your buddies in the lanes on either side and swim a couple more laps. Another hundred yards. If you stay in the pool until you start to go wrinkly, you may find that you've swum thirty-five laps without realizing it. Thirty-five laps happen to be one mile. So let's not get hung up on the m-word. This was not competitive swimming as we know it.

I adjusted my swimcap and goggles and slipped into the pool. I had arrived half an hour earlier than usual so there were no swim buddies around yet. And the pool had just emptied after the busy water aerobics class, so I had a lane to myself. I pushed off the wall and glided forward in the tranquil water. I would start with five laps of gentle breaststroke to warm up.

The reason I had had so much time on my hands for the last three years was because I didn't have a green card. I had arrived from the UK with my husband on an "Accompanying Spouse Visa." I could accompany my wage-earning husband as much as I liked, so long as I didn't enter into paid employment myself. I filled my time with volunteering for two nonprofits, shopping, lunch and swimming.

This was the opposite of my usual Type-A, frantic, city lifestyle. For the previous six years, I had run the London head-hunting practice of a large, pan-European company. Life had been demanding, fast-paced and fun. Now life was one nonstop, laid-back vacation that unfolded in the warmth of near year-round California sunshine. Except that a great vacation requires a re-turn-to-work date to contrast the indulgence of doing exactly what you want with the hectic pace of the rest of your life. My laid-back lifestyle had been bleached into boredom. It lacked a finite end.

I touched the wall after lap five. Time to switch to ten laps of freestyle. I had only started swimming because I was bored. My coaching friend Elaine had said she would teach me how to swim freestyle to give me something to do. I remembered how I had struggled to put the arm strokes together with the breathing. I smiled at how much chlorinated water I had unintentionally consumed for two whole months. Then I cracked it. Three years later, I could glide forward for lap after lap without consuming a drop of pool water.

I reached the end of my third freestyle lap and said "hi" to Jenny, the first swim buddy to arrive. But I wasn't in the mood for chatting. I wanted the water to cushion my body while my mind went into free float, searching, listening, reaching inside for the reason I was being dragged towards the triathlon. I lowered my face below the water line as my arms pulled water past my body, the sounds of real life muffled by the gurgle of bubbles streaming past my ears.

So what was driving me towards a triathlon? First to surface in my consciousness was my resilient, competitive nature. When I joined the UK's largest recruitment consultancy in 1989, there were eighty-six consultants. Four years later, at the end of a brutal recession, I finished sixth in the fee earnings table out of the remaining twenty-seven. The nonprofit world in the US had provided me with the satisfaction of contributing time and effort, but it hadn't exactly hit the spot when it came to the buzz of pushing myself hard. I craved a huge challenge to flush the frustration of enforced leisure out of my system. I needed to put myself on the map, to show people who didn't know me well that I was capable of a whole lot more. I was hungry for recognition and the satisfaction of achievement.

Next, I'd been inspired by the American can-do spirit. I now told myself that I could do anything if I wanted it enough. It's not that Brits lack ambition, motivation or the will to win. There have been countless British winners in sports, entertainment, science, you name it. The British just view achievement differently. We applaud people who make wise choices and dedicate themselves to the pursuit of greatness. We look with slight suspicion on people who make dramatic changes of direction, as though they made an error of judgment first time around. A reaching-the-pinnacle mentality is far different from a do-anything-you-put-your-mind-to mentality. I was now ready to do anything I put my mind to.

Third, I was angry. A year after I arrived in the US I had my first-ever annual physical exam, something that the UK's over-burdened nationalized health service doesn't often have time for. I learned that the age of forty is a turning point in women's health. From now on, I should take a daily calcium supplement to guard against osteoporosis. Forty is the magic age when the annual mammogram kicks in. And I should watch out for night sweats and hot flashes, just in case I was one of those women who turned menopausal in their early forties.

How dare my body do this to me? Mentally, I felt about 28, but my body had continued to age in real time. The electric shock of reality brought me right up to date. What would be next? The walker and the hip replacement? I was fast approaching 42. I would get fit, eat a healthy diet and wage war on the aging process for as long as possible.

No. The lack of challenge, a can-do spirit and a mid-life crisis weren't strong enough reasons, individually or combined, to force me into doing something so out of character that my friends would think I had lost my marbles. Besides, I had secured my green card a couple of months earlier and gone back to work four days a week. Learning to sell business services in the US market, with different business norms and conventions than I was used to in the UK, was challenge enough.

When I ran out of reasons that might be pushing me towards the triathlon, Rational Me couldn't keep quiet any longer. It dragged me back to the one heavyweight reason that spelled disaster for the triathlon. I hate failure.

I go out of my way to avoid any project that plays to my weaknesses. I learned a long time ago what some of those are. I'm weak at activities that require ongoing, steady effort, like taking minutes at meetings or giving someone a ride every week. I thrive on well-defined, short-term, high-energy projects. Like the time I stepped in with one week to go and turned a poorly organized nonprofit fundraiser into a high-profile success. I need a goal with a clear path rather than repetitive activity with no end in sight.

The triathlon played straight to my weaknesses. Regular training would require me to commit to that boring, repetitive effort that spells failure for me. Progress would be imperceptibly slow. I'd have to start something with no idea whether I'd even make it to the end. And the goal would be so far out of sight that it wouldn't do anything for my motivation.

"Hey, Jane! You swimming for England today?"

I touched the pool wall, my concentration broken by Jenny's call from the next lane. My arms were aching and I was breathing heavily. Great. I leave my body on autopilot for just a few minutes and Rogue Code reprograms my arms to swim one mile as fast as possible without stopping.

An hour later, after countless laps of energetic swimming, I was still none the wiser. No matter how hard I tried to dig deep, the real reason driving me towards the triathlon wasn't fessing up. I decided to change tack. I would go on a fact-finding mission to prove to Rogue Code that it was asking the impossible.

I arranged to have lunch with Kevin Kennedy, who I had met a few weeks earlier through business networking. I had heard through a contact that he was a very experienced triathlete. Dishes clinked around us as we settled at the table. I ordered a chicken and avocado sandwich. Kevin opted for a BLT. I took a sip of sparkling water. Should I open the conversation by telling him that I was considering doing a triathlon?

Are you CRAZY? Rational Me interjected so fast that I blinked in surprise. I was here to find evidence to convince Rogue

Code to pull out of this whole thing before I started. I'd look foolish in a few weeks when I told Kevin that I'd changed my mind.

I took a bite of my sandwich. Better than I expected. The chicken breast was lightly smoked and had a tangy, sun-dried tomato dressing.

"Kevin, I hear you're a triathlete?"

Yes, he was. A very busy triathlete, by the sound of his event schedule.

"So what's it like, swimming in open water?" I asked in my most nonchalant voice.

"Very different to the pool," he said. "You're surrounded by a bunch of guys all swimming like crazy to get to the first buoy, so it can be, shall we say, hectic. The water temperature's a little colder. And you're usually wearing a wetsuit."

"A wetsuit, huh?" I sipped more water. "Is the water really that cold?"

"Yes and no," he said. "Sometimes it can be real cold. But the wetsuit gives you extra buoyancy, so it actually helps with the swimming."

"And it's a one-mile swim?"

I took a bite of my sandwich and tried to look diffident.

"It's 1.5k, which is a shade off one mile. Then it's 40k on the bike, about twenty-five miles, and then a 10k run, just over six miles." I appreciated his courtesy in using kilometers, the standard measurement in Europe. "But there are shorter events like the Tri for Fun series in Pleasanton. That's about a four-hundred yard swim, an eleven-mile bike and three-mile run."

Even in yards and miles, that sounded a long way. And I failed to see how any length of triathlon could be described as "fun." But I was here on a fact-finding mission. Time for the deal-breaking question.

"Is there an age limit for such a physical sport?"

"Triathlon only started about twenty-five years ago," he said. "A bunch of those guys were in their forties then and they're still competing today in their seventies."

It got worse.

"And triathlon's become real big since it was in the Olympics for the first time in 2000. A huge number of people of all ages are taking it up."

Oh dear.

I continued fishing right through lunch for evidence to silence Rogue Code. Afterwards, I thanked Kevin for his time and strode back to my car. This lunch had backfired. Instead of confirming that the triathlon should remain on my List of Things in Life to Be Avoided at All Costs, I had failed to find any credible reason why I shouldn't give it a go. My "if it ain't broke, don't fix it" philosophy of life was under threat. Time to resort to drastic measures.

I persuaded my husband David to come with me to the San Jose Triathlon on the flimsy pretext of watching Kevin and our dentist, Brett Hofmann, cross the finish line. That should bring me to my senses once and for all and permanently uninstall the pernicious Rogue Code.

I congratulated Kevin when he came in, smack on the two-hour mark. The results board showed he was a top ten overall finisher. Brett finished in 2 hours, 48 minutes, well up the field in his age group and a great result for his first event. I walked back down the course. Athletes powered by, the anticipation of a great finish illuminating their faces and driving them forward at full speed.

Round the corner, out of sight of the finish line, I got a glimpse of reality. This was more like what I'd experience when I'd swum one mile, cycled for twenty-five and run for over six miles. Here, without the motivation of the finish line in sight, some athletes screwed up their faces in last-ditch determination as they forced their aching legs to run on empty. I had trumped Rogue Code. No way would I subject myself to such pain and exhaustion.

I turned and strolled back towards the giant inflatable arch at the finish line. The last hundred yards were lined with advertising banners, rippling stars-and-stripes flags, spectators, strollers, kids, and athletes cheering home their buddies. A barrage of finishers' names streamed over the loudspeakers. The play area overflowed with bouncy children. The stalls selling swim, bike and running accessories teemed with people. Dozens of athletes queued up in the Competitors Only area, swapping stories of their experience as they waited to collect their post-race food.

I stopped at the finish line. I glanced towards the digital clock as time froze for that split second that each competitor would claim as their own—their time for completing the San Jose Triathlon. The heat of the sun bounced off the pavement, the noise from the loudspeakers swarmed around my head, and all the while more athletes pounded down the home stretch and across that finish line. I breathed deeply. Then in my mind's eye, I crossed that line myself.

No way! I won't let you do this to me! Rational Me made one final, desperate plea. Then silence. That was the moment it realized it had lost this battle. Rogue Code had made the decision and there was no going back. A tremor of fear rippled through me. Somehow, I would soon start training for a triathlon.

"What about some brunch?"

David's voice snapped me out of my private time warp. That Sunday morning, he had dragged himself out of bed at some un-mentionable hour, without complaint, to pursue my hare-brained idea of watching a sporting event he'd never heard of. He had left me to myself as I indulged in the strange behavior of wanting to be alone with the finish line. He had coped with even stranger behavior of near total silence for over two hours. Now he was hungry.

"Sure," I said. "Brunch. Let's go."

I headed to the car, thankful to leave the noise and heat behind and seek out a quiet space to deal with the shock. We headed off to our favorite diner.

By the time the tea and toast arrived, I couldn't wait any longer.

"I'm going to do that event next year," I announced.

David's toast-laden hand paused halfway to his mouth.

"What, the triathlon?"

His face registered that this idea had just moved from the hare-brained to the total fantasy category.

"Yes, the triathlon," I said, with as much conviction as I could muster. "I'm going to train and I'm going to do it."

"No you won't," he replied in a matter-of-fact tone. "You'll give it all up in a couple of months."

I was stung, but I wasn't surprised. David and I had been married for nearly nineteen years. He was a most supportive husband, but he was also honest with me. He knew that my life was littered with projects that I had abandoned because I had become bored or lost sight of the goal. Part of me wanted to agree with him. I had no idea if I'd make it to the end either.

"We'll just have to differ on this one," I said, pulling on my most determined face. "I know why you think I won't do it. But I'm going to surprise you."

The lid was sealed tight shut on my decision. I couldn't back out. I was still no closer to understanding the real reason why I had to pursue the triathlon. I just knew I had to. I was unsettled, even scared that I was going to start something for a reason I didn't fully understand.

"I'll believe it when I see it," he said with a smile.

That evening, I dug out some old trainers from the back of the closet, found a faded T-shirt and some shorts and put them all at the end of the bed, ready for my first run round the block. I was about to start training for a triathlon.

The Triangle of Misery

Number of miles I have jogged in my entire life to date: about 14

Number of miles I intend to jog this month: 14.4

I detest running. Always have. In my school days, I loathed it even more than the utterly loathsome school needlework classes, where I spent an entire semester hemming a pink gingham apron and scored a historic twenty-nine percent on my term paper, the lowest of my school career. Running plowed new depths of loathing. Running was punishment for staying in bed too long and being late for the school bus.

The bus left at twenty to nine on the dot from the Railway Inn pub at the end of our road. If I was still at home at twenty-four minutes to, I had to leg it as fast as I could down the road. Halfway to the bus stop, just outside my friend Catherine's house, my legs would turn wobbly and my lungs would be ready to burst. But I had to keep going. Run now, or miss the bus and walk three miles to school.

Sprinting, on the other hand, did not count as proper running. Sprinting was any distance that was not as far as Catherine's house. I tolerated it because I could launch myself forward in one huge burst of effort and stop just before my legs wobbled. Sprinting was over in less than thirty seconds. I never trained at it, though. I just did it in preference to high jump or javelin at my school's compulsory track and field practice. My best time for the hundred meters was 14.7 seconds. Well behind the fastest girl, but fast enough to say I was a reasonable sprinter.

I was reminded of the difference between running and sprinting on School Sports Day. Everyone in the school had to take part in at least one event. My class had faster hundred and two hundred meter runners than me, so our class captain put me in the four hundred meters. I burst off the starting line and stormed ahead of my competitors. Six hundred high-intensity teen voices screamed from the sidelines, fueling my triumphant dash past the two-hundred meter mark. Then I reached Catherine's house. I staggered round the bend into the home stretch on drunken legs, determined to hang on to my lead. After all, class points were at stake. I burned up with shame as every runner but one surged past. The bus had most definitely left without me.

I tried running again at college. Half a dozen undergrads in my student residence halls started an informal evening run through the streets of the well-heeled commuter town of Guildford. Running was cool. I wanted to be cool too. So I bought some red Nike running shoes that matched my red sweatshirt and sweatpants, and joined in.

Each time, I would watch the receding forms of Katy from my German class and Ravi the mechanical engineer until they disappeared out of sight. Andy, the only freshman on our floor, would be next. Steve, a sweet, bespectacled, sandy-haired guy who fancied me would always slow down to run alongside, just so I wasn't running on my own.

Unfortunately, Steve wasn't the reason I started running. My real reason was dark-haired, blue-eyed, totally fit Paul, who was on the cross country team and always led from the front. Three weeks later, I admitted to myself that he would never notice me for my running ability. My Nikes were consigned to the closet.

After I left college, I did my best to give running one more chance. I was newly married and flat broke. Running would get me fit on the cheap. No membership dues to pay. I could run as much I liked, whenever I liked. Come January 1, motivated by a New Year's resolution I intended to keep, I dug out my nearly new Nikes and ran round the block with my husband. Neither of us was any good at running as I didn't in the end marry either the cross country knee-trembler or the bespectacled guy who fancied me.

We set off past rows of terraced red-brick houses, built for the middle classes of the 1870s, and that now constituted our happy but down-at-heel neighborhood in the army town of Aldershot. We wore gloves to protect our hands from the frosty cold. The sky was leaden gray. I couldn't remember a New Year's Day that wasn't gray.

I expected to complete one run round the block, a distance of barely half a mile, even if I had to slow down almost to walking pace. I used to be a sprinter, for goodness sake. In less than four gray January minutes, I had used every shred of energy my legs possessed. Then I walked the rest of the way home. I usually gave up entirely by January 6. David didn't last much longer. After three failed New Year resolutions, the running shoes were demoted to gardening shoes.

Twenty years later, what had possessed me to consider doing a triathlon when I thought I had banished running from my life forever on Shoe Demotion Day? Now I would have to run a whopping 6.2 miles, which sounded suspiciously close to a quarter of a marathon. What's more, I'd have to run on legs that had just pushed me twenty-five agonizing miles up hill and down dale on a bike and were about to collapse. This was a thousand trips to Catherine's house rolled into one.

The alarm woke me up at 6:45 a.m. I forced myself straight

out of bed, even though I have never broken my teenage habit of burying myself under the goosedown silo of my duvet, right up to the moment when my day threatens to implode if I don't make a move. I pulled on the scuffed trainers, faded yellow T-shirt and khaki shorts I had laid out the night before.

"Have a good run," David called from the bathroom. "Are you sure you don't want me to come with you?"

David had taken up running again when he was bitten by the midlife fitness bug a year earlier. Without me alongside to moan and groan or the miserable English winter to contend with, he had made good progress. He now ran for half an hour, three times a week.

"Thanks, but no need," I replied, with more haste than I had intended. The last thing I wanted was for him to witness my first, puny efforts at running. "Bye for now!"

I flew downstairs and out of the front door before he had chance to reply. He didn't know my route, so he wouldn't be able to follow me.

I took my first, curious peek at what the day looked like when I was usually asleep. The soft gray layer of summer marine fog that settles overnight around the San Francisco Bay area had not yet been burned off by morning sunshine. Fog dulled the colors of trees and houses to a matte finish and blunted the temperature to a tolerable level. Still air lay undisturbed by traffic noise, the void filled with a dawn chorus of birdsong that bounced and echoed round the houses. I felt like a gatecrasher in a parallel, early-morning universe.

I crossed the starting line by the mailbox and set off running along the gentle uphill road. Concentrate on putting one foot in front of the other. Running is like walking, only faster, right?

At two hundred yards, the gradient turned sharply steeper. I slowed to a walk, fighting for breath. A one-hundred-fifty-foot eucalyptus tree towered up ahead, its branches arching across to a cascade of split-level houses built into the hill on the other side. The road leveled off beyond that point. I gave myself permission to walk to the tree. But once past its thick red trunk, I must run. Triathletes don't walk. A couple of minutes later, I walked over long strips of peeled bark that released a faint, tingling aroma of crushed eucalyptus. The signal to run.

My new goal was to reach the end of the road without another stop. I breathed two paces in, two paces out. Twenty-four breaths later, my heart hammered against my chest and my lungs fought to grasp the meager air and drag it past the sandpaper lining my throat. Painful inhalations blocked out everything round me except feet connecting with tarmac. The voice in my head took over. It yelled out to my legs to STOP RIGHT NOW. My legs obeyed. I would never run 6.2 miles if I carried on like this. Life had turned from hope to misery in ninety-six paces.

I walked to the end of the road and turned left. A tall wooden fence on my left bordered a short level stretch with no sidewalk. Eighty yards to recover. Don't expect miracles on your first day, Jane. Take it easy. I turned left again and ran down the road that completed the third side of the triangular block I lived on. Past a patchwork of California ranchers, ten-year-old mock Tudors and the ubiquitous, anonymous style of West Coast, stuccoed suburban, their irrigated gardens overflowing with purple petunias, pink hydrangeas and white impatiens. Running downhill was easier. I didn't use as much lung capacity and my legs found their own way down the slope without me having to push them.

The final four hundred yards. The road tipped upwards in a short, steep uphill. After only a few steps my forward momentum evaporated, my legs filled with lead and my heart pounded again. The insistent voice that monitored my pain threshold hit override and brought my heavy legs to a standstill. I walked up the rest of the hill and down the final slope towards home. Our mailbox came into view.

My heart had now eased off to a moderate beat. Come on, Jane. Run the last hundred yards. I cranked my legs up one last time and ran. When I arrived outside our house, I looked around to see if David was watching. He wasn't. But just in case he ever was in future, I made a mental note to make sure I always finished by running rather than walking. No matter how bad I felt.

I stepped under the invigorating jet of a hot shower and spent several minutes reviewing my progress. Now I had a benchmark. Fifteen minutes to do 1.2 miles with three stops. Not exactly a great athletic base to build on. But it was a start. I hadn't expected my body to hit the pain barrier after a few paces. Athletes were supposed to fight through pain. I resolved to try harder.

I ran twice more that week. Same routine. Out of bed at 6:45 a.m. On with the gear. Off round the Triangle of Misery.

Breathe two paces in, two paces out. After two hundred yards, I would hit the aerobic wall and come to a forced stop. I would seize the air to pull each breath to the very bottom of my lungs. But there just wasn't enough air out there to grasp. Surely I couldn't be that unfit? All that swimming must have given me some benefit. Fifteen minutes. 1.2 miles. Three long stops.

My progress was far worse than I could have imagined. Maybe I was never cut out to be a long-distance runner. Maybe I was right not to tell anyone about my stupid triathlon idea because I may never be able to conquer the running. Maybe I would have to give up after all. And then David would have the last laugh.

Week Two, Run Six. I set off up the gentle incline, knowing that the two-hundred-yard roadblock lay in wait farther up the road. I approached meltdown point. No energy left to keep up with breathing two paces in, two paces out. I dropped back to breathing two paces in, three paces out. Something changed. But what? My legs and lungs screamed out to stop when I ran past the two-hundred-yard mark. But deep down, I still had a few lungfuls of air left to pull me through.

I chugged my way up the steeper incline. No matter how painful this was going to be, I refused to give in. By the time I reached the top of the Triangle my head was buzzing, my legs were trembling and I was almost ready to collapse. Yet I had made it to the top without a single stop. I punched the air and let out a jubilant yell.

Now I understood what was wrong. Back in the early days of swimming, I would run out of air in exactly the same way after a twenty-five-yard length of the pool. Elaine, my swim-coach friend, spotted that I was hyperventilating. I would try to take in too much air and get into a vicious circle of the more I breathed in, the more out of breath I felt. She made me slow down my breathing. That cured the hyperventilating. I had adopted the same tactic on this run. Longer, slower breaths. Breathe two paces in, three paces out.

I walked the eighty yards along the top, then set off down the last side of the Triangle. Excitement tingled through my veins. Elation pushed me downhill and farther up the last incline than I'd ever gone before. I walked for a hundred yards, then ran for home.

I rushed inside to tell David what had just happened. He celebrated my victory with a big hug. He was still convinced that I would give it all up in a few weeks. But that wasn't the same as not wanting me to succeed. Then he told me that he was taking me shopping.

When David started running again, he had bought new shoes designed to absorb impact and give proper support to his feet. I'd mentioned to him after I finished my last couple of runs that my feet and ankles hurt. He thought the problem could be caused by wearing shoes that weren't designed for running. Before I went any further, he wanted me to have proper shoes.

David walked up and down the women's running shoe aisle of the sporting goods store, pulling out boxes with names like New Balance, Nike, Mizuno and Saucony. Soon I was surrounded by a dozen open boxes of size 8 shoes. I tried each pair on. Some had labels like "medium stability" or "high motion control." But I had no idea if I was dangerously unstable or had any motion that needed controlling.

Eventually, I went with a pair of Asics that seemed comfortable and were reasonably priced. I also bought two pairs each of navy running shorts, pale gray sports bras, white socks and red tops, all made of a man-made fiber called *Coolmax*. The fabric wicked away moisture and kept skin feeling dry, unlike cotton, which retained sweat and dried slowly.

I couldn't believe the difference when I ran the next day. It wasn't just my feet, which were cosseted in a pair of proper running shoes. It wasn't just the *Coolmax* fabric, which was so comfortable that from that moment on, cotton was forgotten. It was everything about me.

I dressed the part. I was a runner. I might be an inept runner, but I was a runner in training instead of someone who had pulled on some old clothes and was struggling round the block. And who could tell how inept I really was when they saw me glide past in my new gear, looking the part? They had no idea how far I had run. Or how far I had left to go. They saw a runner.

For the next couple of weeks, I ran three times in the mornings and swam three times in the evenings. My running goal was to reach 1.2 miles without stopping. My swimming goal was to eliminate breaststroke from my mixture of freestyle and breaststroke for the whole triathlon distance of one mile.

When you run at the same time every morning, you see familiar faces—Man with Baseball Cap, Three Women Friends, Man with Two Small Dogs. One day, I encountered two thirty-something men I hadn't seen before running towards me. And they weren't just running, they were running *and* chatting. How did they have enough breath left over to do that?

They floated towards me like two finely tuned Porsches, hardly breaking a sweat. I maintained my solid impression of a spluttering, bright red Beetle (old style). At least they caught sight of me when I was running and not walking. They drew level.

"Hi," said Porsche Number One as he purred by.

"How's it goin'?" said Porsche Number Two, with a nod in my direction.

Aargh! The Porsches were talking to me. What on earth should I do now? I had no spare breath left to say "hi" back. I made a split-second decision to attempt a casual wave. But somewhere between my brain and my hand, the message got corrupted. I ended up looking like I was swatting a fly. I seriously considered changing my route next time.

After two weeks, I managed to run my 1.2-mile route with only one stop, halfway up the last steep hill. Another break-through. On the home stretch, I ran past a tall stranger wearing a Giants baseball cap, walking a golden lab dog.

"Enjoy your run," he called out.

"I am," I replied. And then before I could stop myself I add-ed, "I'm training for a triathlon!"

I was stunned. What had I just said? I had told someone other than David that I was in training. It felt good. I was ready to load the pressure on myself by telling people that I was going to do something big.

That day at work, I oh-so-casually mentioned to everyone I bumped into that my triathlon training had gone well that day.

I did the same the next day and the next. Within a week, nearly everyone who knew me, and several who wished they didn't, had found out about my triathlon ambitions.

What surprised me most about my first four weeks of training was that I had stuck with it. The swimming was shaping up nicely. I had almost eliminated breaststroke from my one-mile swim. I had forsaken my goosedown cocoon and had voluntarily got out of bed forty-five minutes early to run, even though I needed every shred of willpower to overcome the pain barrier that inflicted such physical and mental hurt. Yet I still got out of bed and went running.

I hadn't quite managed to run the Triangle without stopping. But I had pushed beyond my comfort zone and not backed off. Early mornings still felt strange but I no longer felt a stranger. And I was learning something new about myself for the first time in a very long time.

The Accidental Cyclist

Number of years elapsed since I last rode a bike: 31

Number of seconds elapsed before I decided to give it another go: 30

They say you never forget how to ride a bike. But ever since I'd started running four weeks earlier, I'd been wondering, off and on, who "they" were. And why is it that we never hear from the ones who did forget? I knew I'd have to put myself to the test sometime and get on a bike. I just hoped I wouldn't belong to the group you never heard from.

My parents gave me my first bike for my eighth birthday. A gleaming, brand new Raleigh *Relex*, painted deep aquamarine—without a crossbar, of course, because this wasn't a boy's bike. I practiced so many figure eights on the wide concrete strip behind our garage that the training wheels were removed in record time. Or so my mum claimed.

I rode my smart aquamarine bike along the quiet cycle trail, through the traffic-free park, down the deserted canal towpath, everywhere that didn't take me on busy roads. My Raleigh *Relex* took me through my Cycling Proficiency Test, that rite of passage for British kids, where I had to negotiate round orange traffic cones in the school playground to demonstrate that I could look over my right shoulder, signal, move to the middle of an imaginary road and execute a perfect right turn. I took my certificate home, showing it off as though I'd just won Olympic Gold.

Another proud moment for my mum. But I still stuck to the cycle paths. I loved that bike as much as I hated traffic.

By the time I turned eleven, my knees would bang against the handlebars when I pedaled. The bike was passed down to my middle sister. I didn't ask for another. By then, boys were more interesting than bikes. And boys were more interested in girls who hung around nonchalantly at the school bus stop than those who still rode bikes.

I was musing over my beloved Raleigh *Relex* and the never-forgetting theory of bike-riding one Saturday morning in July while David and I were driving south on coastside Highway 1. We were treating ourselves to a long weekend near Mendocino, on the Northern California coast, and planned to spend a day hiking the Fern Canyon trail in Van Damme State Park. Just after we crossed the bridge over the Big River, I spied a sign for a bike rental shop.

"Dave, pull over," I said. "Want to find out if you really never do forget how to ride a bike?"

"Works for me," he said.

Nineteen years of marriage have acclimatized David to my hare-brained schemes and last-minute changes of plan. He responds to the good ones with "works for me" and the bad ones with "gosh, I'd never have thought of that." Most times, he manages to steer me away from the Gosh ideas by making me believe that I alone had made the decision to drop them.

Renting bikes worked for me, too. When I least expected it, I'd found a way to test the never-forgetting theory without the added pressure of buying a bike. Cycling didn't hold quite the apprehension that running did. But would I still harbor that childhood fear of traffic? Exploring cycle paths on rented bikes allowed us to test out if we liked cycling enough to make such a big financial investment. After all, we would be buying two bikes, not one. David wasn't about to pass up the opportunity of acquiring a new toy too.

We turned off the highway down a quiet country lane shaded by large trees, and pulled into the rental office car park. A small wooden cabin with a "Bikes for Rent" sign was tucked away down a gravel road leading to the edge of the Big River. A large van parked to one side had its rear doors open, exposing two racks of smart, gleaming bikes just waiting to be ridden.

The rental guy picked out bikes for David and me. This bike was nothing at all like my beloved Raleigh *Relex*. For a start, I would have to contend with gears. A small lever near my right thumb switched the chain between a small and big gear ring right by the pedals. The bike handle in my left hand operated like a motorbike throttle. When I rotated it towards or away from me, the chain moved one notch up or down the group of seven gear rings on the back wheel. That made a staggering fourteen different gear combinations to choose from. Today could get complicated.

The tires were wide and rugged with deep tread on them. Had I hired a mountain bike by mistake? No, Rental Guy explained, this was a hybrid bike. It had wide-tread tires and smaller wheels like a mountain bike, combined with a conventional frame and padded saddle more suited for gentle recreation. The brakes were still where I remembered them. But which lever operated the front and which the back brake? A long-lost memory surfaced. Something about braking hard with the front brake catapults the rider headfirst over the handlebars. Great. Today could get complicated and dangerous.

Before Rental Guy would let me ride the bike, he asked me to pick out a bike helmet. I wandered over to the helmet rack in the van. We didn't have helmets thirty-one years ago. Were they all one size? And which way round should I wear it? In an instant, my most important goal in life was to make sure I didn't try the helmet on back to front.

David strolled over. We stood side by side at the helmet rack. He knew straight away why I hadn't picked out a helmet. He didn't have a clue either. But he soon worked out that the piece of plastic clipped onto one end resembled a sun visor. That must be the front. We tried on our helmets and he fastened mine up for me.

"Thanks," I mouthed silently. He smiled back.

After we signed the paperwork, Rental Guy gave us a map of local cycle paths. We planned a route that started with a right turn north on Highway 1, back over the bridge across the Big River, then right again down a narrow lane that came to a dead end at the water's edge. Then we would take the cycle path that flanked the river for about twelve miles.

Rental Guy then directed us to a nearby private road where we could practice gear changing in seclusion. He went over the gears one more time and encouraged us to come back for more help if we needed it.

To reach the private road, we would have to pedal back up the gravel slope for a hundred yards or so. I wasn't sure if I could even remember how to push off on a bike. The slope had major potential for an embarrassing fall. We walked our bikes up with as much dignity as we could muster.

"Ready to give it a go?" David said, when we reached level ground.

"I am if I find out which lever is the front brake," I said. David squeezed my left brake lever. He smiled in encouragement. "Ready now?"

I sucked in my top lip and said nothing.

"Come on," he said in his most persuasive voice. "They say you never forget how to ride a bike."

I decided against asking him if he had spoken with "them" recently.

David set off for a trial ride down the single lane road. I had run out of delaying tactics. I took a deep breath, straddled the bike, put my left foot on the pedal at the bottom of the arc and pushed off three or four times with my right foot, as though I were on a skateboard. When I built up enough momentum, I sat back on the saddle and pedaled. A bit wobbly, but I was moving. My heart pounded. Despite warm sunshine, my skin felt cold. I could feel the helmet straps running past my ears and the fastener under my chin. My head wasn't used to being encapsulated in plastic. Was the helmet secure? Would it slip down over my eyes?

I concentrated on pedaling to the end of the road. A big turning circle came into view. A brand new white truck, still with dealer license plates, was parked on the right hand side. I just needed to angle the handlebars a little to the left and I'd turn full circle. No need to slow down. I couldn't cycle any slower. Within ten feet of the truck, I turned the handlebars. But not in time. The bike tipped and almost dumped me off. My hand reached out to steady myself on the truck. Another six inches and my handlebars would have scraped the paintwork.

I planted both feet on either side of the bike and shuffled it round so that I was pointing back down the road. Remember Jane, after a fall, or near-fall, get back on the bike. I cycled back to the starting point.

"Hey, look at you!" David called out when I stopped. "I knew you'd get the hang of it."

I furrowed my brow and shot him a glance.

"How about if I ride next to you?" he asked. "Would that help?"

"No, it's OK." I shuffled my bike round again to point back down the road. "My steering is so shaky, I need the road to myself. And there isn't room in that turning circle for you, me AND the truck. You go first."

He zoomed off up the road.

After four laps, I settled on a "one size fits all" gear setting that would allow me to concentrate on steering rather than pedaling. I could now move intentionally to the left and right to avoid potholes in the private road. But I still hadn't managed to turn round at the end. That meant I could avoid riding over road kill on the highway, but I ran the risk of ending up halfway to Oregon by the end of the day.

Time to leave the safe haven of the private road. Just three hundred yards of highway, over the bridge, then we could turn off right and head for the cycle path by the river. David led the way.

We stopped at Highway 1. I reached up and touched my helmet to check it hadn't slipped. The hairs on the back of my neck prickled. I couldn't stop myself taking quick, shallow breaths. Remember, triathletes push the envelope and venture into the unknown! Four weeks ago, I'd have got off the bike and walked. But the last four weeks' running had toughened up my willpower. I pursed my lips and turned right.

Deafening traffic raced past at warp speed about three inches from my left elbow. Did car drivers realize just how scary fifty miles an hour felt to a cyclist who was only an arm's length from eternity? I gripped the handlebars. A wake of fume-filled air from each car blasted me closer towards the flimsy barrier lining the bridge. I looked over the edge. At least a twenty-mile drop to the bottom. I swallowed hard. One more blast of air would blow me right off the bike and straight over the side. I shivered. Dear God, I just wanted to be a triathlete. Instead, I'm going to die.

David rode ten yards ahead of me. I imagined I was attached by a rope to his bike. He was pulling me along. I couldn't go back. I couldn't turn left or right. I certainly couldn't look down. I pointed the handlebars straight ahead and kept going.

We crossed the bridge and made a wide, right sweep down the lane towards the river. I let the bike find its own speed down the slope. I coasted to a halt at the end, just before the river. My legs shook. I planted both feet on the ground, leaned over the handlebars and took several deep breaths.

David circled round, pulled level with me and stopped. He put his hand on my shoulder. We stood in silence, watching the wide, languorous river meander onwards to the sea. The bridge was way above us. The traffic noise had receded. Smooth, silent water slid past, its gentle pace measured by the occasional leaf floating by on the surface. A group of voiceless kayakers about ninety yards away on the opposite bank fell into line and set off paddling upstream.

"See that barrier over there?"

David broke the silence. I looked in the direction he pointed. A metal field gate stretched across the entrance to a gravel cycle path about two cars' width wide, running alongside the river.

"There won't be any traffic because it's blocked off to vehicles," he said. "You'll be fine once you're past that point."

I nodded, fiddled with my helmet strap once again and checked which gear I was in. A pointless exercise. I hadn't a clue if I was in the right gear or not for the terrain. But I used those few seconds to convince my don't-do-it voice that I was going to ride again.

We walked our bikes round the side of the gate. Time to cycle. Wide river vistas opened up through breaks in the trees. Families played on the beach. Toddlers paddled in shallow water. A group of teens played an impromptu game of water polo. Way off in the distance, kayakers reduced to orange fluorescent ants in matchstick boats diminished upstream. I kept them in sight as I rode, until they disappeared beyond the bend in the magnificent, Amazon-like river.

The path turned inland, then began a gradual climb through the trees. I tried out the gears to find the best one for riding up the incline. The sound of gravel scrunched by deep-tread tires echoed louder under the trees, now that the kids' laughter had receded. Tension eased from my shoulders. I plucked up courage to pedal a bit faster.

We rode in dappled sunlight through bowers of large birch trees, then emerged into bright sunshine before plunging once again into the green coolness of canopy cover. We followed the twists and turns of the path, leading us first to the river and then back inland, down to water level then back up again. I was safe from traffic. I could control the bike. My earlier apprehension dissolved.

An hour later, we stopped at a small promontory overlooking the wide, majestic sweep of the river. David wedged the bikes between two large bushes to make room for us to sit down in the shade of a California oak. He took off his backpack and removed the picnic lunch we'd bought earlier when we had planned to hike in the State Park. We swapped halves of sandwiches. My honeyroast ham on ciabatta and roast beef on wheat tasted extra good because I'd worked so hard to earn them.

Lunch also fed my confidence. I was ready to explore more of the cycle path. This time, I led the way. I built up speed on the flats, cranked the gears when I approached a hill and felt the breeze on my face as I coasted down the other side. Warm sunshine bathed my skin. The perfume of flowers wafted in the air. The rich texture of birdsong, voices, water and rustling leaves was no longer smothered by the drone of a car engine. Cycling connected me with my surroundings in a way that could never happen in a car.

Four hours after setting off, we arrived back at the field gate barrier across the cycle path where we had regrouped after my bridge moment. We walked up the slope back to Highway 1. When the red light held up traffic for us, I pedaled across the road and turned left. Three hundred yards to the rental office turning. Cars continued to fly past at warp speed. Apprehension formed a knot in my stomach. But I refused to be intimidated. I had my cycle lane, they had their highway.

When I reached the rental office turning, I pulled over. I would need a lot more practice dealing with traffic before I would even consider crossing a four-lane highway. We walked the bikes across the road, then cycled back to the bike van.

"Good ride?" asked Rental Guy.

"Very pleasant, thank you," I said. "And you know what they say. You never forget how to ride a bike."

The next day, David and I had a long talk about buying bikes. We had enjoyed ourselves on our Mendocino trip, but one pleasant bike ride didn't turn us into cyclists. We had looked at bikes on our initial shoe-buying trip to the sporting goods store. They would set us back at least $500 each. We decided to do the sensible thing and hold off for a couple of months, just to see if we still wanted to buy them after I'd done some more training. We both knew it was a secret code for seeing if I still wanted to do the triathlon by then.

One week later, almost by accident, we bought the bikes.

Kids with New Toys

Worst thing that went wrong with my first bike: flat tire

Things that could go wrong with my second bike: twenty-seven gears, just for starters

---

That Saturday afternoon, as we walked through the door of Chain Reaction Bicycles in Redwood City, David and I reminded each other that we were on a bicycle fact-finding mission only. We would enforce the strict No Purchasing Under Any Circumstances Rule. If either of us was seen to waver, the other was to make the secret sign. If that failed to break the spell, step two was to drag the offender out of the shop and apologize to the sales staff that one of us had been struck down with temporary insanity. Step two had never thus far been invoked when the No Purchasing Rule was in effect. The embarrassment was threat enough.

Greg from Massachusetts, the bike mechanic who had been pressed into service as sales specialist on that hectic afternoon, drew the short straw. We had a lot of facts to find. He worked his way patiently through every dumb question. Then he took us through Bike Riding 101 in the bike shop car park. He showed me how to tilt the bike pedal upwards and then slip my foot into the toe clip, a cage of straps that hugged my foot from the toes to the arch. But why did I need my foot strapped to the pedal? And what would happen if I couldn't wrench my foot out in time when I wanted to stop? I contemplated possible scenarios resulting from getting my feet stuck in the toe clips. I could only come up with one painful one. Toe clips did not strike me as a good idea.

Before I had chance to discuss the possibility of removing the toe clips, Greg moved on to the brakes. On each side of the handlebars was a large, silver, aluminum lever with a little black lever attached to it. If you squeezed the left silver lever towards you, it operated the front brake. The right lever operated the back brake. Greg demonstrated the brakes.

"Now for the gears," Greg said. "If you click the right aluminum brake lever from side to side, it will take you down your rear cogs. Click the black lever, you'll go back up again."

My rear cogs?

"And it's reversed on the other side," he continued, hardly able to contain his zeal for all things mechanical. "Left brake lever moves you up the chain ring, black takes you down. Got that?"

He clicked away at the levers with furious enthusiasm as he whirled the pedals round. I was supposed to be taking this in.

"So I have four levers?" I said, the consternation in my brain spilling over into my voice. "And they're the opposite way round? And brakes and gears use the same lever? What happened to the bike throttle?"

"Excuse me?"

Oh dear. I longed for the simplicity of the gear mechanism on the hybrid bike, even though at the time the left throttle and right little thumb lever had seemed a most complicated way to handle fourteen gears. And I'd have to learn bikespeak if I were to have any chance of understanding Greg.

He went over everything a gazillion more times until I sort of grasped that the three large gears positioned by the pedals were called the "chain ring." I moved the chain from gear to gear, or ring to ring as I was supposed to call them, with the left silver and black levers. The nine gears bunched round the spindle of the back wheel were called cogs. I moved the chain over those with the right levers. I thought a cog was the name for a tooth on a gear. But no, cogs were cogs and teeth were teeth. And neither of them were gears. Just to finish me off, I calculated that if I had three rings on my chain ring and nine cogs on my rear wheel, I had a staggering twenty-seven options to choose from. It was bad enough on any given day choosing between three pairs of shoes, let alone twenty-seven gears. I sighed.

The handlebars had that curved-down style like bikes in the Tour de France. I'd only ever ridden bikes with straight handlebars that I could reach while sitting upright. To reach the bottom of these curved handlebars, I had to lean forward and down. I tried reaching down a couple of times as I rode figure eights round the car park. I wobbled dangerously close to a pristine bronze SUV whose unfortunate owner hadn't realized that the car park doubled as the Bike Riding 101 arena.

But at least it wasn't compulsory to grip the lower curve of the handlebars. I could rest my hands just above the levers on the straight part of the handlebars and operate the gears and brakes from there. That is, if I unraveled the difference between a brake, a chain ring, a cog, a large aluminum lever and a small black lever that were knotted together in my brain like kids' shoelaces.

I cycled round the car park for over an hour, practicing gear changing and slipping in and out of toe clips on two different bikes. Once in the saddle, I moved into denial about the No Purchasing Rule. It was simply a matter of choosing between the LeMond and the Trek.

Both bikes were priced close to $1,000. Greg assured me that either would keep pace with my abilities until I was at least an intermediate cyclist. Then I could come back and buy an expert bike, one that had superior gear shifters and was made of lightweight carbon fiber. A lighter bike would go faster.

But the basic LeMond or Trek was good enough for me. Why pay for design technology on an expert bike in order to shave a couple of minutes off my event time? I could shave a much bigger chunk off my event time by improving my cycling technique than by buying a carbon fiber bike. If I ever reached the point when a couple of minutes made all the difference, I would reconsider.

I settled on the Trek because the ride felt more comfortable. David had set aside the Rule a long time before me and had already decided on the Trek. He was now inside the shop, choosing extra goodies.

We left with two correctly sized Trek 1200 bikes, two each of cycling jerseys, shorts, helmets, pairs of gloves, bottle cages, water bottles, bicycle locks and tire inner tubes, plus one bike rack for the car, tire pump, set of tire levers in case of a flat, multi-tool, tire repair kit and saddle bag. I also had a little speedometer fitted to my bike that would tell me how fast I was riding, average speed and how much distance I'd covered. If I was going to train properly, I wanted the lowdown on how much punishment I had endured each day.

We spent $2,419 in total. This blew our original $1,000 budget right out of the water. But by then we had stopped caring. This was an investment in our future healthy lifestyle.

I sneaked into the garage three times that Saturday evening, just to take a peek at my brand new, shiny black, Trek 1200 bicycle. Once I even sat astride it and imagined myself racing towards the finish line.

By Sunday morning, I wondered how I would even reach the start line. My sleek, gleaming Trek was a serious machine designed for racing, with lots of things that could go wrong. What had I done? It was like waking up to find that your favorite toy pedal car had been replaced by a Jaguar.

That morning I also faced my first sartorial dilemma. Does one wear underwear or not beneath one's bike shorts? Even if I had thought about this yesterday in Chain Reaction Bicycles, I was hardly going to ask Greg. And I couldn't exactly stare at the posterior of every properly dressed cyclist, looking for evidence of Visible Panty Line. I'd just have to experiment and ride once With and once Without.

David and I drove down the San Francisco Peninsula to Cañada Road. This fresh-paved road runs through seven miles of open countryside, along the line of the San Andreas Fault, from Highway 92 to Highway 84. Every Sunday, county sheriffs close off a 3.8-mile stretch at either end and hand it over to cyclists, walkers, runners and in-line skaters. A sheriff waved us through the temporary barrier. We were cyclists. We belonged here.

We unloaded our bikes. My brain remained trussed up in confusion over toe clips and gears. I ignored my stomach that churned in panic over all the mishaps that could befall me. My brand new, shiny bike cried out to be ridden along 3.8 miles of wide, newly paved road that was blissfully devoid of vehicles. My fingers curled round the handlebars and my feet itched to connect with the pedals.

"Ready, Dave?"

I looked behind me to check where David had got to.

"Yep," he said and straddled his bike. "But you go first."

"Don't worry about me. I'll manage."

"I know," he said, pulling on his gloves. "I just want to give myself a challenge to catch you up."

Even though he didn't say so, the real reason was that he wanted to keep an eye on me in case I got into difficulty. Even though I didn't say so, I was reassured that he would be right behind me.

I straddled my bike and checked behind once more to rule

out any collision with an unsuspecting cyclist, baby stroller or other human being. I slid my left foot into the toe clip and pushed off with my right. I pedaled a couple of times to build up some speed, scrabbled to flip the right pedal over to bring the toe clip to the top and wiggled my foot into it. I laughed with glee as I rode my first hundred yards on my new bike, looking out across the calm expanse of Crystal Springs Reservoir.

After about four hundred yards, the road took off down a long, sweeping hill. My bike freewheeled at its own pace. The speedometer showed that I was flying along at eighteen miles an hour. My stomach churned again at the thought of falling off at eighteen miles an hour. I willed myself not to think about it.

At the bottom of the hill, I hit a gentle upward incline. The bike slowed. Time to unravel my gear confusion. One set of levers operated the rear cogs and the other the chain ring. But which was which? And the left levers worked the opposite way from the right, but which way round was it? I wanted to try out the nine cogs on the back wheel because they would provide some fine adjustment to match the gear to grade of slope. I opted for the right silver lever and clicked it. The effort required to pedal uphill eased off a little. I had made the right choice.

"Silver, easier: black, harder," I chanted in time to the pedal strokes. "Silver, easier: black, harder."

I changed gear every few seconds, repeating the silver/black mantra to learn which lever took me up the rear gear cogs and which took me down. My legs sensed how one gear change, up or down, affected the amount of effort required to pedal.

The familiar road scrolled past at unfamiliar, slow-motion pace. I approached the Pulgas Water Temple. This folly of Greco-Roman pillars and dome marked the end of the 160-mile pipeline bringing water from Yosemite's Hetch Hetchy Reservoir to the Bay Area. I noticed for the first time the avenue of tall poplar trees framing the Temple at the far end. The two lines of trees shielded the Temple until I drew level, then unfurled to reveal its tall pillars and dome in perfect perspective. The moment I cycled ten yards past, the avenue closed its protective arms round its charge, hiding the temple from view. This revelation happened too fast to see in a car. I cherished the brief glimpse I had been granted from the perfect vantage point of my bicycle seat.

"How are you coping?"

I heard David's voice and glanced to my left. He had pulled level with me. I had expected him to catch me up. His legs were stronger than mine.

"Do you want me to ride with you?" he called out, with a concerned look.

"I'm fine. Just working out my gears." I smiled back and nodded. "You go on ahead."

"Are you sure?"

"Absolutely sure. Go for it."

I watched him pull ahead until he was about fifty yards in front. I went back to gauging how the power from my legs translated into the whirr of wheels. I plowed in greater effort on a larger gear. The bike responded. The wheels ate up yards of pavement, transporting me past unfolding vistas of straw-colored fields singed with sunshine. The breeze caused by cutting through the air cooled the reflected heat off the road.

At the twenty-two-minute mark, I approached a short incline at the end of the 3.8-mile stretch. Within a few yards, the pedals became so stiff they almost seized up. I changed down my rear cogs as fast as I could. But the gradient was steeper than I had expected. I wasn't strong enough to keep the pedals turning round. I wobbled. In an instant, my perspective changed from measuring how fast I was moving forward to how long I could balance on a bike that was barely moving forward at all.

Loose gravel at the side of the pavement came into sharp focus. Survival instinct took over. Both feet ejected simultaneously from the toe clips and plonked themselves on the ground. I shuddered to an abrupt, ungainly halt about twenty yards shy of the top. But at least I was upright.

"Well done on the hill!" David called out from the sheriff's water station.

He took a last gulp of water, tossed the empty paper cup into the trash and freewheeled down to where I had stopped. He put his arm round my shoulder.

We swapped stories. I had soothed my gear lever headache, even though I had muffed the final hill. David had survived his gear changing and toe clip moments without a murmur. He took new experiences more in his stride than I did.

We discussed the return route. We faced an easy freewheel down the hill we had just climbed. Then a long haul back up the first hill we had coasted down on the way out. That hill must have a tough gradient if my bike had reached eighteen miles an hour without me having to pedal. But I was determined to ride the whole way back. I would not resort to walking.

When David was a hundred yards ahead, I turned my bike round and set off down the hill. I clicked through to my topmost gears to push the bike speed as hard as it would go. The speedometer showed twenty-four miles an hour. My stomach churned again. I could hurt myself badly if I fell off now. I cut through the still air at such a pace that I could hear the breeze whistling past my ears.

A dip in the road. The point where the gradient switched from downhill to uphill. My legs found an extra ounce of furious pace, pushing me up the grade like a long jumper hurtling towards the sandpit. I needed as much advantage from the downhill speed as possible to carry me uphill.

I covered the next fifty yards at red-hot tempo. Then the hill began to bite. I clicked rapidly down the gears. The hill pushed back at me, forcing each pedal stroke to turn over slower than the last. I clicked down more gears. Creaking, groaning pain built up in my thighs. Within eighty yards, the speedometer showed five miles an hour.

I had reached my lowest rear wheel cog forty yards back. How much farther to ride? I looked up. The hill stretched ahead for half a continent and rounded a corner out of sight. I couldn't see the end. Waves of panic washed over me, leaving my limbs weak in their wake.

I glanced down to the pedals. The chain was on the middle ring. I had to switch to my smallest ring because I needed that extra power. I knew I had to use the left levers, but which one? Silver or black? If I picked the wrong one, the chain would land on the biggest ring and bring me to a dead stop. A dead stop meant that I would be trapped in the toe clips and hit the ground. Think, woman! I went back to the mantra for the right levers. Silver, easier: black, harder. So the left side must be . . . silver harder: black easier. Black EASIER! Do it now, before you grind to a halt on the hill.

I clicked the left black lever. The chain clunked from the middle to the smallest ring, sending vibrations up through my feet.

The payoff was that I could turn the pedals round with a microscopic reduction in effort. But changing rings had made no difference to my labored breathing or to the burning sensation in my thigh muscles. Every ten yards piled on pain and sapped my dwindling energy. The bike couldn't help me any more. It was down to me alone to fight this hill.

I stared at the two yards of road in front of me. No matter how much I was tempted, I refused to look up. A second panic wave would dump me off the bike in an instant. Left, right. Left, right. Each stroke was one stroke closer to the top.

Pain turned seconds into minutes and minutes into days. I gasped for breath. My legs cried out to stop, drowning out everything in my life except left, right, left, right. Some day, things would change and I would go back to walking, talking, eating and sleeping. But at this moment, all I had was left, right, left, right.

When I had almost given up hope of returning to normal life, the gradient flattened out. No warning. I changed up a gear to stop my feet from spinning round too fast. I dared to look up. The peaceful vista of the reservoir and hills opened out on my left. I'd made it back.

I eased off down the flat and released the tension out of my legs with some gentle pedaling. I breathed in the serenity of my surroundings, laden with the heady scent of relief at weathering the worst that the hill could throw at me. I coasted to a halt next to David.

He swigged from his water bottle and offered me some. I drank three large gulps. We leaned on our handlebars in the July heat and looked out in silence across the reservoir to the amethyst haze on the farthest hills.

We turned to each other. A wide, infectious grin spread across David's face. I grinned back. We shared a high-five and a loud holler of congratulation. Far too demonstratively American for our reserved British upbringing, but so right for the moment. We had got the better of our toe clips. We had tackled the gradient and not been found wanting. We had taken the Jaguars out for a test drive and piloted them home without mishap.

From that moment on, we would dash home from work a couple of nights a week, load up our bikes and take off for the bike trails along Crystal Springs Reservoir or at Coyote Point on the San Francisco Bay. We reveled in our freedom to reach a destination without the encumbrance of a car. We craved the endorphin rush generated by muscles that had worked hard to take us there and back. We were addicted to our bikes.

The second weekend in August, we planned a couple of days' cycling along wine country back roads near Healdsburg, seventy-five miles north of San Francisco. We had only ridden Cañada Road when it was closed to vehicles on Bicycle Sunday. Our regular trails were limited to bikes and pedestrians. This trip would be our first encounter with cars.

The Healdsburg hotel car park was deserted at 8:30 a.m. that Saturday morning. We unloaded the bikes from the car and checked tire pressures. We each bolted down a bottle of organic orange juice and a blueberry muffin. Neither of us had the patience for a proper breakfast.

Our ride would begin with a left turn straight out of the hotel entrance onto Dry Creek Road, a four-lane highway that headed northwest out of Healdsburg towards the vineyards. I didn't trust myself to maneuver into the left-turn lane, stop at the lights, set off, deal with toe clips and steer left when there were a dozen cars in the way. I walked across at the pedestrian signal.

Once past the junction, I reminded myself that I had just used up my one free walking pass. Now I must tough it out with the traffic. I didn't have to grit my teeth for long. The volume of cars thinned out when the road narrowed to two lanes outside town. Yes, I could handle this amount of traffic.

Two miles later, we came across a decades-old general store complete with wooden sidewalk and hitching posts for horses. Inside, the deli counters were packed with cold cuts, salads, olives and desserts. Roasted vegetable sandwiches and Greek salad would make the perfect choice for lunch. We stored them in David's backpack.

We turned left off the highway onto the quiet serenity of

Lambert Bridge Road, a gateway to winding byways that led to nowhere urgent. Our bikes coasted over gentle switchbacks, passing legions of fruit-clad vines marching up each sun-baked hillside. Bursts of dark red roses stood sentinel by rows of zinfandel grapes. We breathed in rich grass and wildflower scents, intensified under fruit-ripening sunshine. Hazy vistas stretched to infinity. We reveled in a festival for the senses.

We reached Geyser Peak Winery smack on lunchtime. The cool, vine-shaded patio beckoned us in and invited us to unwrap our sandwiches next to the gurgling fountain. Two glasses of chilled Sauvignon Blanc followed us over to a corner table. We drank them. And then we drank the refills.

Our bikes waited patiently for us to return. They didn't complain that we had left them out to bake while the temperature edged up to 98° in the shade. But from the moment my knee recoiled when it brushed against the searing crossbar, I knew that I was about to pay my penance for spending two wine-mellowed hours on a shady patio.

Fourteen miles lay between us and our hotel. Fourteen sun-bleached miles, elongated by blistering heat into a crushing slog across the desert. We ground out each mile, powerless to cycle using anything more challenging than our lowest cogs on the middle ring. The oasis of the general store appeared through the haze, where we gulped down two pints of water each. We ran the gauntlet of tar-melting sunshine along Dry Creek Road, stopping to shelter in the shade of every straggly bush and half-grown tree for respite from the oppressive glare. My bright red face stung as I stared back into the frying pan of reflected heat off the pavement.

When we reached our hotel room, David and I peeled off our sweat-drenched clothes, tumbled into the bathtub and collapsed together in a confused tangle of sun-scorched limbs. The soft, cool rainfall of the shower soothed our fiery skin. At that moment, we resolved to enjoy lots of wine and lots of cycling, but never, ever again at the same time.

Oh, and I did complete the With and Without experiment. Just in case you're wondering, in order to avoid glowering red lines caused by sitting on knicker elastic, I strongly recommend Without.

"Needs YMCA"

Achievements so far in cycling, running and swimming: 15 miles, 1.8 miles and 1 mile

Achievements in stretching: bought book, put book on bookshelf

In all the three years I had been swimming at the YMCA, I had never once set foot inside the weight room. This had nothing to do with the fact that a roomful of contraptions more resembling instruments of torture than aids to fitness might be the tiniest bit intimidating. And absolutely nothing to do with a roomful of people who knew exactly how to use these contraptions and who could spot a newcomer a mile away. No. I just didn't need any additional weight work because swimming exercised all my muscles, thank you.

Now that I was a triathlete in training, I had to face reality. My body required a major overhaul. That meant revising my opinion of the weight room and doing some regular training to develop more strength. I also secretly hoped that weight work might make my body look more like that of an athlete instead of a woman who enjoyed strolling around in sports gear.

After six weeks of training, I already juggled a weekly schedule of a fifteen-mile bike ride, comprising two laps of Cañada Road on Bicycle Sunday, two morning runs of 1.8 miles each and two swims of one mile each. Somehow, I would have to squeeze a regular visit to the gym into my schedule. I started by booking two different sessions. First, a fitness test to provide a benchmark on my current strength, flexibility and cardiovascular capability. Then an hour with a trainer who would set me up with a weight program.

Karen, the Fitness Center Coordinator, administered my fitness test. I was expecting some lifting and jogging exercises. Instead, she first brought out a pair of calipers and used them to pinch together spare fat on my upper arms, thighs and stomach.

"This will give us a good index of how much body fat you currently have," she said, pinching away.

Karen was my height with short, dark hair and a taut, wiry body. Five feet seven inches of packed power. I surrendered to the calipers. She calculated the measurements.

"You have 22.3 percent of body fat," she announced. "So you're in good shape."

This was probably 22.2 percent more than Karen had. I wondered if I would ever achieve such a lean body.

We moved on to the cardiovascular test. I had to step up and down on a stair-height step while Karen timed me and monitored my heart rate. Heart rate would indicate how efficiently my heart pumped oxygen to my muscles, which in turn affected how much endurance I had. For the strength exercises, I completed as many sit-ups as I could manage in one minute, then lifted a bar above my head in time to a metronome. For the flexibility test, I sat on the floor with my legs outstretched and tried to touch my toes.

The six results categories ranged from *excellent* to the rather euphemistic *needs YMCA*. My cardiovascular and strength results came in right on the cusp of *above average* to *good*. Both results were much better than I had expected. Three years of swimming must have counted for something. My flexibility, however, was only one point above the very bottom of the scale in the *needs YMCA* category.

"Hmm," said Karen. "Do you do any stretching?"

"Well, I stretch after I run," I replied. I gave her my best angelic gaze in order to hide the awful truth. I stood up. "I do this stretch," I said, grabbing hold of my ankle and pulling it up behind me. "And I do this one too."

I rested my straight leg on a chair and leaned forward to touch my ankle.

"Stretching your quads and hamstrings is a good start," said Karen.

I trusted her description of whatever I had been doing. I was just copying what I had seen other runners do at Crystal Springs Reservoir.

"You might not think stretching does much for your running," she continued, with almost psychic perception. "But if you're not that flexible, you'll be a lot more prone to injury. You can easily pull and tear muscles if you push it too hard when your muscles are tight."

Karen had chosen not to ask if I did any other stretches. I suspected that was because she already knew the answer.

She reached into a drawer and pulled out a leaflet with stretching diagrams on it.

"Take this," she said. "Try these few basic stretches. And you might want to buy this book."

She scribbled the name "Bob Anderson" and the word "Stretching" on the leaflet. I promised her I would buy the book.

"And you should stretch every day," she said, saving the worst news until last. "If you stop stretching for a couple of weeks, your muscles will tighten up again and you'll be right back where you started."

My face fell. Great. Sentenced to boring, repetitive stretching for as long as I wanted to be an athlete.

"Thanks, Karen," I said. "I'll see what I can do."

I returned to the gym the next week for my appointment

with Shelley, the trainer. We went through some stretches in order to warm up. I didn't tell her I had bought a book on stretching. She would have gleaned from my puny efforts that I hadn't read it yet. Next, I pedaled for five minutes on a cardio bike to push my heart rate up. I couldn't understand what cardio had to do with strength work, but I did as I was told. Then we moved onto the assault course.

The exercise machines were towering, intricate structures of green seats, white metal bars, levers and pulleys, each one designed to work a different set of muscles. Each machine also had a computer screen attached. Shelley explained that if I logged on at each piece of equipment I used, the screen would flash up my pre-programmed settings, such as how much weight I should be lifting and various seat adjustments. The computer would also count the number of repetitions for me.

Shelley lined up exercises on eight machines—four for my upper body and four for my legs. We started with a machine called a leg press. I had to lie flat on a backrest with my legs hunched up in a squat position and my feet flat on a vertical plate. She adjusted the backrest so that I wouldn't be too close to the footplate and showed me where to adjust the weights. Then I pushed the plate away until my legs were straight, and returned to the squat position. I repeated the exercise for twelve repetitions, pushing fifty pounds of weight each time. Not that hard. But while I listened to the machine beeping every time I pushed the plate down and back, I couldn't help wondering how I would make all these weight and seat adjustments on my own. And there were seven more machines as complicated as this one.

We worked our way round machines with names like "lat pull," "chest press," "leg curl" and "seated row." Some needed a seat adjustment, some both seat and bars. The levers to make those adjustments were all hidden in the most awkward places.

If the machines were hi-tech enough to play a victory anthem when I reached my pre-programmed goal, surely they could spot a user in trouble and have a voice program call out, "The lever is behind the tall pillar six inches off the floor!" I dismissed that idea when I imagined the voice program prefacing its comments with "Hey, stupid!" I'd just have to learn where to find the levers on my own.

Once I had tried out each machine with Shelley, she watched me do a second circuit. Should I grab the handles in front or to the side for the seated row? Did the seat on the chest press need adjusting or not? And where would I find the half-plate for the leg curl? Did it even need a half-plate? When we finished, Shelley said she would write the whole program out for me and leave it in my folder in the exercise drawer under my new client number, which she would assign to me in the next day or so.

Whoa, so I now had a client number? And my client number was different from my logon number? She explained everything again. I was still baffled.

When we went round the conversation loop a third time, I knew that I was having a Common Language Moment. Remember that quote about England and America being two countries separated by a common language? It's true. But it isn't simply a matter of switching vocabulary, like ensuring my American friends avoid embarrassment by reminding them that "pants" in the UK refers to underwear only. The real problem occurs when the British and Americans use the same words without realizing that each side interprets them differently in the same conversation. Take my first visit to the supermarket in the US.

"Paper or plastic, ma'am?" the cashier said.

"Oh, I'll pay by cash," I replied, bagging my own shopping.

"Excuse me?"

"I said I'll pay by cash."

"Excuse me?"

"You do take cash, don't you?"

When Shelley repeated the exact same words in the gym, I knew we were in the middle of a Common Language Moment.

This wasn't Shelley's fault. She thought she was helping. My usual solution to repeating conversation loops was to find a way for us to back up and explain ourselves using different words, in order to reach a meaningful conclusion. Today, I'd been bombarded with so much information that I was too tired to get to the meaningful-conclusion part. I would take a breather and work it all out my next visit.

I returned to the gym two evenings later, refreshed and ready to conquer the weight program. My first setback was that today was Shelley's day off. Never mind. I went through the exercise drawer and found everyone's plan but my own. I would have to ask for help.

Karen, who had conducted my fitness test, was on duty in the gym today. She first had me log on to *FitLinxx*, the gym's computer that sent all those instructions to the weight machines about personal settings and the like. The screen had a box next to my name for notes from the YMCA to me. That was where Shelley had typed in my client number and the exact location of my exercise plan. We found the plan. I thanked Karen at least three times.

But when I read it, I found that the plan was only a paper version of the computer's list of personal settings. It said nothing about where to find the levers or how to use the equipment.

I refused to give up. Remember, triathletes push through adversity! I decided to start with the leg press. I was sure I could remember this one. Something about lying on my back, adjusting the backrest and leg-pressing fifty pounds twelve times. I found the weight and back rest adjustments, set them to the correct settings and positioned myself to do the exercise. Now all I had to do was log on to the computer so that it could count my repetitions.

I punched my logon number onto the touch-sensitive screen.

LOGON NOT RECOGNIZED.

Surely I couldn't have forgotten the number? I checked my exercise sheet. The number was correct. I tried again.

LOGON NOT RECOGNIZED.

Keep calm. There had to be an explanation. The room was filled with beeping noises of counted repetitions. So other people were logged on. The computer was working. I tried the logon one more time. Still not recognized. I tutted in exasperation. What did this computer expect? A formal introduction?

Seconds stretched out to epic proportions. I was supposed to be doing my leg-press exercise and instead I was just lying there without moving. My face flushed deep red. OK Jane. Breathe deeply. Either you can keep repeating an action that obviously isn't working, or you can ask for help again. Everyone already knows that you haven't a clue what you're doing, but you'll look even more stupid if you continue to lie here not doing the leg-press exercise.

I went back to Karen. She knew what to do. Was I logged on centrally to *FitLinxx*? No, I wasn't. She had logged me off, at my request because I didn't know any better, after we looked for the exercise sheet. No problem. I simply had to log on again at the main terminal so that the computer would know I was in the gym. Then it would recognize me when I used the machines.

I thanked Karen again for her help. I made my way back to the leg press, muttering that computers attached to exercise machines were a tiny bit of overkill in my humble opinion. But now someone else was using the leg press. Just when I'd geared myself up for a machine I knew how to operate, I would have to change tack.

I moved on to the leg curl. An instruction board positioned above the weights displayed a perplexing diagram that purported to show somebody demonstrating the exercise. I stood by the board, studying the diagram intently.

"Say, are you using the leg curl?"

A woman in navy running tights and red T-shirt stood at my elbow, her head tilted to one side.

"No, no, you go ahead," I said, stepping backwards out of her way and bumping into a guy who was waiting for the chest press machine next door. Apologies all round.

I stood next to the leg curl machine and made my best attempt to copy the guy's waiting-for-the-equipment pose—arms folded, left leg bent, faraway look. But I watched the leg curl woman out of the corner of my eye. I wanted to remind myself how to do the exercise.

Six o'clock. Peak time at the gym. I anchored myself to the instruction board at the leg curl machine while a sea of humanity swirled around me on the way to its next port of call. I would never cope on my own today. Karen floated past. I bobbed in her wake as she navigated to starboard by the treadmills.

"Karen, sorry to ask again, but any chance that you could go through the set-up routine with me? I'm having problems remembering what to do."

"No problem," she said with a smile. "But I'm booked to do an orientation in five minutes. How about Friday?"

We agreed on a time. I accepted with thanks.

A man wearing a brown leather weightlifting belt strutted past with his hands on his hips, his neck and shoulder muscles bulging out from under his Oakland Raiders jersey, his chalky fingers leaving fingerprints on his black shorts. He cast a brief sideways glance in my direction. My panic meter tipped into the red zone. I couldn't bear all these people judging how useless I was. Especially not Strutting Weight Belt Guy.

I had had enough. I took a deep breath and opted for a nonchalant stroll to the exit. Think body language, Jane! Think "I've remembered I have other plans for today" thoughts and whatever you do, don't bolt.

As soon as I left the gym, I tore off to the locker rooms. I changed into my swimsuit and slipped into the pool. I had swum up and down this pool so many times that my muscles knew what to do without me having to tell them.

Reassuring ripples of water soothed my skin. Water doesn't tell me that my logon is not recognized. It doesn't strut. It doesn't have an attitude. It just accepts me as I am, envelops me in silence and cushions my body as I glide forward.

Once the anger had seeped out of me, my mind had room to work out what had just happened. I usually expect to nail a task after a couple of attempts. This time I hadn't. Anger was my reaction to stepping outside my comfort zone and ending up out of my depth.

I was physically capable of lifting weights at the levels Shelley set for me, once I learned how to set up the machines. But this weight program was less about a physical limit than a mental limit. I wasn't fluent in the language of movement. In everyday life, I sit, stand and walk. I perform actions I've learned and repeated thousands of times, like brushing my teeth or driving a car. I'm not used to giving unfamiliar commands to my body to lift, hoist, push and pull strange objects round a weight room. And my spatial reasoning is weak, so I struggle to recognize patterns and shapes, like the layout of weight machines. This was unfamiliar territory that I didn't like one bit.

Learning to find my way round the weight machines was

going to take me longer than I had anticipated. I would have to ask for a lot more help than I usually do. But I reminded myself that asking for help did not signal weakness, only a desire to learn.

Long, repetitive strokes through cool water restored my perspective on life. I resolved to go back to the weight room and deal with the discomfort head on. But not right now. I'd faced up to my problem. My bruised ego had had enough for one day.

I went back two days later for my appointment with Karen, but I moved the time back from evening to early afternoon. The gym users on my last visit probably weren't making judgment calls about my lack of knowledge. They were just busy people who wanted to get through their program and go home for supper. But I could take my time in a quiet gym. With Karen's gentle reminders and tips, I drummed the sequence of maneuvers into my head. By the end of the one-hour appointment, I could complete a circuit on my own and only had to ask two questions. Karen had given me confidence to go back and practice.

On my sixth visit, I steeled myself to go at rush hour. I toughed it out, finished the whole session and strolled back to the locker room. I had nudged my personal boundaries back a little further. I slipped into the pool. This time, my sense of accomplishment fueled some of the fastest lap times I'd ever recorded.

Gail Force

Number of cars encountered on my bike before I met Gail: 7

Number of cars encountered on my bike during
one hour with Gail: 7 million (or thereabouts)

I remember the exact moment that Gail DeCamp announced her presence in my life. I was dashing across the San Jose Central YMCA car park straight after work one hot, sunny Wednesday evening, cursing under my breath that I was late for my appointment with the trainer. I juggled my bag of training gear and a bottle of water in my left hand as I fought to stop my purse strap from slipping off my shoulder with my right. We reached the entrance at the same time.

"Hi," she said. "Looks like you enjoy working out."

She held the door open for me. She was about my height, dressed in black cycling shorts with a pale yellow, sleeveless top.

"Hey, why don't you try my spin class? It starts in twenty minutes."

She smiled in encouragement and fixed me with a direct gaze. Her build was slight, but was composed entirely of toned muscle. I like bold people, especially those who can segue from introduction to invitation in five seconds.

"Today's a bad day for me," I replied, stating the obvious. "The weight room guy is about to set up my exercise program on the *FitLinxx* computer."

We walked together towards the locker rooms and introduced ourselves. I told Gail that I had only been cycling for three weeks and wanted to do a triathlon next year. She told me she had been competing in triathlons for seven years and had worked as a personal trainer for three. She gave me her mobile number, the times of her classes, the email of a guy who ran cycling courses and some tips on managing traffic. All within ninety seconds.

"Is your class suitable for beginners?" I asked.

"Sure," she said, with another encouraging smile and fix of the brown eyes. "Come a few minutes early next week and I'll go over your bike set-up and the basics with you."

I had to see this woman in action.

I had first heard of spin classes when Karen, the San Mateo YMCA Fitness Center Coordinator, had mentioned that spinning was a good way to build up leg strength. A spin class was indoor cycling exercises on stationary bikes that closely resembled road bikes. Each exercise was accompanied by music to stave off the boredom of pedaling to nowhere. The bikes had resistance meters attached to the front wheel that you could adjust to mimic churning up a tough hill or spinning along on the flat. I could "dial in" a much steeper hill than I might find out on the road, with no fear that I might fall off if the gradient became too steep.

I had already been to one spin class at the San Mateo Y. First, I had to rely on a classmate to help me set up the bike. Once the music started, I was on my own.

"Intervals!" the instructor shouted.

"Get ready for jumps!"

I tried to copy what the others were doing, but I didn't have a clue. The one thing I did learn was that spinning was about keeping the wheels turning at a fast, even pace. While everyone else did intervals, whatever they were, I'd practice spinning, which was new enough for me. I didn't even recognize most of the music that we exercised to, except for *Message in a Bottle* by The Police. When they got to the line about "sending out an SOS," I wondered if I should sing along. That way, maybe someone might get my message.

I set aside my squirming recollections of jumps and intervals as I walked towards the spin class studio the next week. I focused instead on Gail's parting comments that she would show me the ropes before the rest of the class arrived. It was bad enough being the new kid on the block without being excluded by not knowing what to do.

"Hey Jane! Good to see you."

We were off to a good start. Gail had remembered my name.

She showed me how to adjust the spin bike seat so that my legs were slightly bent at the bottom of the pedal stroke. That way, I would transfer most power to the pedal stroke without injuring myself. We adjusted the saddle and handlebars so that I was not leaning too far forward. She explained the resistance meter and told me what kind of exercises to expect in the class. Seated spins with low resistance to practice sprinting to the line. Climbs standing on the pedals with high resistance to strengthen hill-climbing muscles. Jumps, a mixture of four pedal strokes seated and four standing.

"Anyone else here today who is new to spinning?" Gail asked as she looked around.

I was the only newbie that day.

"Jane, just attempt those exercises you're comfortable with," she said. "Forget the rest until you get the hang of it. And you might want to leave out the jumps. They can be brutal for a beginner. OK?"

I nodded and forced a wan smile.

Behind me, the room had filled up with a dozen classmates during my orientation. I had positioned myself right at the front of the class, so my only connection with them was the whirr of front wheels. I stared forward and watched Gail. She put on today's music and asked us all to warm up with a five-minute gentle spin. Then on with the first exercise.

"So that's a four-minute standing climb for everyone except Jane. Jane, crank up the resistance meter as though you're climbing a hill, but do it seated. After two minutes, spin it out."

I did as I was told. Passed on the jumps. Survived the class. Even enjoyed the odd music track. I would be back for more.

Within a couple of weeks I was doing some of the more challenging exercises, including jumps, although each time I would curse Rogue Code for insisting that I develop enough leg strength to cycle up Everest. I got to know Gail's favorite music and the types of exercise she had planned for certain tracks. Outside the class, the sound of Queen's *Another One Bites the Dust,* one of her favorite tracks, would immediately transport me back to that excruciating five-minute standing climb on the hardest hill I could manage. My quads would tremble in time to the music to remind me that they hadn't forgotten how much I punished them every Wednesday evening.

After each class, Gail and I spent a few minutes chatting about my training while we packed up our gear. She always offered a few words of encouragement. And after only four spin classes, I could already see results out on the road. I now tackled the final hill on Cañada Road without being reduced to that last gasp, all-or-nothing lunge for the top.

"Gail, would you give me some coaching on my bike out on the road?" I asked after the fifth class. "I'm not sure my trial-and-error method of dealing with twenty-seven gears is the best way forward."

What I didn't tell her was that if I spent all my time training alone, how would I know if I was training correctly?

"Sure," she replied. "How about next week?"

We met in the car park at the Rancho San Antonio County Park, just off the 280 Freeway near Mountain View. I had checked out the website map beforehand. The park was covered in a network of cycle paths. While we went through the pre-ride ritual of checking tire pressures, Gail talked about the route she had planned along the hectic, four-lane Foothill Expressway.

"So we're not riding on the cycle paths in the park?" I asked.

"No. This is just a convenient parking lot," she said, loading her bike pump back into her car. "What's the point when you have to dodge visitors and there's a speed limit of fifteen miles an hour?"

How could I have made such a silly mistake?

"Gail, I'm only used to riding on roads with a maximum of one car every five minutes," I said, trying to remain calm.

The Foothill Expressway, one of the Peninsula's main commuter thoroughfares, was on my map of Routes to Be Avoided at All Costs.

"And I don't do left turns," I said, the words speeding up out of control. "I can't even look over my shoulder. When I want to turn left, I get off my bike and walk." My voice rose a notch. "I just don't want to end up as automotive sandwich filling, that's all."

Gail put her hand on my shoulder.

"Hey, I hear you! It's OK. We all go through our first traffic moment."

My teeth ground together and my jaw tightened at the thought of my impending Foothill Expressway encounter.

"Here's what we'll do. When we turn left on the Expressway, stick tight on my wheel, and I'll look out for both of us. And I'll teach you how to switch lanes safely when there's a pause in traffic, OK?" I nodded. "And remember, it's not in my interest to kill my client. I want you to come back for more coaching. You can't do that if you're dead."

I laughed. She laughed. I was going to be OK.

We approached the junction. My first challenge was to move from the curbside across one lane to the left-turn lane. Gail looked behind. I didn't dare look. She could look for both of us. She held out her arm to signal left. I watched her back wheel. She moved across the lane. I followed, lashed to her slipstream by an invisible safety cord. I heard a car. Seconds later, a silver Jetta slipped by us on my right. All three of us came to a halt by the red light. A black Camry pulled alongside on my left.

I had to trust Gail. She said she would get me though this alive. But car drivers were encased in protective, fourteen-foot boxes of glass and metal. My head was encased in a flimsy plastic bike helmet and the rest of my body in fresh air. Totally unprotected from the hurtling, 1.5-ton trajectories around me. It wouldn't take much. A wobble. A slip of the pedal. A tip of the bike. Then squish. Jetta 1, Jane 0. Do limbs squash flat like the old Tom and Jerry cartoons?

The lights turned green. Do or die.

Gail looked back to issue last-minute instructions.

"Stick tight on my wheel, Jane. You'll do fine."

I took a deep breath. I pushed off with my left foot in the toe clip. I didn't bother finding the right toe clip. I put my foot straight on the pedal and built up speed. The right toe clip scraped the ground every time I pedaled one full turn.

The junction was the size of a football stadium. The Jetta shot by my right elbow and turned right. A huge white SUV followed with an accompanying roar. The Camry brushed by inches from my left elbow and turned left. More engines revved behind me. Who knew how many more cars were waiting to splat me?

My right foot found the toe clip. I pedaled faster across the junction. Gail's bike swung left and straightened up alongside the curb. We reached the Foothill Expressway. I breathed out.

Gail and I rode side by side, with her on my left. Cars and trucks blasted past but she protected me in my own safe space. We rode in silence for several minutes. By the time we reached the third traffic light, my elbow joints had unlocked and my shoulders had released their tension.

"Don't worry," said Gail. "We'll build up your confidence with some basic skills. Once you know what to do in traffic, you'll be able to deal with it on your own."

The traffic had eased off. We were well past peak morning commute. First we practiced looking behind and crossing lanes to make left turns. I had learned to look behind over my right shoulder at the age of nine, when I did my Cycling Proficiency Test in the UK. Now that I was cycling on the "wrong" side of the road, I had to look over my left shoulder. I coped, but not without a precarious wobble each time. Once I had managed to spot a gap without veering into the line of traffic, crossing lanes was straightforward.

Next I learned how to stand up on the pedals when riding up a hill. I could deal with a standing climb on a spin bike. Whenever I had tried the same maneuver on Cañada Road, I had nearly fallen off. Gail showed me how to select the correct higher gear, then stand up and steady myself by pulling on the handlebars.

We moved on to pedaling technique.

"Pretend you're scraping mud off the sole of your shoe at the bottom of the pedal stroke," Gail said as she cycled alongside me. "That's the first stage in learning to use all of the pedal stroke and not just the down stroke."

Finally, I understood why toe clips were better than standard pedals. Without toe clips, I could only push down on the pedal from the twelve o'clock to six o'clock position. With toe clips, I could push down and pull partway up to the nine o'clock position. Pushing and pulling from twelve o'clock round to nine o'clock transmitted more energy to the bike.

I looked down at Gail's pedals. She didn't have toe clips. Her bike shoes had cleats underneath that clipped directly into a socket on the pedals. So her shoes were riveted onto the bike. She could transmit even more push/pull power through riveted shoes. A fleeting vision of the future flashed before my eyes. Toe clips were like training wheels. One day I would graduate to riveted shoes. I didn't dare contemplate the learning curve those would demand. I should enjoy the training-wheel phase while I still could.

Then we worked on gear selection. I would cycle faster by selecting a smaller gear and pedaling faster than by choosing a larger gear that required more effort and a slower cadence. This was what the essence of "spinning" was all about: choose a gear where I could turn the pedals over about ninety times a minute. She demonstrated a ninety r.p.m. spin and had me match her foot speed. Then she showed me how to work out ninety r.p.m. for myself using the clock on my speedometer.

Next, we worked on drinking from the water bottle when cycling. After all, I didn't want to stop, either in training or in a race, just to take a drink. First, I should practice just touching the bottle for a few moments and reach back to the handlebars. Then move on to pulling the bottle out of its cage and putting it straight back. If something happened urgently that I needed both hands for, I could throw the bottle aside and grab the handlebars. Better a safe rider and squashed bottle than the other way round.

I managed to touch the bottle briefly before reaching back for the handlebars. With practice I would be able to take out the bottle, drink and put it back. But not yet. I asked Gail to pull over so I could take a drink. I wasn't ready to experiment with squashed bottles or riders.

I had learned a lot in my first session with Gail. She had boosted my confidence. She had praised my determination in sticking with my training. She recognized my problems and frustrations and explained solutions in a way I could understand. As we coasted back to Rancho San Antonio car park, I knew I'd teamed up with the right coach for me.

I eased to a halt by our cars. I took my right foot out of the toe clip, ready to steady myself when I stopped. But instead of the bike tipping slightly to the right, it tipped to the left. My left foot was stuck in the toe clip. In an instant, I saw clear, unobstructed space open up between me and the ground. I knew what was about to happen. My mind recorded every thousandth of a second of my inevitable journey towards the tarmac. My bike, with me attached, hit the ground with a thud.

Gail turned round just as I assumed the horizontal.

"Ouch!" she said, her face screwing up in sympathy. "Are you hurt?"

She set about extricating me from my toe clips and bike. I was shaken up but otherwise uninjured, apart from a grazed knee. She could barely slip in a word edgeways as I explained over and over that this was the very first time I had ever fallen off my bike. She congratulated me on getting my first fall out of the way. She recounted her top two most embarrassing low-speed falls in front of friends. She opened up her first aid kit and helped me clean up the mild graze. Then she reset my bike chain, which had become dislodged from the chain ring in all the kerfuffle.

We said our goodbyes. Gail drove off. But the session wasn't over for me yet. Gail had asked me to bring my running shoes. From now on, every time I rode my bike, she wanted me to run for ten minutes. After spin class, I should run for ten minutes on the treadmill. Gail had warned me that running straight off the bike would be a lot tougher than my regular running, but it would prepare me for the bike-to-run transition.

My legs were always ready to stop after my usual morning run. But they had never so stubbornly refused to move as they did this morning. I goaded them into action with the threat of telling Gail that I had failed in my mission. I dragged them, step by step, along the pancake-flat path. I struggled on for seven whole minutes. I gave in to walking for forty seconds. Then I forced myself through the agony of kick-starting my lead-filled legs again. I nearly expired after the tenth minute. I hadn't given a moment's consideration to the bike-to-run transition before today. Gail was right. The transition was an element in itself for which I would have to train.

After my next spin class, I headed straight for the treadmills. I wanted to make a good impression on Gail. And as the spin bike room and treadmills were separated only by a sliding screen, I couldn't very well escape from under her nose and slope off.

I had never been on a treadmill before, so I asked the gym supervisor to show me the controls. Running on a treadmill was entirely different from road-running. My feet sank deep into the rubber belt on each step, as though I were running over a foam mattress. I thought I was going to fall over. But I soon adjusted to the spongy sensation and didn't notice it after a few minutes. I hit the emergency stop button with a flourish, right on the ten-minute mark. The belt stopped dead in its tracks, nearly catapulting me headfirst over the controls in front of me. I had forgotten about slowing the speed down to a walk before I stopped. No harm done though. And I'd run for ten whole minutes. I'd won the battle with the obstinate legs. I turned round with just the tiniest hint of swagger and stepped off the treadmill.

What the gym supervisor hadn't warned me about was that

in the ten minutes I had been on the treadmill, the entire floor of the gym had metamorphosed into the same huge foam mattress. Everyone else had been warned about this. They could all walk without problems. What's more, I could have sworn that I was standing still while the ground slid by underneath me. I glided along, each foot sinking deep into the surface.

My reflection in the floor-to-ceiling gym window mimicked me. I looked like an astronaut on the moon. Careful – steps – in – slow – motion. One quick movement would send me bouncing about five feet in the air. How could I avoid the embarrassment of showing all these people that I couldn't deal with the foam mattress? I concentrated on looking normal by putting one foot in front of the other as carefully as possible, checking my window reflection for signs of bouncing. I took the shortest route back to the ladies' locker room, by which time the floor had returned to earth.

The next week, Gail reviewed my weight program in the gym. First she checked out the exercises I had been given by the Y trainer. I had made good progress. I had overcome my initial confusion with the *FitLinxx* system in the gym. Now I had reached the point where I didn't like to work out without it. I was addicted to the beeps that each machine made when it counted my repetitions and the *diddle-ee-dee!* victory fanfare when I completed the exercise.

Every time I completed the required number of repetitions at the specified weight, the computer would flash up a message of congratulation on the tiny screen. Then it would ask if I wanted to increase the weight limit on my next visit. Every time I had hit "yes." I was now leg-pressing 160 pounds after starting at fifty pounds. That had to be a sign of improvement.

"If you go on like that, you'll end up with tree-trunk legs," Gail said. "Extra weight builds muscle and strength. Repetition builds endurance. You want some strength, but your objective is endurance."

Gail redesigned my program to cut back on weight and increase repetitions. She introduced me to a couple of extra exercises using free weights, the traditional dumbbells, bars and plates that I associated with weightlifting. Free weights required more control. They could be more dangerous for beginners like me, with weaker muscles and less control. But free weights toned more muscles because there was no machine to take the strain and limit the direction of the weights. Gail supervised me carefully to make sure that I was lifting correctly and choosing a weight within my limitations.

She also diagnosed that I had a number of muscle imbalances. I needed to strengthen my abdominals. I had strong shoulders but weak pectorals, the muscles across my chest that I would need for endurance swimming. I had strong quad muscles up the front of my thighs but weak hamstrings down the back of my thighs. From now on, I had to incorporate extra exercises into my program to balance up my muscle groups. Gail reminded me once more that this was doing me good. She would check in with me in a couple of weeks.

I spent most of each weight session imagining all the more enjoyable things I could be doing instead of trudging round the gym. But every time I was tempted to leave out a particular exercise or miss out the gym altogether, I reminded myself that I didn't want to end up with a lopsided body. I had to tone all the muscle groups I'd been told to work on. I also reminded myself that triathlon training was about addressing my weaknesses. And one of those weaknesses was losing interest if I didn't have the immediate fix of instant results. I would wean myself off the instant fix and persevere.

Another excuse to abandon the exercises was that I had to

venture into the lair of the Free Weight Kings. You could almost smell the testosterone in this grubby, windowless backroom lit by stark fluorescent lights. The Kings, all of them likely under thirty, dressed in a quasi-uniform comprising baggy shorts and basketball jerseys. They held fast to their belief that they ruled the free weight room between the weekday hours of six o'clock and eight o'clock. They treated this space as their exclusive domain, where they showed off to each other by heaving oversized weights around. They took particular pleasure in dropping the weights on the floor and yelling while they watched them bounce. And, of course, they strutted. Let's not forget the strutting.

I was usually the only woman there at that time in the evening. Several weeks ago, I would have fled. Now I refused to be intimidated. I had paid my membership. I was entitled to use this facility. Anyway, I wasn't in their way because I used equipment they considered too puny for their needs. We made an uneasy truce. They ignored me by giving me a wide berth in the baby weight corner. I ignored them and strutted my own stuff, thank you.

After ten weeks of training, everything was coming together. I had switched over entirely from breaststroke to freestyle for my one-mile swim. My gym program was shaping up. I loved the challenge of the spin classes. I cycled fifteen miles of Cañada Road from Highway 92 to the town of Woodside and back without a break, often adding a victory lap to Edgwood and back. But my running was stuck in a rut.

Five weeks earlier, I had finally run the 1.2-mile Triangle of Misery without stopping. After the euphoria had settled, I extended my route through the neighborhood to 1.8 miles. This new route had a short, sharp, shock of a hill just before the home stretch. The hill was no more than forty yards long, but it came after a gentle downhill and lurked without warning round a blind

corner. I compared running notes with David. We didn't run together because he ran farther than I did. Nor did I want him to
see what pitiful progress I was making. He instantly recognized
my description of the hill as the nasty little kicker at the end of
his own route. He had named it Hell Hill several months ago. The
name stuck.

I had persevered on my 1.8-mile loop, ever hopeful that I
would score a breakthrough and run this loop without stopping.
But each time the sudden, steep gradient of Hell Hill would beat
me down—my one and only stop on the 1.8-mile loop. I had
also expected that running would become easier after ten weeks
of practice. It didn't. The only bit that didn't hurt was the first
couple of minutes. But mentally that was just as bad. I was filled
with a sense of foreboding that things were about to get a whole
lot worse. For most of the remaining nineteen minutes, my inner
voice battled my body as the agony piled on. Aching legs. Rasp-
ing breathing. And the constant fight with an overwhelming urge
to walk.

There were occasional stretches, usually on gentle downhills, when running didn't feel quite so bad. My labored breathing
would ease a little and my creaking legs appreciated the rest from
churning their way uphill. But those were the most dangerous
times. If my concentration lapsed for just a few seconds, an alternate persona would nip past the defenses and hijack the communication channel to my legs. The next thing I knew, I would
find myself walking. How did that happen? How could I have
an alternate command center in my brain that told me to do the
complete opposite of what I was supposed to be doing?

On those gentle spells, my mind also spent a few moments
mulling over why I was training for the triathlon at all. I had
wrestled with this conundrum almost daily since my first training
run. I still didn't know why. Now and then I would even scream

in frustration, knowing that the answer lay somewhere deep inside. Yet it refused to rise to the surface. I was being driven forward with relentless certainty by something I wasn't in control of. At the same time Alternate Persona, the part most definitely not responsible for this decision, was doing its best to sabotage my plans. This internal duel became so exhausting that I resolved not to think about it and just train.

But ten weeks after I had started running, the bald truth was that I was stuck at 1.8 miles. If I couldn't run 6.2 miles, I couldn't do a triathlon. I didn't know what to do next, so I emailed Kevin Kennedy. I'd checked in with him several times since that lunch when I had interrogated him about triathlon. I had come to rely on his upbeat, supportive emails that were filled with common sense, experience and encouragement. Within ten minutes of my desperate plea, his reply popped up in my inbox.

> **Don't worry. Virtually every triathlete has their "nemesis" discipline. For you it's running. For me it's swimming. It takes so much more willpower to push myself into the pool than it does to go out for a run or ride. But in many ways it makes me even more motivated to conquer it. And it makes the successes in swimming more meaningful than those on the bike and run.**

So it was OK to find one discipline tougher than the rest. I might not progress as fast as I had hoped but at least I was "normal." I bounced straight back and planned to go running the next day, motivated to conquer. Unfortunately, my enthusiasm was in inverse proportion to my experience. And it was about to land me in a spot of bother.

Going Long

Last month's gripe: inability to run farther than 1.8 miles

This month's gripe: wondering how a water bottle could cause me grief

Determination is a great asset. It's the fuel that pushes me through barriers. Kevin's reassuring email about my running problems had topped up my fuel tanks and got me back on track. I resolved to persevere and take each milestone as it came. But I was also determined to prove that I could blast through the 1.8-mile barrier.

I took the day off work to run at Sawyer Camp Trail by Crystal Springs Reservoir, halfway down the San Francisco Peninsula. The morning was sunny, peaceful and tinged with that indulgent glow that comes from devoting time to myself when I would usually be working.

I'd never run at Crystal Springs before, although I had ridden my bike there several times. The trail was level until mile five. I reasoned that if my only stop on my 1.8-mile running route was at the beginning of Hell Hill, why not eliminate hills altogether and run without stopping on the flat?

At 9:30 in the morning, the summer temperature was still in the mid 60s. I looked down to the reservoir on my left, sitting above the sharp dip of the San Andreas Fault. The long, serene body of water curled out of sight round the hills, its surface reflecting clear morning sunshine and the wooded slopes on the other hillside. The reservoir exhaled a warm, gentle breeze that brushed over my skin. I soaked up the vista. How lucky I was to live in this part of the world.

I pulled on my new hat, picked up my water bottle and set off to run. I passed moms with toddlers in strollers and senior couples walking arm in arm. The paved road wound its way between the reservoir to my left and a steep hill to my right. I ran on the gravel path alongside the road, listening to the satisfying scrunch that each footfall made as it landed. My objective was to run three miles, a large but manageable step up from 1.8 miles. The path had route markers every half mile, so I would know exactly how far I had left to run. I didn't own a watch, so I carried a tiny travel alarm clock in the pocket of my running shorts, stuffed in alongside the car key. That way, I could check how many minutes I took to run one mile.

I passed the twenty-yard section of path where sandbags held back erosion from the hill. Then round a sweeping left-hand bend. On my regular running route, I recognized every house, road sign and turn in the road. I knew almost to the last step how far I had left to run. On this route, I had no idea how many more twists in the trail I would have to pass before I reached each half-mile marker. Running blind unsettled me.

Past the first half-mile marker. Another mile before I could turn round. But how much farther was the next marker? Five minutes? Eight minutes? The alarm clock was wedged too deep into my shorts pocket to fish it out while running. I needed to create my own half-mile tape measure. If I knew how many paces I took to run half a mile, then counting my paces would tell me how far I still had left to run.

If only I had thought of the counting idea before I passed the half-mile marker. Now I would have to wait until the one-mile marker to begin measuring. I cursed under my breath. Through a shady tunnel of trees. Right-hand bend. Where was that marker? Another bend. A small, rectangular, brown sign with the numerals "1.0." At last.

I passed the sign and started to count each pace. I wasn't running that fast, but the steps rolled by too quickly. I couldn't keep the numbers straight in my head. Instead, I switched to counting my breathing. Two steps in. Four steps out. One breath equaled six paces. I could manage that.

My legs had now been running non-stop for over a mile and were beginning to tire. I had no idea how many minutes I had been running. I could do with a break.

That moment of weakness was the signal for Alternate Persona to start up its insistent, stop-stop-stop chant in my head. I knew that voice. That was the voice that urged me to quit whenever the going cranked up one notch above easy. Alternate Persona was in charge of the easy life and the sworn enemy of Rogue Code.

I fought off Alternate Persona by convincing myself that counting was vital to the cause of world peace. The tape measure project was just a by-product. As I neared thirty-seven breaths, I heard running footsteps behind me. I didn't dare look round. The steps followed me but didn't pass. Great. How could I count for world peace AND shut out Alternate Persona AND wait for the dread moment when I would have to put on my how-much-I-love-running face when the runner overtook me? My counting wobbled under the strain.

Sixty-two breaths later, a woman with shoulder-length brown hair drew level with me. I fixed my game face. She overtook me thirty yards out from the 1.5-mile marker. Her T-shirt had a purple and green Team In Training logo on the back. My legs clamored to stop. But I was too proud to let her see me walking. I ran off the scrunchy gravel and onto quiet pavement. She was only five yards ahead of me but she wouldn't hear my footfalls. I slowed down to a walk the moment I passed the marker.

Now that I had saved civilization and seen off the other runner, I returned to my tape-measure project. The half mile had taken 117 breaths. I unscrewed the cap on my water bottle and gulped down a third of it. I walked round in circles, not daring to cross the invisible line by the 1.5-mile marker at the start of the route back. After two minutes, I put the cap back on the water bottle and steeled myself to run back down the path. I had 117 breaths to get through before I reached my next marker.

But the dread of setting off again held me back behind the invisible line. I weighed up which was worse: the agony before I stopped running, when my screeching body revolted against taking another single step, or the agony when I started up again. That was when my legs remembered the hell I'd just put them through and took revenge by ratcheting up the aching to double strength. Every time I restarted, I had to go through this spell of double-dose aching before it receded to mere miserable aching. I was so fearful of what was about to happen that I dragged out the calm, gentle respite of walking until it was almost impossible to run again.

I paced round in circles. Three miles was less than half the distance I would have to run in the triathlon. Today's run was a small stepping stone. The moment I crossed the starting line by the 1.5-mile marker, I must lock myself into running. I pushed myself over the edge and headed for home.

My legs crescendoed in complaint until they screamed at full volume. I knew the drill. Legs ached, breathing hurt. Then Alternate Persona would start up. You have to stop. It hurts. Stop the hurting. Stop the running. Stop hurting stop running stop hurting stop running why are you doing this to me release me from this right now stop stop stop stop STOP NOW. The real misery came from fighting back, from refusing to obey the stop commands, from blotting out the deafening megaphone of Alternate Persona who had other plans for me. And I wasn't even at the next half-mile marker.

A tiny thread of reason wrapped itself around my thoughts. I couldn't be in that bad a shape physically if the agony in my legs eased off within a couple of minutes of walking. I just had to toughen up my willpower to push me through the grim times. But telling myself to toughen up didn't help when one minute I was running and the next I was plunged into a mental abyss with no route out. I had two options; I could drag myself forward to the next marker or I could surrender gracefully to the seductive calm of walking.

How could I find willpower in the depth of the abyss? I always thought willpower was about turning down that second portion of chocolate cheesecake. But that wasn't in the same willpower league as pushing on with something I didn't want to spend another second of my life on, ever again. And I simply didn't have enough of the stronger kind to fight back. I passed the half-mile marker. Not even halfway home yet. The lead weight of another 117 breaths hung round my shoulders. You can't do this you can't you can't stop stop stop right NOW.

Amidst the megaphone ranting of Alternate Persona, I sensed more than heard a weak voice pleading with me to hang on, to gather up the few remaining threads of determination and knot them into a lifeline. This voice reached out to me from somewhere deep inside, from that unreachable part that had made this triathlon decision without consulting me. Maybe this voice knew why I was doing this. Maybe this voice was Rogue Code.

My only link with the voice was my running. I had to keep running. I wanted to connect, understand, communicate. If I offered an olive branch of continuous running, could I open a dialogue so that it could tell me exactly why it was making me do this? It might not tell me today, but I had nothing except this tenuous link under extreme stress to connect me with my unknown self. With my elusive Rogue Code.

Keep counting. Don't think. Just count. I passed the second half-mile marker. One final lot of 117 breaths would get me home. Blot out Alternate Persona with numbers. 46. 47. Willpower equals numbers. Nurture my willpower. 84. 85. Fight the urge to stop, ignore the pain.

112. 113. I rounded the bend. I saw the post that marked the start of the trail. A rush of adrenaline took over and blasted me down that final stretch, past imaginary crowds lining the route. I waved my arms in the air as the tape broke across my chest. A couple nearby smiled and called out, "Well done!"

I dug my alarm clock out of my shorts pocket. My run had taken forty-one minutes, including the walking. My breathing slowed down to normal. I drank some more water. I took an inventory of my body. The tide of agony was already receding. Did I imagine the pain? Or was the run really that tough? And what about that faint voice urging me to keep going? Was that part of my imagination too?

I went through some cooldown stretches for my quads and hamstrings, then sat in the shade. An in-line skater in her twenties strapped up her kneepads. Two moms pushed strollers, one supervising a three-year-old girl on her pink bike with tassels streaming from the ends of the handlebars. A group of four smiling Asian women seniors wearing large-brimmed hats chattered away in a foreign language, the tone of their voices and their body language indicating that they were long-time friends.

Eight minutes after stopping, my body had rebooted its regular energy settings. No more pain. I leaped to my feet. Surely I had more running left in me? Why stop at three miles?

I picked up my half-full water bottle and set off again down the path. I would battle through one more mile. I ran slowly, counting my breathing from the get-go so I knew how far I had to go. This was a bonus mile. I gave myself permission to stop if I got too tired.

I was still chugging along near the half-mile marker when the Team In Training Girl rounded the corner and ran towards me.

"Hi there," I called out as she drew level. "Can you wait for me at the end?"

"Sure! No problem."

She waved as she passed me. I turned round and followed her about fifty feet behind. After nineteen breaths, Alternate Persona clamored for attention. I hadn't imagined the whole counting lifeline first time round. I needed it now. I clung to the numbers to pull me home. I was also pulled along by the potential embarrassment of finishing a long way behind Team In Training Girl after I had asked her to wait.

When I reached the end, I introduced myself. Her name was Elizabeth. We did some cooldown stretches together. She told me she was training for her first triathlon at Pacific Grove, near Monterey, in September. This morning, she had just completed her six-mile run.

"Running is the absolute worst for me because I'm one of the slowest runners in the group," she said. Excitement radiated from her smile. "Everyone always overtakes me. But today, I got to overtake you. I knew one day I'd find someone slower than me!"

I was thrilled for her, even as I tried hard not to think about the dubious honor of being overtaken by one of the slowest runners.

I asked her about the Team In Training program. It was run

by the Leukemia and Lymphoma Society. In return for raising sponsorship, the program provided all the coaching, training sessions and race planning needed to complete a triathlon, marathon, long-distance bike ride or other endurance race. Elizabeth was attached to a group in Palo Alto with roughly a hundred members. The program had a lot of weekend workouts and several hard sessions during the week. Although she had missed a few workouts, she felt ready for the triathlon. She had made lots of friends and couldn't wait to take part in the event. I thanked her and wished her luck. We said our goodbyes.

On my drive home, I thought hard about the Team In Training program. I was attracted by the huge amount of support their coaches could provide to help me build up skills in all disciplines. I would meet people just like me—people with no prior athletic experience who wanted to take a step outside themselves. I wasn't put off by the sponsorship. I worked in sales and was sure I could raise funds if I put my mind to it, especially as that money went to an excellent cause.

But I've never been one for team colors and team decisions. A group of one hundred seemed overwhelming. The triathlon was also my personal odyssey. I didn't want to follow someone else's structured plan to get me there, even though that training plan might be far superior to my own. No matter how much I would benefit from Team In Training's goodies of coaching and of meeting athletes at my level, I couldn't overcome my irrational aversion to "joining," to submitting my personal will to a large group. I would have to pass.

The next day, my whole body ached. I expected my legs to protest after running twice as far as I had ever run before. I hadn't expected my left upper arm to hurt. It throbbed so much that I took some ibuprofen to calm the pain. How had I hurt my arm by running? After a couple of days my arm stopped hurting quite so much, but now my shoulder ached. Or maybe my shoulder had ached all along and I hadn't noticed because I was preoccupied with my arm. Whatever. I was still puzzled by the problem.

I tried to train as normal the following week, but my body was shot to pieces. My legs were still exhausted. I ended up stopping three or four times on my usual 1.8-mile route. I held off my upper body exercises in my weight program, just in case they weren't good for my shoulder. I could swim freestyle without pain but breaststroke hurt. Leaning forward on the handlebars for forty-five minutes in Gail's spin class aggravated my shoulder. The pain didn't improve. Two weeks later, after spin class, I told Gail about my problem.

Gail rotated my arm and shoulder and asked me some questions. She thought the pain stemmed from the rotator cuff, the joint where the round socket of the arm joins the flat plate of the shoulder. The Physical Training Director at the San Mateo Y had also diagnosed the rotator cuff after she saw me wince when I tried an upper body exercise.

Gail recommended I go for physical therapy if the shoulder didn't improve soon. In the meantime, she showed me how I should lie on my side and lift a one-pound weight with a straight arm in different directions. These exercises would strengthen the muscles all round the rotator cuff. I could use a one-pound jar of jam rather than buy a tiny weight I probably wouldn't use again. And I could do the exercises in front of the telly every night to stave off boredom.

On subsequent visits to Crystal Springs, I noticed that other runners ran with a water bottle strapped to a belt. Or they left a water bottle under the bench at the park entrance and retrieved it at the end of their run. They didn't do what I had done, which was to run for fifty-one minutes, my sweaty hand gripping my water bottle tightly the whole way to stop it slipping. Only then did I realize the cause of my shoulder injury. I must have tensed my left arm and shoulder all the time I was running, carrying the equivalent of a one-pound weight for most of the way. I had been so locked onto breaking my 1.8-mile barrier that I had never noticed other runners' water strategies.

The water bottle episode taught me a sobering lesson. Determination can override common sense. Injuries can happen easily and thoughtlessly. From now on, I would have to learn to exercise with more care. Next time, I may not get away with a rookie mistake so easily. I may land myself in serious bother.

Worth Consideration

Number of endurance sports workshops I attended this month: 1

Number of endurance event websites I discovered and then wished I hadn't: 1

By the end of August, my one-mile swim time was down to thirty-eight minutes. I could cycle fifteen miles on the flat and run nearly two miles without stopping. I hadn't tried stringing them all together yet, but I was making progress towards the one-mile swim, twenty-five-mile bike ride and 6.2-mile run of the Olympic-distance triathlon. I also lifted weights and went to spin class. I let it drop in conversation wherever I could that I was on my way to or had just returned from a training session of swimming, cycling or running to prepare for my triathlon. "Wow, a triathlon? That's awesome!" Maybe people were genuinely amazed. Or maybe they were just astonished that someone who didn't look the slightest bit like an athlete thought she could pull this off.

Their reaction fed my ego. And I began to believe my own publicity. I was going to do a triathlon. Every time I ran, I pictured myself powering towards that finish line. When I rode my bike, I saw myself cycling out of Lake Almaden Park entrance at the start of the bike route at the San Jose Tri. When I swam, I imagined working my way past the bright orange buoys marking the quarter, the half, the three-quarter points in Lake Almaden. Then one day, when I climbed out of the pool, the thought crossed my mind that if I really had just swum one mile in a lake, I'd be getting on my bike and cycling twenty-five miles right now. I looked down at my swimsuit and the water puddle forming round my feet. So how exactly would I get there from here? Dry off? Get changed? All in front of fifteen hundred other competitors and spectators?

That was my moment of conscious incompetence. The moment when I moved from unconscious incompetence—bumbling through my training, thinking I was making lots of progress—to knowing all too well that I was bumbling along without the slightest idea if I was training correctly. I had to find out what I didn't know.

I went online and googled "triathlon training." The top search result was www.active.com, a site listing hundreds of races in every discipline possible. The website also featured a twenty-one-week training plan to take complete novices like me from the barely walking stage to finishing a race.

The first couple of weeks in the training plan required me to run four or five times for twenty minutes at a time. I could do that already. Week three added in two swims of three hundred to one thousand yards. I could do that already too. I read through the entire five-month program. The training was manageable and well-structured. I still had almost ten months to go before the San Jose Tri next June, so it was too soon to start a five-month program now. I would return to the training plan early next year and complete the remaining four months in the run-up to the Tri. But the twenty-one-week structure had reassured me that I was on the right track.

I continued to browse. Next, I came across a workshop at Sports Basement, a retail store in San Francisco.

Curious about triathlon? Seasoned coach and sports psychologist Michelle Cleere introduces you to the basics of triathlon, from training and nutrition fundamentals to tips for making a quick transition between the swim, bike and run legs of a race.

This workshop would explain how to change from wet swimsuit to dry cycling shorts with a degree of modesty. I signed up on the spot.

The following Sunday morning, I joined thirty-two other triathlon hopefuls in the middle of Sports Basement's triathlon gear section. A more-or-less even split between men and women, most of them in their twenties and thirties. All of them looked a lot more athletic than I did. Maybe I was sub-beginner level. Never mind. We all had to start somewhere. The Hopefuls gathered in a semicircle round a bike with a wetsuit draped over it. Several pieces of clothing were scattered over the floor.

Michelle Cleere took the stage. She had bright blonde, close-cropped hair and a firm, strong face. She sported the finely tuned body of a superior athlete. Just like Gail. Just like Karen at the Y. That level of fine-tuning spelled hours and hours of training. I wondered yet again if I would ever reach that level of fitness.

Michelle began with her Training Gear Check List. The list was divided up into "musts" and "worth consideration." Even the "musts" column listed a staggering twenty-nine items. I concluded that triathletes must be gearheads.

The most obvious "must" was a triathlon wetsuit. On the warmest days, the water temperature in San Francisco Bay doesn't get much above 65°—and can fall as low as 50°F in the winter—so a wetsuit was essential. In contrast to a surfer's wetsuit, which had elbow and kneepads to protect against knocks, the surface of a triathlon wetsuit was smooth and built for speed.

A tentative hand raised itself above the heads in the audience. Michelle paused. A tall, thin girl with long dark hair was slouched back in her seat, as though she were trying to hide. Her brow furrowed in apprehension.

"Can you explain how you get from the wetsuit to the bike?" she asked. "I mean, is the transition area full of naked people?"

Thank goodness she had been brave enough to ask.

"Good question," said Michelle and nodded in reassurance. "I want to make sure we get all the questions answered that you were afraid to ask."

I shot a glance of sisterhood towards the girl who had asked the question.

"There's no nudity allowed at a triathlon," Michelle continued. "So you wear a triathlon suit underneath your wetsuit. Or you can choose a tri swimsuit instead, which has extra padding round the seat. But let's just say I always found that the padding never stayed between me and the saddle for the whole twenty-five miles."

The disappearing swimsuit sounded most uncomfortable, so I opted straight away for the triathlon suit. This consisted of shorts that have just enough padding in the seat to spend an hour and a half on the bike without too much discomfort, plus a top and sports bra. All three pieces were made of very fast-drying material because they would get soaked underneath the wetsuit. The price of modesty would be to cycle in wet clothes. They should dry off by the time I finished the bike leg and started running. But just in case they didn't, I made a mental note never to compete anywhere with a wind chill factor less than 70°.

Another hand shot up, this time from a tanned thirtysomething guy in a black T-shirt.

"So what if you, er, need to pee in the middle of a race?"

Another vital question. Michelle cleared her throat.

"If you gotta go, you gotta go," she said. "It's up to you, but if you've already got your wetsuit on, it just means you have an extra layer of warmer water inside your wetsuit. If you're on the bike, then multi-task and keep pedaling. Your legs will soon dry off. And I've never, ever needed to go on the run. Your kidneys have stopped working by then."

I rather hoped my kidneys would stop working earlier than that. I've never been the outdoorsy type.

Michelle moved on with the gear requirements. The "musts" list continued with sunscreen, two pairs of goggles (in case the first pair broke as you were lining up for a race), a swimcap plus a "hothead," a swimcap made of thick neoprene to combat the icy Bay water. Then bike paraphernalia of shorts, jerseys, helmet, gloves, water bottles, bike shoes, tire repair kit and more besides. Running gear included shoes, shorts, tops and a hat, an essential item to avoid sunstroke. Apart from the tri suit, most of the gear would be used for training, rather than competing. I began to understand why this workshop was taking place inside a sporting goods store.

The "worth consideration" list contained some interesting items. The bike that Michelle had brought along for the demonstration had aero bars, two horizontal bars attached to the handlebars pointing directly forwards. Experienced cyclists crouched lower on the bike frame and leaned on these aero bars with their forearms to achieve a more aerodynamic shape. The paint on parked cars was still under threat if I dared to reach down even to my drop handlebars. I doubted that aero bars would make it onto my "worth consideration" list for a long time.

Next were EZ laces, springy pieces of elastic that when threaded through your running shoes would allow you to slip your feet straight into your shoes without losing precious seconds tying laces. The number of seconds I would lose on the swim, bike and run through lack of training or experience would dwarf the seconds I lost in tying laces, so there didn't seem much point in buying any. And I certainly didn't need to go hi-tech and measure my heart rate with a heart rate monitor. My heart already knew that it was pumping itself inside out when I ran.

Michelle continued with a gold mine of tips, tricks and insider info about competing. I should lay a bright towel beside my bike to help me identify my transition spot amidst hundreds of other bikes. I should smear *Bodyglide* lubricant round my neck, wrists and ankles to stop the wetsuit chafing. I could spray cooking oil on the outside of the suit to help it slide off more easily. But I should never spray oil on the inside or else the California sunshine would fry the layer of oil left on my skin when I cycled.

Then came tips on preparing for race day. Plan ahead. Prepare all my gear the night before. Eat high carb/low fat/low protein foods before the race. Drink plenty of water to top up on hydration. Stay off my feet as much as possible. Familiarize myself with the race course.

Michelle finished with a fascinating insight into the mental side of training, her specialty as a sports psychologist. I should train my mind as well as my body. My mind would surprise me by pushing me on more than I expected. If I believed I couldn't do it, I wouldn't. If I told myself I could, positive self-talk would improve my performance. She made a lot of sense. I vowed from now on to practice lots of positive self-talk.

After the seminar, I began my own odyssey towards gear-head-dom. Reflective swim goggles (two pairs), another swimsuit (without padding), cool sports sunglasses, three tops, two sports bras, two pairs of running shorts, another pair of cycling shorts, countless pairs of socks and a hat. I wasn't ready to buy the triathlon suit or wetsuit just yet, but I'd be back to Sports Basement when I was.

Over the next week, I was consumed with soaking up as much knowledge as I could on endurance sports. First, I read *To The Edge: A Man, Death Valley and the Mystery of Endurance,* Kirk Johnson's story about running the Badwater Ultramarathon, a 135-mile race from the lowest to the highest point in Death Valley in the height of summer. I identified with Kirk not knowing why he found himself gripped by such a grueling physical challenge. I marveled how he found the answer in the depths of himself at the end. I hoped that Rogue Code would let me know what this was all about well before it forced me to Death Valley. Alternate Persona would surely stage a revolt if things ever headed that way, even though it had failed to block the triathlon first time around.

Next I struggled through Dean Ottati's *The Runner and the Path.* Running put Dean in touch with his inner self. It gave him a channel to explore life, the universe and everything. How did he glide along effortlessly for mile after mile? Never once during my painful, begrudging battle with running had I even remotely enjoyed it, let alone found myself transported to running nirvana. I envied Dean. I wanted to glide along in touch with my inner self too. I concluded that I detested running so much that it would never happen for me.

Then I picked up Paula Newby-Fraser's *Peak Fitness for Women.* I learned that the training plan itself was an art form. I had to train smarter and give myself a structure. I should build up my strength and endurance in a Base Training Phase. Next, add in some faster workouts to increase my speed and prepare myself to race. I followed Paula's advice, planned a mix of easy and hard workouts and started a training log.

But I was still confused. The blurb described Paula as "the greatest women's Ironman champion." Kevin Kennedy had also talked about taking part in Ironman Germany. I thought "Ironman" was Germany's way of describing a zealously tough triathlon course. Not so. Paula described an Ironman race as a 2.4-mile swim, 112-mile bike ride and 26.2-mile marathon—a race lasting four times longer than the standard "Olympic" distance of one-mile swim, twenty-five-mile bike ride and 6.2-mile run that I would be racing at San Jose. The Ironman race was in a class of its own. This was endurance beyond my worst nightmare. I couldn't begin to grasp how many months and years it would take to train to that level. I appreciated Kevin's achievements in a whole new light.

I now had a training plan from Paula's book and confirmation from the twenty-one-week website program that I was on the right track for San Jose in ten months' time. But right now, plenty of time was a problem rather than an advantage. I was stranded in a no-man's-land that would play to my weaknesses. The San Jose Tri was too far off in the future to motivate me. Yet I couldn't stop training because I had so much ground to cover.

A couple of days later, Rogue Code took control of the situation. The trigger was the active.com newsletter that appeared in my inbox. I enjoyed my weekly browse through newsletter topics I had absolutely no use for, such as "Marathon Tapering: Why Less is More." Then, in mid-browse, before I had a chance to argue, Rogue Code navigated me to the current events section. I found myself clicking on a one-mile open water swim in four weeks' time, at the end of September.

The tantalizing prospect of testing myself over one mile in open water seeped up through my fingertips. Why not go for it? I was already swimming one mile on every visit to the pool, so I could manage the distance. I had to swim in open water at some point. The event was close by, at the Sacramento River Delta near Antioch, in the East Bay.

More temptation lurked on the next page. The same organizers also listed another event called the Salmon Duathlon, a three-stage combination of three-mile run, nineteen-mile bike ride and a final 1.5-mile run. The duathlon was to take place at a tiny blip on the map called Knights Ferry, about ten miles east of Oakdale along Route 120, on the way to Yosemite. The course description read,

> . . . two loops round the old Knights Ferry
> Duathlon course over the famous covered
> bridge . . . the bike is a paved out-and-back
> over rolling hills.

The race was scheduled for the first weekend in November. Why not go for that one too? I had nine weeks to build up my running from 1.8 miles to 4.5 miles. Even if I could run only the first three-mile stage and have to walk most of the final, 1.5-mile run, I'd get round. And I was cycling fifteen miles already. I had only to step up another four miles and build up some extra strength for the hills. This race would be a good measure of the progress I was making. It was stretch, but it was certainly worth a shot.

My stomach churned and my palms sweated as I filled in my details on the screen. I ignored Alternate Persona that questioned how I could compete in two races after only three months of haphazard training. I went back and forward between the credit card page and event descriptions, just to make sure one more time that I was signing up for the one-mile and not the two-mile swim. I triple-checked that the distances for the duathlon had not metamorphosed from three miles, nineteen miles and 1.5 miles into something impossible when I wasn't looking.

I couldn't put it off any longer. I hit *send*. The confirmation screen came up. A tremor of excitement rippled through me. I had enrolled in my first events.

Making Friends with My Wetsuit

Number of wetsuits I currently own: 0

Number of times I had swum in open water, with or without a wetsuit: 0

I am impulsive, visionary and creative. These are all euphemisms for coming up with great ideas and leaving the planning to others. That usually falls to my husband, who is thoughtful, analytical and practical. Our contrasting skill sets make for a happy marriage because we play to our strengths. Or in less kind moments, contrasting skill sets is another euphemism for my husband pulling me out of the hole I have dug for myself.

What had I been thinking when I clicked the "send" button on the sign-up page for a swim race in barely four weeks' time? That because I could swim one mile already in the pool, I would simply jump in the Sacramento River Delta and swim one mile in open water, just like that? And all in a wetsuit I didn't yet own?

Rogue Code flashed up error messages in my brain. It would not let me revert to type and allow my creative tendencies to prevail. Never mind that planning was an alien concept. I would plan what needed to be accomplished. I would buy the wetsuit, practice swimming in open water, reserve a hotel room close to the race site and impress my husband with my forethought. I would not need him to bail me out of this one.

My first stop was the wetsuit rack at Sports Basement in San Francisco. Buying a wetsuit is a tricky business. To begin with, suits are measured by height and weight, not by regular clothes sizes. I'm 5 feet 7 inches and weigh 156 lbs, which put me in a size 6. When Jeannie, the wetsuit expert, found out that I regularly swam one mile in the pool, she dropped me down to a size 5, which she called an "elite" fit. Me, elite?

"Most beginner triathletes are new to swimming," Jeannie explained. "There's more neoprene in a larger wetsuit and that's what provides buoyancy. And buoyancy is good because it helps beginners float on the surface and maintain a more horizontal body position."

"So a smaller wetsuit means I'll sink faster?"

"No!" she laughed. "But a smaller fit enables a more experienced swimmer to move faster through the water. It's a trade-off between buoyancy and speed. I think you're ready for a smaller fit and the wetsuit will match your experience for longer."

I still doubted that I qualified as "experienced," just because I stayed in the pool long enough to swim a mile.

"Here, put these on," she said, handing me a pair of large, fluffy woolen gloves. "These will stop your nails from tearing the neoprene."

I glanced at my carefully trimmed nails.

"We ask everyone to do it," she said in a conspiratorial whisper. "Even guys who bite their nails right down."

I did as I was told. We headed to the changing rooms.

Trying on a wetsuit was like squeezing my entire body into a bicycle inner tube. The moment I got my feet through the bottom of the legs, the neoprene shackled itself to my ankles as though it was never going to relinquish them again. I edged the suit up inch by inch, hopping on the spot while the neoprene fought with my calves to show who was boss. Once I negotiated it past my knee joints, I wondered at what precise moment my thighs had ballooned up to whale-like proportions.

I eventually yanked the suit up to my waist. I was sure Jeannie would agree that it was way too small because the crotch was sitting about three inches below the top of my thighs. See! The legs were too short. No, they weren't. Jeannie told me to grab hold of the neoprene somewhere around mid calf, pinch it between my oversized, woolly fingers and hitch it up a couple of inches. Then hitch the neoprene a couple of inches above that, and so on, until I'd edged the suit up to its proper position. Then repeat for the hips and body, because the shoulders were still sitting four inches below where they should be. Then finally for the sleeves, so that they fit snugly round my armpits.

After ten minutes, when I'd succeeded in imprisoning myself in a rubber straightjacket, Jeannie took me by surprise and zipped up the back. My shoulder blades were pulled to attention and the top of the suit gripped my neck. Good grief, I could barely do an impression of a Frankenstein walk, let alone breathe and swim.

"Jeannie, are you absolutely certain it's meant to be this tight?"

I staggered round the changing room, limbs outstretched in my Frankenstein pose. Jeannie assured me that it was. An elite fit, remember.

Peeling off a dry wetsuit was also a tricky business. I'd just exhausted myself fighting my way into the wretched thing. Now, without a lubricating layer of water between me and the suit, it refused to cooperate. With Jeannie's help, and after a lot more pinching and pulling, I prized myself out of the size 5. Then, just for my own peace of mind, although I wasn't doubting Jeannie's excellent advice about the size 5—of course not, she was the expert—I asked her to help me go through the whole rigmarole again and try the size 6.

I bought the size 5.

It was nearly noon when I returned to the car. I sat for a good five minutes, looking at my wetsuit in its new travel bag. I knew what had to happen next because it was written into my master plan. But I took an extra few minutes to remind myself that triathletes were not wimpy. They pushed the envelope. My envelope was about to get very soggy indeed.

I drove along Embarcadero to San Francisco Aquatic Park, just beyond Fisherman's Wharf. This small harbor is located right next to the cable car turnaround, another of the city's top tourist haunts. Parking is a nightmare. But Aquatic Park was a safe place to swim because the harbor walls shielded it from currents. And Gail had said that there were always several other swimmers around to help me if I got into trouble.

I usually have good parking karma, but not today. Nothing was available in the free four-hour or two-hour spots. I growled in frustration when several cars that arrived after me took spots that became vacant. The only spot available was a one-hour meter. I would barely have enough time to walk to the beach and change, let alone swim. The multiple parking misses compounded my foul mood. Everything had conspired against me swimming today. I pulled onto Van Ness to drive home.

"Call yourself a triathlete in training?" Rogue Code was so insistent that I found myself shouting out loud in the car. "Then stop pretending and get back there RIGHT NOW."

I turned round and parked on a meter near Ghirardelli Square, a five-minute walk from Aquatic Park. I didn't have a single quarter on me, only nickels and dimes, but they would buy me fifty-four minutes in total. Before I could give myself time to back out, I squished all my spare coins in the meter, opened the car boot, grabbed the bag with the wetsuit and marched down to the water.

Warm September sunlight illuminated the curve of the walls

that enclosed the safe haven of Aquatic Park. Small dinghies dotted around the harbor swung lazily on their mooring buoys. Ripples lapped against the hulls of historic ships moored along the wall to the right. Today was one of those rare summer days in San Francisco when the sun shone instead of being shut out by a cold, clammy layer of thick marine fog.

A dozen passers-by strolled along the esplanade. A handful of families played on the sand. Several people in wetsuits swam in the water. Little piles of clothes were lined up along a wall by the pier to the right of the beach. But I couldn't find any locker rooms. What was I supposed to do now? Get changed on the esplanade and provide a free cabaret to all these people on how efficiently I could squeeze into my size 5? If I put my purse out with a few coins on top, they might even mistake me for a street performer and I'd earn a few bucks.

No way was I sharing my wetsuit wrestling match with anyone. I had my dignity. I spied some restrooms set back from the pier and went in to investigate. They were reasonably clean. I would change in the large, wheelchair-access cubicle.

I moved straight into the pinching-and-pulling routine. After only six minutes, I had squeezed all of me, including the balloon thighs, into the suit. All I had to do now was zip it up. The zipper ran from the small of my back up to my neck, with a two-foot long cord attached to the fastener. Jeannie had told me that I simply had to grasp the cord, pull it over my shoulder and yank on it to pull up the zipper. But when I tried, the sides of the suit were stretched too far apart for the cord to pull the zipper up. I didn't have a spare pair of hands to hold the sides together. I was stuck.

Had I really bought the wetsuit, fought bad parking karma and got this far, only to give up? I had been outside my comfort zone for well over an hour now. But it was cast in stone in my master plan that today was the day for my first open water swim. I gathered up my gear, stepped outside the restrooms and prepared for my next outside-the-limits moment.

The British are a people that like to keep their distance. We're polite, even friendly, but we don't perform anything more intimate than a handshake with someone we're not related to. When I moved to California, I'd had to learn to hug complete strangers. By and large I'd acclimatized. But not to the extent of asking a stranger to move into my personal space and zip up my wetsuit, even if I was wearing a swimsuit underneath. This time, I didn't have a choice. I comforted myself with the thought that I'd never see the stranger ever again.

I weighed up likely targets on the esplanade. A man and woman in their late forties sat on a bench looking out over the harbor. He had a camera round his neck. She had a guide book on her lap. Even better. Strangers who didn't live in San Francisco. I would ask her.

"Excuse me," I said. "I wonder if you'd possibly mind zipping up my wetsuit? I can't quite seem to manage."

I rushed my words in an effort to get this over with as fast as possible. I didn't want to risk getting on hugging terms over a zipper.

"Of course," said the woman. She leapt to her feet and stood behind me. "These zips are a right nuisance, aren't they?"

I immediately recognized her flat vowels as an accent local to me. That is, local to somewhere in the North West of England. She even used "right" as an adjective, a Northern trait that my Southern husband had picked up from me and had been teased about ever since by my in-laws.

"We do this all the time. We're water-skiers." The zipper shot up my back in one swoop. "There you go. Is that all right?"

"Just fine," I replied.

I need have no fear of overzealous hugging from a Brit.

"Sounds like you're from back home," the man said. He too had leapt to his feet and stood grinning in front of me. "Where do you come from?"

"The North of England," I said.

"Where exactly?"

Three times I answered the "where exactly" question. I'm from near Manchester. I'm from a village near Stockport, which is near Manchester. Finally, I'm from Romiley, a tiny place of a couple of thousand people that no one has ever heard of.

"We have!" they both chimed in jubilation. "We live there!"

I smiled back at them. We became near best friends in two minutes. We talked about the street I grew up on and the street where they live now, about the school I went to, about the playground where I did my Cycling Proficiency Test as a kid, about which shops had gone and which were still there. They told me about their water-skiing at Abersoch, a town on the North Wales coast close by where I had spent childhood holidays. I confided in them that this was my first dip in open water. They said they'd look after my gear and cheer me on.

I pulled on my swimcap. But when I searched through my new wetsuit bag, I discovered that I had left my goggles and *Bodyglide* lubricant stick in the car. If I swam too far without applying lubricant, the wetsuit would leave big red chafe marks round my armpits and neck. And I hated getting my eyes wet, especially in stinging salt water. What more could go wrong?

I had already taken twenty-four minutes to get this far. It would take me another five minutes each way to retrieve the goggles and *Bodyglide* from the car. And I would look unbelievably stupid, walking round the streets of San Francisco in a wetsuit and strappy sandals. I might even get arrested. Or maybe not. That was quite mild on the San Francisco Rubber Outfit Scale.

I stood looking at the line of swimmers stretched out from the pier on my right to the farthest buoy way over on the left side of the harbor. My willpower had nearly left the building. I raced after it and corralled it back into line with the threat of an embarrassing tactical retreat from the beach in front of the Romiley couple. I had to stride into that water right now as though I meant business.

I detest cold water. David had had plenty of fun at my expense on a Bermuda beach one year, when he watched me take twelve minutes to wade waist-high into 76° water. I recalled the agony of anticipation as inch-high, menacing waves encroached insidiously on my trembling flesh, my skin awaiting its fate at the hands of thermal shock. This water was much colder—around 64°—which was warm for the Bay in September, but arctic for me. Rogue Code gave me a nudge. The slower you walk, the worse it will be. I steeled myself.

I strode down the beach and into the water without breaking my step. My feet and hands registered the cold, but I didn't flinch. Chilly water reached my knees, then my waist, but my wetsuit protected my body from contact. Coolness pressed against the suit, as though I were leaning against a freezer.

The water reached chest height. I couldn't wade out much farther without losing my balance. Time to swim. I took a deep breath and launched my feet off the bottom. As soon as my neck dropped below the water line, cold water trickled inside my suit and curled its way down to my waist. But this wasn't the full freezing onslaught that my skin was expecting. After a few seconds, my body heat took the cold edge off the thin layer of water trapped under the suit.

Today's objective was to swim in the wetsuit, not put miles on the clock. A white buoy rocked gently back and forth about forty yards out. My goal was a slow breaststroke lap round the buoy, keeping my head above water to protect my eyes. My arms pulled a few clumsy strokes.

Holding my head up changed my entire body position in the water. Instead of resembling a streamlined, horizontal arrow shooting across the surface, my body tilted at an awkward 45° angle. My back arched outwards and my legs kicked well below the water line. Every kick took me a short distance forwards but also a short distance upwards. After months of well-trained, horizontal form on my favorite stroke, I was reduced to this unnatural bobbing forwards and upwards.

To compound my discomfort, I had no line on the bottom of the pool to follow. I was cut adrift in an expanse of opaque gray-green water that was so cloudy I could barely make out my hands in front of me. And I was very low in the water in relation to the buoy. One minute the buoy seemed within touching distance, the next I lost sight of it as I dropped below a wave. My concern edged its way up towards panic level. Was I even moving forward?

Calm down, Jane! You swim much farther than this in the pool. And stop worrying that you can't touch the bottom. You're too strong a swimmer to drown.

But without poolside lifeguard chairs or any other familiar object to measure my speed against, I had no idea how fast I was swimming. My body rocked gently back and forth with each small incoming wave. I thrashed towards the buoy. Two waves forward, one wave back.

I zigzagged round the buoy, the water pulling me first left and then right, backwards and then forwards. I struck back for the shore. My neck ached from holding my head up at such an unnatural angle. My arms were fatigued from fighting the neoprene with each stroke.

But now the direction of the ripples confused me into thinking I was swimming backwards. Or maybe I was. The shore wasn't getting any closer. And the Romiley couple on their bench were a lot farther to the left than I remembered. Had I drifted sideways? Maybe Aquatic Park had currents after all.

I stopped to tread water for a few moments to plan my survival strategy. If I aimed farther left than the Romiley couple, then whatever was dragging me sideways should compensate and dump me on the shoreline in front of them. My new sight point became the far left side of the pier, towards the historic ships. I counted my strokes to take my mind off the waves' forward and back motion. If I kept swimming, I should make landfall before sunset.

The shore grew closer after what felt like ten hours but was probably ten minutes. The opaque water lightened. When I could see sand on the bottom, I stood up and sloshed through knee-high waves. The Romiley couple waved. I strode up the beach and esplanade towards them, leaving a trail of splashy footprints on the pavement. Even though my legs dragged with the exertion of all that breaststroke kick, I held my head up high and walked tall. I'd just completed my first open water swim, right on target in my master plan.

The Romiley couple sat me down and peeled the suit past my knees. My limbs were too confused to tackle the ankle-shackling routine. The couple each took a wetsuit leg and gave one last wrench to release my feet from bondage. She folded my suit up and popped it down next to me on their bench. We chatted some more about their plans to motor down to Big Sur on Highway 1. After a few minutes I regained my equilibrium and stood up. I thanked them. We shook hands, said our goodbyes and I wished them a good holiday.

As I toweled off in the restroom, I realized I didn't know their names. I smiled. Brits rarely bother to find out the name of a chance acquaintance when we'll never see that person again. Striking up a conversation with strangers is a North of England trait, something that reserved British Southerners find in turn irritating or endearing about us. But best do the chatty, friendly thing without the intimacy of names.

I pulled out my clothes from my wetsuit bag. Then I discovered one more niggle to add to the day's list—my underwear was missing. I had flung it in the car boot after I decided in Sports Basement to leave my swimsuit on. Never mind. Who's to know what's on, or not on, under my khaki capri pants and red polo shirt, unless they look very closely?

I drove home, had a shower, got dressed and rinsed the suit off in the bath. Then I made myself a congratulatory cup of tea to celebrate completing my master plan. I had not wimped out when presented with lots of opportunities. Today was a Good Day.

I May Be Some Time

Total number of minutes spent swimming in wetsuit to date: 29

Total number of minutes it takes me to swim one mile: 38

Throughout those last couple of weeks of September, time winched me minute by minute towards the Open Water Swim. I was tethered by an unbreakable cord to the last Sunday of the month. Each day dragged me closer to the appointed hour. No escape. But no surrender either.

I hadn't swum in open water since my Aquatic Park debut. My master plan called for one more swim at Coyote Point in San Mateo, a safe swim spot in the calm, inner San Francisco Bay. I took my sister Sue along as stand-in lifeguard. She was a British Airways crewmember and was in San Francisco on a two-day layover. She'd been trained how to rescue hundreds of passengers from a plane that crash-landed on water. Rescuing me, if I needed it, would be small potatoes.

We devised a plan. If I got into difficulty, I would wave my arms. She would then summon help from the guys setting up a canoe expo in the beach car park and exhort one of them to paddle out and rescue me. As I swam up and down, I remembered snippets of the poem *Not Waving But Drowning,* by Stevie Smith. I hoped that Sue would recognize the difference.

With visibility down to two feet in murky water, I couldn't help but wonder what was down there. Do electric eels frequent the Bay? Might the Great White Shark sighted recently off the Marin headland have taken a wrong turn, or maybe a right turn, on the way to its next meal? I thrashed up and down the inlet for seventeen frantic, fright-fuelled minutes before my imagination got the better of me.

"I didn't know you could swim that fast," Sue said as I scrambled out of the water.

"Neither did I," I replied, although I omitted to mention the driving force behind my speed.

Three days before the race, I reminded David that I had booked a room for Saturday night at a Best Western Hotel in Antioch. This was the closest city I could find to the event location at Bethel Island, on the Sacramento River Delta. I asked him if he still had the race on his calendar. He put his arm round my shoulder.

"Nothing's going to stop me from being there to support you," he said.

His mouth smiled but his eyes looked bemused. By this time, he was almost certain that I would follow through with the triathlon. His expectation that I should have quit by now lay unspoken between us.

On Saturday afternoon, I packed and repacked my event bag of wetsuit, swimsuit, *Bodyglide* lubricant, swimcap, goggles, extra goggles, towel and shower toiletries. My body was convinced I was about to go into hospital for a minor operation. I sensed the dread of something unpleasant that had to be endured, but knew that I would be in better shape once I had come through the other side.

David drove. I had lapsed into silence by the time we arrived around 8:30 p.m. at the hotel. We had reached the hospital waiting room. David unpacked the breakfast cereals and tea ready for tomorrow. I insisted that he set the alarm for 6:15 a.m.

We killed time by watching CNN Headline News until it hit the repeat loop.

When the alarm went off next morning, I was already awake. I edged out of bed, reluctant to acknowledge that the unbreakable cord had made its last turn of the winch. I forced myself to eat breakfast. We packed and left.

David drove and I navigated. I always navigate on road trips. David jokes that I have a GPS implanted in my brain. I always get us to where we need to be. We crawled along lonely highways through flat, reclaimed farmland in the early morning light, looking for a road to nowhere. I drummed my fingers on the map and snapped my head round at every road sign to see if it signposted the road to Bethel Island. Could that be the turn? Or that one? No, it wasn't.

"Relax!" said David. "I'll get you there. I won't let you miss your big event. Trust me."

I sat on my hands and stared ahead.

After another false start, we located the web of narrow lanes that led us past empty fields and wide inlets contained by delta levees. We pulled into the deserted car park at the farthest end of the farthest road. We looked around. We looked at each other. We waited.

Six minutes later, a red pickup pulled up next to us. A man and woman in their twenties stepped out.

"Are you here for the Bethel Island Swim?" the man asked.

"Yes, we are," I said, throwing open the car door and rushing round to their pickup. "Are we in the right place?"

Words tumbled out of my mouth in relief that someone else who knew about the swim had turned up.

"You sure are," the woman said. "We're volunteers. It's right this way."

"Next time, why don't you put me in charge of getting us

here?" David said. He winked. "That way, we'll turn up after the organizers."

I gave him a hug.

We followed the volunteers through the car park and up a slope to the top of the levee. Before us lay our first view of the river, blanketed in the still, calm air of early morning. Pale sunshine picked out glowing sheaves of straw-colored reeds lining the breakwater that ran parallel to the levee about thirty yards out. Beyond the breakwater, the delta was so wide that I could barely see the other side.

Directly in front of us, a concrete boat slipway led down into the river. I walked to the edge, knelt down and dipped my hand in the cool water. It was crystal clear this close up. At six feet out and barely two feet deep, large pebbles coated with fronds of glossy, bright green weeds lined the bottom. I'd have to find a way clamber over that stuff without slipping. At about fifteen feet out, the water clouded over to an opaque gray-green. Hopefully the water was deep enough to swim in by that point, or else I risked damaging my feet.

I needed to settle my nerves. David and I walked along the levee to our left. After five minutes, we came to a halt by a gate that blocked the path. We stood and watched boats towing fluorescent orange buoys work their way out along the channel between the breakwater and the levee. One buoy was way out in the distance, well past even the end of the breakwater. Once I swam past the breakwater, I would be fighting choppy waves blowing in from the delta. My stomach fluttered and my arms felt weak. Thirty-five laps of the pool unwound into one straight mile looked an extremely long way.

By the time we returned to the slipway, the organizers had set up the registration table. I picked up my very first race T-shirt, plus goody bag containing toiletry samples and advertisements for other events. Then a volunteer directed me to the bodymarking queue. When David and I had visited the San Jose Tri, we had puzzled over why competitors had race numbers written on their arms. Now I understood. I turned to David as a woman wrote my race number on the back of my hand in indelible ink.

"I don't plan on drowning today," I told him. "But if I do, tell them to look for a body with 225 written on it."

"Are you sure that's why they do it?" David said, his mouth open and eyebrows puckered in incredulity.

"She's right on that one," the volunteer said. "We don't want any unidentified bodies left over at the end."

We still had over an hour to go before the race start. I thought about the dozens of times I'd swum a mile. About clean, strong arm pulls, about settling into a steady rhythm of breathing every three strokes. The first ten minutes of warming up were always the worst, when the ache in my arms would build to such intensity that I would doubt I could maintain that pace. Then the ache would ease off, numbed by endorphins. A confident surge of energy would take over and push me forward. I would settle into a mantra of one-two-three-breathe. I hoped to stay in that groove for the whole race, emptying my mind of all but the mantra.

With thirty minutes to go, the registration area buzzed with activity. Several swimmers pulled their wetsuits on. Others already in wetsuits walked back and forth on the slipway, waving their arms in circles like supercharged windmills. Spectators chattered. Volunteers brought more T-shirt supplies to the registration table. I found a quiet corner and worked my way into my wetsuit, taking care not to rip the neoprene on its first serious outing. David zipped me up and pinned a waterproof slip printed with my name and number to the zipper cord. The organizers would remove this slip when I crossed the finish line to record my result.

What would swimming alongside a hundred other people feel like? A few days earlier, I had emailed Kevin to find out what to expect. He told me that there would most likely be a mass start in the water. I should position myself towards the back to let the fast swimmers get out of the way. Then find someone swimming close to my pace and draft off them, which meant slotting in behind them and swimming in their bubble trail. The swimmer in front would cut down resistance in the water, so I would use less effort to swim. And the drafting strategy should also take care of the navigation.

The lead organizer called all swimmers together to issue course instructions. Not one but three races were taking place that morning. The half-milers would race first, starting in the water in front of the slipway between the orange cylindrical start buoys. They would race along the channel to the right of the slipway, turn round a buoy, swim back and then run back up the slipway to the finish line. When they were finished, the one- and two-milers would start together from the same buoys but race to the left of the slipway. The one-milers should turn round at the first cylindrical buoy and the two-milers should proceed to the farthest buoy.

Two pieces of good news. First, when David and I had strolled along the levee, the huge distance to the farthest buoy had unsettled me. But I had mistaken the two-mile buoy for the one-mile buoy. I wouldn't have to swim that far out after all. Second, I wouldn't have to swim against choppy waves past the end of the breakwater on my way to the mistaken two-mile buoy.

We would all finish by climbing out of the water and running up the slipway to the finish line. I turned round to look at the huge "FINISH" banner. Only then did I notice an enormous race clock about five feet wide. Foot-high yellow numbers would turn over every second to record elapsed time. I pictured the clock showing my finish time when I crossed the line. A shiver of anticipation ran through me.

David and I watched the start of the half-mile race from the end of the wooden jetty that ran alongside the slipway into the water. We waited in silence for the half-milers to come back.

"I think I'll have one last walk to settle my nerves," I said.

"Lead the way," said David.

"No, I need to go on my own this time," I replied.

I was withdrawing into my own mental cocoon, leaving David on the outside. I had to do this alone. Time to move on.

"Good luck, I'll be rooting for you all the way," he said and gave me one last hug.

I wandered down to the registration table and back in my bare feet, then paused at the top of the slipway. The half-mile swimmers emerged in bursts from the water and raced towards the finish line. The crowd cheered. I wanted to cheer too, but I couldn't manage more than weak applause.

The last of the half-milers crossed the finish line.

"All one- and two-mile racers to the start, please!"

The wait was over. An army of black neoprene thundered into the shallows, the water turning white with bursts of spray. I waded out with a more cautious group alongside the jetty, hanging onto each wooden post for support. But I still lost my footing twice on slimy, weed-covered stones.

Once I could swim without stubbing my toe on the bottom, I struck out with a few pulls of breaststroke to join the waiting battalion. I lined up towards the back of the group between the start buoys. I watched my hands sculling the chilly water in front of me. My fingers were white and waxy, floating almost corpse-like just below the surface of the bottle-green water. I rubbed my hands together. My wedding ring slid up and down my finger, almost past my knuckle.

That ring had been on my finger for nineteen years, two weeks and four days. No way was I going to lose it in the river in some stupid race. I had to save my wedding ring. I swam full-throttle back to the jetty and called out for David. He rushed up to the jetty's edge and leaned down towards me.

"What happened?" he asked, consternation visible on his face.

I reached up with my left hand. He clasped it with both his hands.

"Here," I said, handing him my wedding ring. "I may be some time."

Our eyes met for a second. A moment later, we both creased up with those huge, from-the-gut belly laughs that squeeze tears from the eyes.

"I may be some time" is a shorthand phrase in British English which means "I won't be coming back." They were the famous last words of Lawrence Oates, a member of Captain Robert Scott's failed 1912 Antarctic polar expedition. Oates stumbled out of the team tent into the blizzard to die, so that the rest might have enough provisions and a chance of getting back alive (they didn't). The phrase still has its place in British English to encapsulate that buttoned-up, British habit of massive understatement.

Today, by the jetty, the gallows humor caught the silly melodrama of the wedding ring moment. Our laughter washed away the tension that had been building in my stomach all morning, and instead, left nerves of excitement that I was actually going to do this. Above all, I mustn't forget to enjoy myself. I'd put the work in and I deserved to finish.

David slipped my wedding ring onto his little finger and wished me luck once more. I set off again to line up between the buoys. My game plan played in my head one last time. I recited over and over the exact three-stroke-and-breathe pace I planned to use at the start.

I had almost reached the other swimmers when the horn sounded. The start had caught me off guard. The race was on. I filled my lungs with air, brought my right arm over and put my face in the water to start my freestyle stroke.

No sooner did my skin touch water than I found myself exhaling at double speed. On my second arm stroke, my head jerked back. I snatched a gasp of air. I did the same thing again. And again. And again.

I switched back to breaststroke while I regrouped. Swimmers thrashed forward all around me, each positioned about two arms' length from the next. A couple of faster freestyle swimmers behind me bumped and jostled me as they overtook. I was engulfed in a melee of churning water, flaying arms and fluttering feet.

Why was this happening? When my face made contact with chilly water, my body acted on reflex by forcing the air out of my lungs, jerking my head back and snatching a short breath. When I had swum off Coyote Point, I had thought that the same jerking reaction was caused by fear of the Great White. But it had been caused by warm skin hitting cold water. If I didn't find a way to breathe deeply to the bottom of my lungs instead of these snatch breaths, I would hyperventilate. And then I'd be finished.

I decided to continue swimming freestyle with snatch breaths, but force myself to keep my face in the water as long as possible. I must breathe as slowly as my reflexes would allow. When my skin cooled down to water temperature, I would be able to submerge my face for longer.

After a couple of minutes, my skin acclimatized. The snatch reflex subsided and my breathing slowed to my three-stroke pattern. My heart pounded, partly through exertion but also through the adrenaline rush of dealing with an unforeseen crisis. I gave myself a mental high-five.

I surveyed the swimmers round me. A dozen swimmers behind me, four or five close by and a pack of thirty about fifteen yards in front. The maelstrom had calmed. Time to try the drafting that Kevin had mentioned.

I caught up to the guy in front and watched for his bubble trail. I managed to follow him for a few strokes but then brushed his toes with my fingertips. I backed off a little and tried again. After a few more strokes, I found his toes again. Maybe I was a better swimmer than I thought. I moved to his right, gave him some side room and pulled past him. Three other people swam about seven yards in front of him. I overtook them too.

The open water between me and the main pack of swimmers had now widened to around twenty-five yards. I had pulled about five yards ahead of the swimmers behind me. No one drafted off me. But now I had to do all my own cutting through the water, which was choppy after thirty energetic swimmers had raced through it about twenty-five seconds before me.

The lead group pulled farther away and the following group fell behind. I had no choice but to plow on alone. How was I supposed to navigate with no one to follow? Maybe I should try to keep parallel to the side of the channel. I looked to the riverbank on my left, then to the breakwater on my right. All I could see was a mass of reeds. How tall were these reeds? Were they nearby or far off? With no perspective from the riverbank, I had no idea how to swim in a straight line.

One of the kayakers in the safety team gestured to me that I was well off course. I needed to scoot left. But by how much? I counted ten sets of three-strokes-and-breathe, then stuck my head up to look around. Another kayaker was positioned two kayak-lengths to my left, ready to shepherd me back into line. I scooted right. I zigzagged across the thirty-yard-wide channel for several minutes.

I had passed the point where my arms turned numb after the warmup, but the expected surge of energy had failed to materialize. The lead group was almost out of sight. I became ever more disoriented, cut adrift in this featureless expanse of gray-green water with no way of telling if I was moving forward. Nothing in this race was going according to my game plan. My brain hit a one-alarm panic bell. Maybe I would need a kayaker after all.

I swam breaststroke to take a breather and calm down. A minute later, a couple of swimmers on my left raced past in the opposite direction. They must be on their return leg. I looked ahead and saw a big splash of orange about seventy yards ahead. A buzz of energy shot down to my fingertips. Nearly there.

I switched back to freestyle and zeroed in on the turnaround buoy. Head down, ten breaths, look up for the buoy. It was no closer. I swam another ten breaths. Still no closer. Was this buoy moving away or was I swimming on the spot? My low vantage point over the water had skewed my perspective. I had misjudged the distance.

I finally reached the buoy and struck out on the home stretch. The moment I turned, the swim became easier. I was no longer fighting ripples on the surface but swimming with them, which cut down the resistance. I settled into my homeward freestyle leg.

As I turned to the right to breathe, I caught sight of someone on the riverbank waving to me. David had walked along the path and now kept pace with me on the way back. I waved back. Oops. Shouldn't have done that. Waving was the sign to the kayakers that I needed to be rescued. Moments later, I reassured a concerned kayaker that I was indeed only waving, not drowning.

Just then something entwined itself round my left shoulder and tightened until it restricted my arm stroke. River weed?

Electric eel? A bolt of panic shot through me. I stopped to investigate. The two-foot long cord attached to the wetsuit zipper had wrapped itself round my shoulder. Relief. Nothing sinister. I unraveled the cord and went back to swimming. Six strokes later, my shoulder was bound up again with the cord. I unraveled it again.

When I was swimming upstream, the cord had been swept out behind me by the ripples. Now that I was swimming downstream, I couldn't prevent the cord from being swept forward and tangling itself round my arm every few seconds. Each time I broke my swimming rhythm to stop and unwrap the cord, I lost energy and focus. I would never finish if I carried on like this.

My only option was to ignore the cord and leave it wrapped round my shoulder. I cleared my mind of everything and counted my breathing. Seven breaths is one length of a twenty-five-yard pool. Head down, seven breaths, keep counting. Forget the cord. Ignore the pain. Numbers cancel out distance and time. Focus on the numbers. But I winced as every left arm stroke strained against a taut band of steel.

When the finish buoys came into view, I forced myself to keep calm. No false alarms over skewed perspectives. I'd get there when I got there. But the sight of the buoys quickened my breathing and the pain in my shoulder eased its grip a little.

I passed the finish buoys and turned right to swim towards the slipway. I allowed myself a glance at the clock by the finish line. 33 minutes, 18 seconds. My fastest-ever mile in the pool was thirty-eight minutes. Here I'd been fighting ripples and cords and I'd done a bit of breaststroke for a rest. Did I really swim that fast? I shelved the speculation and swam towards the race steward standing by the water's edge. I stood up a few feet out and waded a couple of steps.

Slimy stones lay in wait under the innocent water. I slipped and stubbed three of my left toes. I cursed in pain and scrabbled on all fours to find a footing. The steward reached out his hand. I grabbed it, stood up, steadied myself and waded out of the water. Pain stabbed through my toes. I told myself to run. The clock was waiting for me. I had to run.

I took off. Spectators applauded. That's for me! They're applauding me! Hot adrenaline flooded my veins. The finish line beckoned. David stood at the top of the jetty with his camera. I ran past him, crossed the line and glanced up at the clock. 34 minutes, 47 seconds. The time I'd always claim as my own for my first race.

Officials swooped down on me, unpinned the paper slip from my zipper and recorded my details on a clipboard. I turned round, disoriented and a little uncoordinated, unsure what to do next. I had focused so hard on crossing the line that I didn't have a game plan for afterwards.

David strode towards me, arms outstretched, a huge smile on his face.

"I'm so proud of you!" he said. "You really did it!"

He gave me a long, jubilant hug.

"Oh, and I think you'll be needing this."

He slipped my wedding ring back onto my finger.

On the drive home, a warm, contented realization settled in that I'd just finished my first-ever race. I asked David if he had really believed I would go through with the swim.

"I still wasn't sure until we got to the hotel," he said. "You were more nervous about this than most of the other things you do. But when I saw that determination you get when you lock onto something, I knew you'd get through it."

"And what about the triathlon?" I asked. I glanced sideways to watch his reaction to my question. "Do you think I'll give up on it now?"

"No, I don't. And I'm proud of you for trying."

I leaned over and gave him a kiss on the cheek. We were back on the same page.

When we got home, I emailed an account of the race and some of David's photos to all my friends. The race results had been posted on the event website. I had finished twentieth out of twenty-four one-mile swimmers. I didn't mind being so far down the field. I had sliced a huge 3 minute, 13 second chunk off my one-mile personal best time. A sign I had turned into an athlete. I kept a record of my personal bests.

When I opened my email next morning, a note from Kevin sat in my inbox.

> **Congratulations Jane! That post-race picture is awesome . . . the look on your face says it all: inner joy and accomplishment. Kudos for keeping yourself together, for not panicking, and for pulling off an impressive performance.**

Absolutely. Kudos to me.

This Hill Is Called Kevin

Number of weeks until my first multisport race: 5

Number of weeks my body thinks it needs before it's ready: 500

O was a tough month. I barely had a moment to savor the success of the Open Water Swim before I found myself dragged into the five-week build-up to the Salmon Duathlon. I had a mountain of training to accomplish. In this race I would have to run farther than I had ever run before—a three-mile run plus a 1.5-mile run, on either side of a nineteen-mile bike leg. Was I even ready to do the race? Over the summer, I had built up my running from 1.8 miles to 3.5 miles with just a couple of stops, albeit without tackling Hell Hill. But I still hadn't ever run 4.5 miles in training.

Running in October was very different from running in the summer. In order to run for longer, I was outside my house by 6:30 a.m., half an hour earlier than usual. The morning sky was pitch black and studded with stars. I triggered security lights when I ran past several houses. No traffic, no walkers, no noise. I could have been running at three in the morning.

Many of the houses were decorated for Halloween. I ran past trees sprinkled with ominous spots of orange light. White chiffon ghosts lurked in bushes. Invisible bodies left their illuminated footprints across lawns, glowing a sickly fluorescent green. When I turned my usual corner at the 1.5-mile mark, I almost tripped headlong over five luminescent skeletons, laid out next to five cardboard gravestones, right by the curbside. I let out a startled yelp.

This would be my fourth Halloween in the US. I was still baffled. What possesses outwardly sensible Americans to cover their houses in tacky junk? And what are parents teaching their children when they demand "trick or treat"? An early civics lesson in extortion? Why didn't more American children grow up into a life of crime?

Trick or treating has gained a foothold in the UK in the last ten years. Except that the British don't really understand that deep down, it's all about the candy. Adults hate handing out something for nothing. And empty-handed teenagers, miffed at no treats, have perfected dastardly tricks such as coating car door handles in honey. Suffice to say that very little candy is consumed during Britain's miserable imitation of trick or treating.

I made a mental note of the cardboard gravestones for my next run and pressed on. The black sky brightened low on the eastern horizon. An intense, rose-pink dawn radiated westwards, dissolving the stars in its path. Sunrise edged the tops of hills in gold. Roof tiles glowed fiery terracotta brown. Swathes of early sunlight wiped away the menace of ghouls at every corner. After sixteen minutes, streetlights switched off. I was thankful for the almost unseemly haste of the sunrise at this southerly 37° latitude. Night-time foreboding melted into daytime kitsch.

At the beginning of October, I found a running buddy. Cristina Sorrentino and I met at a women's networking event. I didn't usually attend women-only events. Why deny yourself the chance to network with half the population? This time, I had decided to keep an open mind.

Cristina and I were both first-timers at the meeting. We chatted about running. She had given up running because of a bad back. Now she had recovered and was ready to take up some gentle jogging. I hadn't wanted to run with a buddy because I was loathe to let anyone else see how poor a runner I was. But I wouldn't hold back a gentle jogger. We agreed to team up in four days' time.

I asked Cristina's permission if we could tackle a hill on our first run together. I wanted to practice running up a long hill, like the one described on the duathlon course. I took her to Water Dog Lake in Belmont. I had walked up to this dull pond of water enclosed on three sides by scrub-covered hills one Sunday afternoon in September. But I had never run here. Difficult access had protected the area from development and it was now crisscrossed with nearly twenty miles of mountain bike trails and paths.

We set out along a wide, gravel-strewn path shaded by a canopy of California oaks. Not much of a gradient. We rounded a right-hand bend. The path snaked upwards. Left-hand bend. Upwards. Trees blocked the view more than fifty yards ahead. Still upwards.

Cristina kept pace next to me. Scrunching feet on gravel. Breathing hurt. What made me think this was a forgiving gradient when I walked up here? My heart beat harder until it pounded against my chest.

I fell back to a walk. So did Cristina. This stretch was tough on both of us. After a couple of minutes, we recovered enough to run again. Last month's gentle stroll under a welcoming umbrella of shade had turned into an anonymous slog through featureless trees. Running a route without identifiable markers unsettled me. How much farther to the lake?

Panic struck. Would I have enough energy to reach the turning? What would Cristina think if I stopped again? Before I had time to weigh this up, Alternate Persona made the decision for me. I stopped. Cristina stopped. She looked as relieved as I did.

We walked another couple of minutes. My heart rate settled down.

"Shall we give it one last push to the lake?" I asked.

"Sure," said Cristina. "We've got this far."

I cranked up my legs to a slow jog and stared at the ground. Breathing hurt again. I measured the distance by counting my breathing between every manhole cover and concrete gully I could find. After all, there were no other recognizable features on this path.

Just when I felt I could push no longer up the unforgiving grind, a break in the trees opened on our left, revealing the welcome sight of an ugly, brackish pond. Water Dog Lake. Cristina and I peeled off to the lakeshore, our legs flooded with relief that we had escaped the gradient. We stood in silence by some forlorn bulrushes sticking out at awkward angles from the water. We looked out over the glassy stillness of the pond. We gave each other a high-five. We had beaten the hill.

When we had recovered our breath, we turned round and set off downhill at a gentle jog. We were well-matched in pace and stature. Cristina's long black hair streamed out behind her as we picked up speed. We started chatting. Cristina had recently moved from New York. We compared notes on living in California. She told me of her postdoc job at Stanford and her plans to train as a psychiatrist. She described her long rehab from her back injury. And we talked of our relatives spread round the world from Europe to Australia.

Wait a minute. What was I doing? Running *and* chatting? I thought back to being overtaken by the chatting Porsche Guys three months ago. About my amazement that they had enough spare breath to do both. I had become so engrossed in our conversation that I had overlooked this turning point in my own running career. I had just joined the Running and Chatting Club. I smiled to myself, chuckling at how such small achievements meant so much.

When we reached our cars, I thanked Cristina for tackling the newly named Hill of Damnation on our first run together. If I had known how tough this hill was going to be, I wouldn't have inflicted such punishment on her.

"No problem," she laughed. "But let's go somewhere else next time."

Thus began my weekly runs with my new running buddy.

The second weekend in October, David went to Europe for a conference. I was faced with a decision. Do I ride my bike on my own or pass this weekend? My first solo wetsuit dip in Aquatic Park emboldened me. I would ride on my own. I had a race to train for. Today would be a No Wimp Out Day.

I drove straight to my usual route along Cañada Road. The road welcomed me as an old friend. Total mileage was 14.7 undulating miles, with only two grim hills. Blue sky, sunshine, gentle breeze, not too hot. Perfect conditions.

I parked at Edgewood Road, at the mid-point of the route. I planned to cycle it as a figure eight, heading out north to Highway 92, then return to Edgewood and finish off with a loop south to Woodside and back.

I set out towards Highway 92. I reached the first grim hill at mile 3.2. I knew I could power up this hill on my middle ring these days. But my legs labored upwards on my lowest gear. Where was all that muscle power I had developed through spin classes? And just what had I done to feel this bad today? When I reached the top, my legs were drained of energy. I could have been cycling this hill for the very first time. Every pedal stroke had sapped my morale.

I coasted back Edgewood. I still felt drained. The thought of the long haul out of Woodside overpowered me. I gave myself permission to cancel the rest of the figure eight and load the bike back in the car. I'd only cycled 7.38 miles, but at least I'd soloed on my bike. And I could still train some more for the bike-to-run transition. I pulled on my running shoes for my ten-minute post-bike run.

There was no paved path to run on, just a trail by the side of the road with sharp ups and downs, pockmarked with stones and ruts. I don't run trails. I only run paved paths. I have a weak left ankle, the result of a nasty sprain when I fell off the curb hailing a taxi on the Champs Elysees in Paris. Planting my foot on uneven ground frightens me with memories of pain and long recovery. After twenty paces, I had to stop and pick my way over rough terrain. I struggled on, trying to find enough smooth, level ground to run. During my ten minutes of wearing running shoes, I must have run for only two of them.

I returned to the sunbaked car, opened its doors to let out the oppressive heat and flung my running shoes in the back. I grabbed my water bottle and leaned against the passenger door in the shade. Today's miserable performance was the result of three months' solid training. I had been kidding myself all along about how much work I needed to do in order to compete in the duathlon. I was nowhere near ready.

What's more, Gail had made a throwaway comment after last week's spin class that had unintentionally raised my anxiety. She had mentioned that a race description of "rolling hills" could mean anything. It all depended on who wrote the description.

What if the writer were Lance Armstrong's training partner, for whom Cañada Road's hills were blips not worth recording? I would labor partway up the hills in the race and then stutter to a halt, my trembling legs beaten by the gradient. I'd be ridiculed by spectators. Other riders would sail past me. If I endured the shame of walking up the hills, I'd finish the race so far behind everyone else that they would have all gone home by the time I reached the end.

Maybe my stressing about the race hills had affected my performance today. But I had swallowed a stiff dose of reality. I couldn't escape the fear that the duathlon still lay far beyond my grasp. I phoned David. No matter that it was eleven o'clock at night in Barcelona.

"I'm sure it's not that bad," he said, calming my panic with reassuring reliability. "Get in touch with Gail and Kevin. They've both got far more experience and they'll have some good advice about what to do next."

"We're going to do a road trip," was Gail's response. "We'll run the run course and ride the bike course. Once you see what the course looks like, you'll know you can do it and you'll go into your race with stacks of confidence."

Kevin's email put life back in perspective.

> Tri-training is subject to some serious ups and downs. Tough days chew away at your confidence. So when you run into a bad day, just forget about it as soon as possible and lock onto the memories of the good days.
>
> Take a look at the course, talk to Gail, see what you think. You don't want to get in over your head. You're going to be nervous about any first race, but the key is to dive in and try, if you think it's even remotely within your capability.

Kevin's email calmed me down. Ups and downs were normal. And a scouting trip with Gail to scope out the course was a great plan.

On the third Saturday in October, Gail and I set out for

Knights Ferry, a tiny hamlet off Highway 120 on the way to Yosemite. The two-hour drive gave us more time to get to know each other. She used to work for Apple Computer as a quality specialist. But she became so consumed with triathlon and promoting healthy lifestyles, she switched careers to qualify as a personal trainer and masseuse. She planned to take classes next year to top up her Biology degree and then return to graduate school to study Physical Therapy. She was a passionate cyclist, owned three bikes and had been training for a half Ironman until she injured her pelvis a few months previously.

We approached the hamlet over a concrete bridge straddling the wide, bustling Stanislaus River. Running parallel to the new bridge was an old, wooden, covered bridge about eighty yards long and suspended about forty feet above the river. That must be part of the run course described on the event website.

We pulled into the Stanislaus National State Park car park and put on our running shoes. We set off towards the bridge.

"Jane, I may be wrong, but I think you might be running faster than you do in training," Gail said after four minutes or so.

I nodded. I was breathing heavily and had no spare breath left to talk.

"You don't have to prove anything," she said with reassurance. "We're here to work at your current endurance level. Let's just warm up, OK?"

I was relieved, not just that Gail had given me permission to ease off but that she had picked up the signals.

We ran over the covered bridge and up the hill. I had to stop twice. We didn't know the exact run course, so we turned round and ran back down. We added a loop on the flat to bring our running time up to thirty minutes, or about three miles. I battled the last half mile every step of the way because I didn't want to give in, regardless of whether Gail was there or not.

My legs were quivering when we returned to the car. We spent several minutes changing our shoes and checking the tire pressure on our bikes. We asked some passing cyclists if they knew the exact route of the duathlon bike leg. They did. We should cycle along Main Street and Orange Blossom Road, then turn right on Sonora and cycle for about eight miles and back. By the time we had said our goodbyes, I was fully recovered and ready to ride.

We rode through the town, then turned right onto Sonora. The first of those "rolling hills" loomed before us and disappeared upwards round a corner. The hill began to bite. I only managed a hundred yards before my lungs gasped and my legs screamed at me. I put my head down. I refused to look up. I counted my pedal strokes. One, two. One, two. The hill sneered back and ratcheted the gradient up one notch. A wave of panic washed over me. Was my worst nightmare coming true? Would I be forced off the bike and have to walk in the race?

It's a brutal moment when you realize you're in a situation that has stretched you to your physical limits and yet still demands more of you. I had been pedaling on the cusp of total collapse for an eternity. I felt like a wounded animal backed into a corner with nowhere to hide and facing the end.

When I felt like I was down to my last few seconds of consciousness, my feet spun round. The hill had leveled out. My legs took the decision to stop, my feet shot out of the toe clips and I came to an abrupt halt. Gail drew level several seconds later. I was on the verge of throwing up. I leaned on the handlebars, dizzy and weak, and took deep breaths to quell my volatile stomach.

When the worst of the nausea subsided, Gail asked me to explain what gears I had used, what personal effort level I had reached and how this compared to regular training. I said that I had gone further into the red zone than I had ever done in training.

"Think of yourself like a car engine," she said.

"Say you're a Honda Civic. You can't drive as fast as a Mercedes, but you have enough power to get round the course. If you rev the engine too hard, you'll blow it up. If you stay within the limits of your available power, you'll get round fast enough. Your long-term training will increase your available power to a Mercedes level. But right now you need to work within the upper limits of the Honda Civic level. Now what were those heart rates?"

Gail had recommended last month that I read an article about heart rate monitoring by Sally Edwards, a world-famous triathlete and champion of women who were new to the sport. On the strength of Sally's article, I had bought a heart rate monitor to help me pace my effort more accurately. I had done some exercises to check my heart rate in my aerobic zone, or as close as I could gauge to where my aerobic zone ought to be.

"I run in training at 162 beats a minute," I said. "According to a heart rate table I found on the Internet, the maximum for a woman of my age should be 178. And it just spiked at 179 at the top of that hill."

"Those tables are just a guide," she said. "We'll work out another time what your true maximum heart rate is. But you need to bring your effort down to a level you can sustain for the whole race. From now on, I want you to work at a rate of 155 and peak at no more than 165. That way, you won't burn out."

I nodded. I looked ahead in silence, wondering what lay round the next corner.

"So what are you really afraid of?" Gail asked.

I bit my lip. No point holding anything back from my coach.

"I'm scared of falling off," I said. "My worst fear is changing down to the smallest ring and finding it doesn't catch."

"Then we'll practice changing down ahead of time," Gail said. "A gentler slope won't put as much stress on the gear change and will cut down the chances of the chain jumping off the ring."

We set off again over large rolling hills. But none of them was as tough as the first one. I swooped downhill and used the momentum to help push me partway up the next one. The hills diminished to easy slopes and finally to level ground after about four miles.

Now we had reached the flat, I wanted to practice reaching down for my water bottle and drinking on the move. I'd got as far as taking the bottle in and out of the holder in training, but I hadn't managed to take a drink yet. I reached down for the bottle. On my second attempt, I succeeded in grabbing the bottle, swigging a long drink of Gatorade and putting the bottle back in its holder. I would be able to drink while riding in the race. At last, something had gone right.

The ride back was calm, controlled and uneventful. I was even beginning to enjoy myself. Gail showed me how to overtake another rider legally. I had to ride at least two bike lengths behind them so that I wasn't riding in their slipstream. Slipstream riding was known as "drafting," and provided a big advantage to the following rider by reducing the amount of effort required to cut into the wind. When I was ready to overtake, I must sprint past the lead rider in no more than fifteen seconds. We practiced the sprint a few times.

"Jane, I reckon you'll overtake at least ten people."

Gail's tone was dead serious.

"In your dreams!" I laughed.

We swept back down the steep hill and pulled into the car park. We loaded the bikes into the car and changed once more into our running shoes for the final run. These last 1.5 miles were tough, especially as we ran the covered bridge and long hill again. Halfway up I dropped back to a walk, but my heart rate didn't explode.

Gail drew up a duathlon race plan for me on the drive home. Go gently for the first mile of the run to warm up and keep within my heart rate limits. Drop down to my smallest ring a hundred yards before the hill. Pace myself carefully up the hill. Walk if I have to on the final run.

We talked all the way home. My head was reeling with nutrition, base endurance building, heart rate training and early triathlon experiences. We had a great road trip.

But the positive memory of the road trip subsided the moment I hit the demoralizing, agonizing pain barrier on my run up the Hill of Damnation at Water Dog Lake. Nothing had changed. I still needed two stops. Those duathlon hills loomed larger than life again. I dropped an email to Kevin. He shot a reply straight back.

> . . . you'll be pleasantly surprised at what
> you're able to do on race day. Just believe in
> yourself and then go out and have fun. And
> remember, that hill is your friend . . .

The hill? My friend? If you say so, Kevin. From now on, Hell Hill will be known as Gail. The Hill of Purgatory on the Triangle of Misery will be known as Cristina. And the Hill of Damnation, that eleven-minute blinder which brings me almost to my knees? That's a no-brainer. That hill is called Kevin.

The next time out round the Triangle of, er, up Cristina Hill I should say, I changed my language. Instead of cursing about how wretched I felt when running uphill, I welcomed the hill as my friend.

"Hello, Cristina Hill! Let's do this together! We'll get there!"

Thank goodness no one could hear me talking to a hill. But the weird thing was that it helped. Positive self-talk, no matter how silly it might have sounded, gave me added impetus to tackle the toughest part of the hill. I wasn't sure what Kevin had in mind, but it worked for me.

As I ran back downhill, I remembered Michelle Cleere's workshop at Sports Basement last summer. I recalled nodding in agreement when she explained that positive self-talk was a key part of mental training. But I had been paying lip service to positive self-talk. I didn't practice it on a regular basis. It was too easy to tell myself that I wasn't yet physically ready for the challenge of a longer distance or tougher hill and allow myself to walk. Today, I finally understood the power of self-talk on a daily basis. My brain tells my body what to do. If I say I can't do it, I'll stop. If I tell myself I can do it, I can push the barrier and increase my performance.

The next day, I went out and bought a new fridge magnet. I took down my wishy-washy Ralph Waldo Emerson magnet of *What lies behind us and what lies before us are small matters compared to what lies within us.* I put up my new, no-nonsense Winston Churchill magnet of *Never, never, never give up.* And "never – never – never – give up" was easier to chant when I was running. From now on, I must train myself mentally on every session rather than waiting until the chips are down in a race.

In the last week before the race, I eased up on the training. My last run was on Tuesday morning and last spin class on Wednesday evening. I did both of them at sixty percent effort. I was as ready as I was ever going to be for this duathlon. Now I just had to go out there, believe in myself and race.

Run, Bike, Run

Number of times I told myself I wasn't ready for a duathlon: two million

Number of times I decided to go for it regardless: two million and one

Duathlon Day. 6:29 a.m. Best Western Hotel, Oakdale, California. I watched the red numbers on the alarm clock flip over to 6:30 a.m. The buzzer sounded. I hit the "off" button within two seconds and nudged David. He grunted in acknowledgment but didn't move.

My race clothes of gray and white cycling jersey and black shorts lay on a chair. My bike stood waiting for me, leaning against the bedroom wall where I had propped it up the night before.

I stepped into the shower. My stomach cramped. My chest ached, as though I were holding my breath. Gentle water cascaded over me but did nothing to soothe the tension. In the swim race, the knots of worry had disappeared the moment the starting horn sounded. The tension would probably ease this time too. And the scouting trip with Gail had given me the boost of confidence I needed that this race lay within my capabilities, even if I was right at the limit. I wrapped my arms round that inner confidence and held it close.

"Breakfast is ready when you are," David called out.

He had made himself busy with support crew arrangements the moment I headed for the bathroom.

I toweled off and pulled on the waiting race clothes. He removed a steaming bowl of breakfast oatmeal from a small micro-wave in the corner of the bedroom and handed it to me. I drizzled the oatmeal with a triple portion of Tate & Lyle Golden Syrup that I had brought back from England. This supersweet, viscous amber liquid had always been one of my top childhood comfort foods. I savored every mouthful. My fuel store for the race lay warm and satisfying in my stomach.

David headed off to Reception. Waiting in the queue to check out would raise my anxiety even further. Instead, I packed the car and did a last-minute gear check. My eyes avoided the clock on the dashboard. I had to be on time.

I sat on my hands for the entire twenty-minute journey to Knights Ferry. Fidgeting would betray my nerves. We arrived at the car park at 7:42 a.m. David glanced over at me.

"So I count nine cars here already," he said. "Which of the remaining hundred spots would you like me to park in, dear?"

We chuckled. Turning up early was becoming our specialty. I delegated the decision to him.

David unloaded my bike and foot pump, then checked the tire pressure. I could have checked it myself, but I was content to let him do it. Besides, there weren't too many other ways he could show his support for me right now. Watching him check the tires reminded me how lucky I was to have his unconditional commitment to me and to my incomprehensible decision to participate in an endurance event.

The car park filled up with SUVs, trucks, RVs and a hand-ful of hatchbacks. Two women in navy sweats jogged down to the registration table. A team of UC Davis athletes wearing their "Aggies" team colors checked tire pressures. A man and woman did warmup stretches next to their black truck. I stood by while David loaded the bike pump back into our SUV.

"Do you want to jog for a few minutes to warm up?" David

asked. "I can look after your bike, if you want."

"No," I replied. Why expend precious yards now when it didn't count? "I've only got four and a half miles in my legs at the most. I'm going to need all of those for the race."

Next task was to scope out the transition area, a section of car park roped off for the race. Twenty rows of bike racks were lined up down the longest side, like teeth on a comb. Each rack held twelve bikes. Should I position myself near the exit or the entrance to the transition area? At the near end or far end of a bike rack? I couldn't determine a pattern, and I didn't want to be stuck in the middle of the really good people. I picked a rack near the entrance to the transition area and took a spot on the inside of the comb, nearest to the spectators. That way, I would only have competitors on one side of me.

By 8:30 a.m., pale sunshine had raised the temperature to a gentle 60°. I still wore my long-sleeved top and running tights over my race clothes. I had bought a new pair of cycling shorts, with thinner padding made of chamois leather, especially for the race. They were easier to run in than my shorts with the bulky foam padding. I hadn't ridden in them yet, so I was a little apprehensive about whether my nether regions would end up completely numb after one hour in the saddle. I had visions of getting off the bike, changing into my running shoes, then wobbling around on drunken legs as the numb parts corrupted the running instructions from brain to limbs. An endurance event hid all manner of perils that I could never have imagined before today.

David and I walked over to the registration table. I collected my race number of 1445 and handed it to him. I would have only rolled and folded and unrolled and unfolded it in nervous anticipation. Best have David look after it. Then the race director called everyone together for the pre-race meeting.

"The run course is a rectangular circuit of 1.5 miles," he told us over a handheld megaphone. "Start on the road outside the parking lot. Run downhill over the bridge across the river. Turn right and run parallel to the river, then right again across the covered bridge. Up the hill, right at the top and back down to where you started on the main road. Then into the transition area and down that path at the back."

He pointed in the general direction of the bike racks.

"Then loop back to the road for a second circuit of the rectangle. That'll be your three-mile run. At the end of the second circuit, transition to the bike. Cycle back down the main road to the river, left at the end, along Main Street and Orange Blossom Road, turn right on Sonora."

My mind pictured the route I had ridden with Gail.

"This is a nineteen-mile out-and-back course, so look out for a steward at the turnaround point," he said. "Then back into transition and out on one loop of the run course. That's another mile and a half. Then you're home and dry."

In addition to the duathlon, a three-mile run would start alongside us. The runners would complete two circuits only of the rectangle alongside the duathletes. Instead of peeling off to the transition area, the runners would finish their race by passing under the banner at the finish line.

"Don't follow the person ahead of you on the first run in case they're a runner and not a duathlete," the race director warned. "We don't want you duathletes crossing the finish line by accident."

The race director wished us all good luck. I turned and walked towards the start line, my arms folded tightly across my chest.

"What's up?" David said.

He touched my elbow and raised his eyebrows.

"I still can't work out where this path is," I said through

pursed lips. "And I've no time to go back and look for it."

A guy with blonde, close-cropped hair overheard me. His gray and white triathlon suit bore the brand name Zoot on the side.

"Don't worry," he said as he walked past us. "It's real obvious when you get there. Just follow the others and you'll be OK."

"Thanks!" I called to his back. "It's my first multi-sport race, so it's all a bit new."

He turned back and waved over his shoulder. "You'll do OK. Good luck!"

I appreciated his good wishes, but he had no idea how slowly I ran. What if I was so far off the back of the pack that I would have no one to follow? And that was without the bit about making sure I didn't follow a runner over the finish line by mistake. I sighed. I could have done without these added complications.

We reached the road. I peeled off my top layers and handed them to David. He pinned my race number to my cycling jersey with safety pins and gave me one last hug. I lined up, about halfway back in the pack behind Zoot Suit Man.

The starting horn sounded. I pushed the button on my heart rate monitor/stopwatch. All chatting and laughter ceased as more than three hundred individual athletes snapped to attention with one purpose. They threaded together into a fluid carpet of bobbing heads, propelled by the soft slap-slap-slap of running shoes hitting the road. I was swept forward, pulled along by the strands of a common goal connecting me to my fellow runners. My brain hit "play." My head filled with *Chariots of Fire* music. I grinned. I had crossed the starting line. I was part of the fabric.

The lead runners unraveled off the front of the pack. Several runners overtook me. I overtook a couple of people. I settled into my place in the overall scheme of things—a guy about five yards ahead, three women a couple of yards behind. I rounded the corner at the bottom of the hill and ran alongside the river. My breathing was a little tight. I checked my heart rate monitor. The display showed 162.

My heart rate shouldn't be higher than 155 beats a minute right now. Gail had given me strict instructions on keeping my exertion level below 155 beats, something I could sustain for the whole race. 165 beats was my ceiling for maximum effort. This wasn't in my race plan. Even in training, my heart rate didn't reached 162 after only four hundred yards.

Work it out, Jane. Something must be causing this. Nerves? Inexperience? Overeagerness at the beginning? Probably all of the above. What about adrenaline? That must be it. Adrenaline triggered by my first road race must be pushing my speed and my heart rate up. So long as adrenaline didn't cause me to burn out, I'd take the additional kick as an added bonus. I recalibrated Gail's marks of 155 and 165 and pushed them up to 162 and 172 to allow for extra kick.

The amplified thunder of athletes' footsteps filled the covered bridge. The hill lay ahead. I burst into the sunlight and hunkered down. This hill is my friend! I've run it before and I can run it again. I pushed myself uphill. My legs fought hard. Another fifty yards. My breathing grabbed the air with just a hint of panic. I glanced down at my monitor. My heart rate read 179.

I had to back off from that dangerous level of exertion that had nearly made me sick on the scouting trip. I walked up the hill to bring my effort under control. By the time I reached the top, my heart rate had settled back down to 156.

Time to run again. I turned right onto the flat and caught up with a woman runner about my age. Her dark, wavy hair bounced with each light step. I fell in beside her. She asked me which race I was running. We began chatting. Good thing I'd joined the Running and Chatting Club with Cristina a few weeks earlier.

Michele, my new running buddy, was running the three-mile race. Forty-four years old and a mother of two, she had decided four years ago to train for a marathon. Now she was training for her second. I told her about my triathlon goals, that this was my first event and that I wasn't the world's strongest runner. Before I knew it, we had breezed through the transition area and looped round the very obvious and well-signposted path back to the road.

Michele coached me every fifty yards on the repeat loop. To encourage me up the hill, she set me a goal to reach the next of the mailboxes positioned at regular, house-length intervals. I hadn't even noticed the row of galvanized steel boxes atop their four-by-four wooden poles first time round. Now I saw them, stretched out like a string of lassos, waiting to grab hold of me and drag me up their section of the hill before flinging me upwards to the next waiting mailbox.

When my heart rate hit 181, I had to go back to my own game plan. I walked. Even the mailboxes couldn't do anything about a 181 heart rate. I thanked Michele for her encouragement and wished her luck as she pulled away.

I started running again near the top of the hill and continued all the way back to the transition area. The clock by the finish line showed 33 minutes, 11 seconds. I ran to the side of the finish banner to loop round to the transition area. Michele stood by the finish. She waved me on as I ran past her. I waved back.

I ran into the transition area. I had no problem spotting my bike. Out of around 180 bikes racked up before the start, I could count the remaining eight by the time I reached mine.

I knelt down to change from running shoes into cycling shoes. I'd finished the part of the race I was most worried about. I'd only run this far about five times in training and never once without stopping. I had now run three miles in about thirty-four minutes. And I hadn't finished in last place either, although I wasn't far off.

David stood several feet away, not making a sound. He crouched down and took a couple of photos. He looked like a wildlife photographer, moving gingerly so as not to disturb a rare species. I had told him before the race not to talk to me because I wanted to focus on making the fastest transition I could. But I was reassured to see him there. After all, he was Chief Supporter.

I put my bike helmet on, unracked my bike, walked it to the end of the transition area and set off cycling towards the main road. I looked down. My bike speedometer registered zero. I clicked the reset button a few times. Still zero. I looked down to check the wheel sensor, a device about the size of a hearing aid battery attached to the spokes. For the first time ever since owning my bike, I had set the wheel into the front bike forks the wrong way round. The wheel sensor was now positioned on the left side, not the right side where it belonged. The device could no longer record wheel revolutions that gave me speed and distance readouts. Switching the wheel round would cost me at least a minute. That was unacceptable. I would have to continue without my comfort blanket of reassuring numbers on my speedometer.

Focus, Jane, focus. Don't waste time on being unsettled. Put the speedometer mishap behind you right now and prepare for the big hill. You'll be there in less than two minutes.

I cycled at a gentle speed along Main Street. Race stewards were positioned at each intersection to hold back vehicles and give cyclists priority. But they didn't have much to do. I suspected that rush hour in Knights Ferry might constitute two pickups and a tractor on a bad day.

Gail's race plan had provided strict instructions on that crucial gear switch on the hill. If I downshifted too late, the hill's steep gradient might cause the chain to jump the gears or even jump off the ring altogether. Or I'd be stuck in a higher gear than I had intended and I'd burn out. Either way, timing was important.

I slowed for the corner and turned right on Sonora Road. I worked my way down the rear cogs as the gradient pushed back at the bike. I dropped down to the little ring right on cue at the bottom of the hill. My speed dropped still further. I shifted down the final two rear cogs. I had reached the lowest of my low gears. Now I just had to grind it out.

Memories of my previous nauseous, dizzy end to this hill floated into my mind. If my heart rate was pumped up with adrenaline, would I pass out before the top? Don't torment yourself with what-if's, Jane. Stick to Gail's plan. Work within your limits.

My legs weakened. I refused to look more than five yards ahead. I channeled my remaining energy into each stroke. I repeated my fridge magnet motto over and over in time to the pedal strokes. Never – never – never – give up. Don't look up or you'll panic. Never – never – never – give up. On the ninth repeat, the pressure of the gradient eased off through the pedals. The gear strategy and the self-talk had worked. I had crested the hill.

I looked up and saw four riders ahead of me. They rode together and turned to each other to chat. A group of friends. I had spent the first seven minutes consumed with the speedometer mishap and fear of the hill. I had almost forgotten that this race had other competitors. This group was ripe for overtaking.

I reminded myself of the overtaking maneuver I had practiced with Gail. I mustn't ride within two bike lengths of the rider in front. That was considered an illegal "drafting" move, where I would gain unfair advantage by riding in the shelter of the lead rider's slipstream. I had only fifteen seconds to pull out, cycle past and pull ahead.

I cranked up the gears on the next downward slope and pedaled hard to build up momentum. I picked my moment and pushed hard up the next hill. I sailed past the group. They couldn't chase me because they couldn't accelerate uphill to catch me. Gail was right. I was going to overtake riders today.

I now wanted to beat as many other competitors as I could. These people were ahead of me because they could run faster than I could. I had to pass as many as possible on the bike leg or they would catch me on the final run. More adrenaline tingled through my body. My goal had shifted. I no longer wanted just to finish. I wanted to race.

I pressed on up the next hill. Out of nowhere, I heard the whirr of bike spokes. I looked up. The first half-dozen race leaders flew towards me at supersonic speed. I was only twelve minutes into my outward leg. Yet the lead group had already reached the turnaround and was on its way back. They crouched forward, leaning on their aerobars in a sleek aerodynamic position, their body postures exuding power and determination.

"You go girl!" the lone woman rider in the group shouted out as she drew level.

I looked round. Who was she shouting at? There were no other women on the road but her and me. Was she giving herself a pep talk? The group shot past. I puzzled over the incident for several seconds.

I rode like a woman possessed, powering past riders uphill and overtaking a few who were coasting downhill. No one overtook me. I rode past sweeping, bare hills that shone golden in the morning sunshine. Returning cyclists streamed towards me on the deserted road. I rode past a field of brown cows. Last time at this spot, Gail had shouted out, "Say 'hi' to the peanut gallery!"

Did cows eat peanuts? I still had no idea what she had meant, but I said "hi" to the cows anyway, to remind me of our great road trip.

I rounded a bend. Fluorescent yellow flashed bright against dull gray pavement. A steward was standing in the middle of the road. I had no speedometer to tell me that I had cycled 9.5 miles already. The turnaround had caught me by surprise.

The stopwatch on my heart rate monitor showed 1 hour, 16 minutes, 7 seconds. I did some quick mental calculations. The outward bike leg had taken about thirty-six minutes. Add another thirty-six minutes for the return leg, plus about twenty minutes for the transition and run. If I carried on like this, I would definitely beat the target I'd announced to everyone of 2 hours, 20 minutes. But I wanted more. I had set a target known only to me of 2 hours, 10 minutes—the very best time I thought I could manage. I attacked the next hill with renewed determination. At this rate, I had an outside chance of hitting my secret time.

"Good job!" a rider called out to me as I overtook.

"Thanks!" I called back in astonishment. Then I added, just in time, "Good work!"

Several more riders I overtook called out too. I swapped a few words of encouragement with each of them. We were racing each other, but we were also racing against ourselves and our personal limitations. Maybe that lead woman cyclist had been calling out to me after all. Encouraging other racers felt the right thing to do.

I overtook my final rider on the long fast sweep back down the Hill of Hills. I had moved up seventeen places in the race. But I still had to wring every last ounce of advantage out of the bike leg before these better runners reached the last run.

I swept back over the river and up the last hill. My heart rate showed 149. I was in good shape. David stood at the top, waving and cheering me on. I grinned but didn't wave back. Taking my hands off the handlebars might risk a last-minute spill. I swung into the transition area and dismounted.

This time, the bike racks were about three-quarters full. Competitors who had already finished the race wandered around, eating orange quarters and drinking water. Congratulatory chatter buzzed in the air. I changed into my running shoes, drank some water and ate a packet of a sticky carbohydrate gel called Gu. The last guy I had overtaken on the Hill of Hills raced past me and disappeared along the trail. Damn. He had the lanky, coordinated look of a fast runner. That was why he had been seventeen cyclists ahead of me. I would never catch him now.

Lanky Guy was the wakeup call I needed. Don't throw away all that bike advantage. I hurtled along the path to loop back to the main road, driven by the instant blast of energy from the Gu. David waved again from his vantage point at the car park exit. I almost tumbled down the hill in my effort to turn my legs over faster.

I rounded the corner to the flat that ran parallel with the river. Lanky Guy was already way off in the distance. But I was gaining on the next runner ahead. I fixed my eyes on his white top and blue shorts, determined not to let him get away from me.

Then my legs stopped running. No warning. One minute I was running and the next I was walking. What did my legs think they were doing? I had one mile to go, I had a runner I could pick off in front and someone closing in behind me. This was my chance to beat Blue and White Guy.

But it's so relaxing to walk, the pain in my lower leg muscles has eased off, why not just walk the whole way back? There's no shame in that, just drift on . . .

Snap out of it. Legs, do you hear me? Snap OUT of it. I won't let you give up on me just like that. You came to race. You've done all that training. You're not going to throw it all away. So get yourselves into gear and run right NOW.

The part of my brain that controlled my legs was having none of it.

OK, then. I'll do a deal with you. If you run 240 paces, I'll let you walk 120. Run 240, walk 120. That's how we'll get through this. Will you buy that?

My legs replied by cranking themselves up into an ambling gait that wasn't exactly running but wasn't walking either. I counted my breathing. Breathe in two paces, out four paces. Forty breaths equals 240 paces. That was all I had to do before I was allowed to stop. Forty breaths.

My lone footsteps echoed through the silence of the covered bridge. Last time, the water had been in shadow. This time, thin slats of bright sunlight shimmered upwards between wooden planks. I ran over moving rods of water. Within ten yards I felt dizzy. Within twenty yards, I couldn't run in a straight line. I slowed to a walk and stared straight ahead.

I emerged from the bridge. The walking break had been unplanned. Now I had to run. I goaded myself into action. Where was that next mailbox?

Past the first mailbox. Legs wobbling from exhaustion. Onto the next. Thirty breaths. Heart rate 176. Enough. I fell back to a walk. I looked behind for my pursuer. He was walking too. I was safe for the moment. I was loathe to see Blue and White Guy gain any more distance on me, but it couldn't be helped. I'd have to let him go.

Well, whad'ya know? He had stopped running. OK Jane, this is your chance. The only way to pass him is to do it now, on the hill. Once he reaches the flat, he'll recover and you won't stand a chance. What are you waiting for? Who's hurting more, him or you? Get ON with it!

I had a fleeting vision of Captain James T. Kirk of the Starship Enterprise on the intercom to Scotty, asking for every last ounce of power out of the engines. I heard Scotty's reply of "Ah canny hold 'er for long, Cap'n," and pictured that dour Scottish look on his face. I allowed myself a brief smile, then cranked up the ailing, creaking engines one last time and directed all remaining power to my legs. The Starship Enterprise always managed to pull itself out of every intergalactic crisis. All I had to do was drag myself up this hill, one mailbox at a time.

Blue and White Guy was still walking. My staggering, foot-dragging pace was barely faster than a walk, but I was gaining on him. Yes you can! Yes you can! I willed myself past him.

"Hey, way to go," he called out as I overtook.

I smiled and waved at him, not trusting myself to speak. Don't think, just count.

My legs picked up straight away when the gradient eased. I had reached the last mailbox. I turned the corner.

Don't stop now or you'll lose your slender advantage. Run the stress out of your legs on the flat. Ease down, keep moving forward.

I rounded the next bend and recovered with some gentle downhill running. I checked my stopwatch. 2 hours, 5 minutes, 23 seconds. Less than five minutes to go to hit my secret time of 2 hours, 10 minutes.

I fixed on the turning into the car park about two hundred yards ahead. Nothing was going to hold me back from my secret time. I reached the turning. Heart rate didn't matter any longer. My old sprinting instincts from my schooldays resurfaced. Push the pace as fast as you can! I saw the finish banner. I flew towards the clock. 2 hrs, 7 minutes, 55 seconds and counting . . .

I crossed the line in 2 hours, 8 minutes and 8 seconds.

Elation ignited my face into a huge grin. I smothered David

in a big, exhausted, half-collapsing hug. He presented me with my victory orange quarters. I ate them, drank a bottle of water and walked around the transition area. Michele must have gone home already. I spotted Zoot Suit Man with his partner and a toddler in a stroller. I dashed over and told him of my 2 hour, 8 minute and 8 second victory. A look of puzzled confusion skittered across his face, but he recovered in time to congratulate me.

The results appeared on the website the next day. I had placed tenth out of thirteen women in the 40-49 age group, thirty-fourth out of forty-two women in total and 134 out of 155 overall. When I checked my email, Kevin's note was waiting for me.

> . . . you conquered both the course and the self-doubts that crept up through the prep. And you discovered a lot of what makes endurance sport and multi-sport so addictive . . . the camaraderie, the personal challenge, and all of the little personal races within the race. Congrats on a stellar performance and on staying so mentally tough late in the race.

His email summed up the pride I felt in my achievement. All those spin classes, those early morning runs and the weight sessions had paid off with a race time even better than I could have imagined. And despite my constant battle with running, I had survived both runs. I still had a lot of work to do. But this result confirmed that I was on track to go for the San Jose Tri. I was going to register as soon as website applications opened on New Year's Day.

Spinning Plates

Number of times I tried to impose order on my chaotic life: countless

Number of times I failed to impose order: countless

I registered for the San Jose Triathlon at 7:48 a.m. on the day the website opened for enrollments. All it took was one simple click. But life would be anything but simple for the next few months. I couldn't wait to get started.

I squeezed eleven training sessions a week onto my busy calendar. On Monday, Wednesday and Friday mornings, I would run. On Monday evenings, swim. On Tuesday and Thursday evenings, swim and lift weights. On Wednesday evenings and Friday mornings, spin in Gail's classes. On Sunday afternoons, a two-hour bike ride with David. And Saturday would be a training-free zone, reserved for real life.

My swim, weight and spin sessions would take place at the San Jose Y, close to work, instead of at the San Mateo Y, close to home. A break longer than fifteen minutes between work and workout caused my motivation to evaporate. But I could move from office to San Jose Y locker room in four minutes flat if all the traffic lights were green.

The first issue I encountered in my schedule was that the indoor pool at the San Jose Y was packed with swim lessons in the early evening after work. I would have to use the outdoor pool in the middle of winter if I wanted to swim laps. I tiptoed barefoot across cold flagstone to the pool, lit from below so that it shone like a beacon in the night sky. The electric-blue water silhouetted the busy colony of swimmers scurrying over its surface.

I found a lane and slipped into the luminescent pool. I turned onto my back and swam some easy warmup pulls of backstroke. Pinhead-sized stars were strewn across the dark half-dome above. Traffic noise receded, replaced by the soothing trickle of water past my ears. I turned over and switched to my thirty-five laps of fast freestyle. My body skimmed along the surface at the intersection of 80° water and 48° air, the water wrapping its protective blanket of warmth around me. Dark sky, glowing blue light, trickling water and fluid warmth combined to surround me in an alternate sensory world, far removed from training. But my shivering, fifteen-yard dash from pool to locker room through chilly air in a wet swimsuit brought me back to the real world soon enough.

My morning schedule of three runs a week was not designed for winter at all. I've always hated getting up. Even worse, getting up one hour early in the dark. Getting up one hour early in the dark and the rain was one step too far.

I reminded myself of the stern British attitude to rain. There was no such thing as bad weather, merely inappropriate clothing. I bought a light, hooded, waterproof running jacket. But I still buried my head under the duvet and indulged in an extra hour of sleep if I heard especially heavy rain beating against the window.

My run buddy Cristina didn't like rainy dark mornings either. Our cure was to commit to a weekly run together along the Bayshore path, past the five looming glass towers of the Oracle headquarters in Redwood Shores. The guilt of letting Cristina wait in the dark was enough to jumpstart me out of bed the moment the alarm clock sounded.

Cristina and I congratulated each other every week on

our outstanding attendance record while we weaved our way amongst slumbering offices and houses. I steeled myself to run in light rain on Cristina-less days, but I struggled to achieve two additional solo runs. Alternate Persona could still pick holes in my schedule when it chose to.

My cycling training schedule was geared to my need to build enough strength and stamina to cycle the San Jose Tri bike course. I had printed out the bike course description from the website on the day I signed up for the event.

> **Approximately halfway through the course, participants encounter a mile-long hill. Bailey Avenue is a steep grade where athletes will start to feel the effects of hammering the flats. This part of the course can be a strategic point where competitors can make or break their day.**

That description had preyed on my mind ever since I first read it. I didn't like the idea that a hill could break my day.

Whatever else was happening in my life, I erected barbed wire fences round the spin class times on my calendar. I had to build leg strength, no matter that each class was so exhausting that I would have to back off from the toughest exercises. By February, I couldn't let the course description torment me any longer. I had to test myself. I called Gail. Would she ride the San Jose course with me?

We met in the car park at Lake Almaden, the site of the Triathlon swim and run courses. A sunny, late-February morning with the temperature in the low 60s. Gail and I cycled along wide, four-lane suburban roads with stops for traffic lights every few hundred yards. After seven miles, the road petered out into a country lane through flat farmland. The sun lit up short, vibrant green shoots that covered the fields. Hills loomed in the distance.

Three miles later, we turned right onto Bailey Avenue. We cycled past the sign for the IBM Research Center. We crossed the little bridge over a stream—and then I saw it. The hill. The road swung to the left before it snaked up and out of sight. Out of sight was not good. Out of sight meant I had no idea how steep the gradient would climb or how long the agony would last.

Gail told me to prepare for a ten-minute climb. Ten minutes? Would I make it to the top? My stomach fluttered and my legs were awash with panic. Then Rational Me stepped in. Who said that I wouldn't make it to the top? That the pain would be intense? Let's wait and see, shall we? No point torturing myself with what might happen.

Alternate Persona wouldn't listen. It screamed at me for getting myself into this mess and insisted I stop.

I pulled off the road by the bend at the bottom of the hill and watched Gail pull ahead. I needed a moment to myself. I looked up. The road stretched up ahead, the summit out of sight. The gradient didn't look that bad, just a lot of it. I hadn't come this far, only to give up. I was strong. Gail disappeared round the corner. I challenged Alternate Persona to shut up complaining and let me get on with this.

My foot slid into the toe clip. I pinged the stopwatch on my heart rate monitor. I set off with a short burst to build up enough speed so as not to fall off. My eyes fixed on the road five feet in front of me. I refused to listen to the cries of Alternate Persona. I had to see how far I could get before this hill forced me to stop.

I counted off the three-foot-high posts with reflective markers that were strung out every hundred yards. Don't panic. Pace myself. This was a scouting trip to check out how long this hill lasted. So what, if I had to stop? Just go back down and try again.

By the third marker, the gradient eased. I rounded the

hairpin bend, maintaining ninety per cent effort on my lowest gear. I dared to look up. Gail stood at the top, astride her bike. Yes – I can – Yes – I can, I chanted in time to my pedal strokes. The gradient eased a fraction more. I passed two more markers. My legs poured effort into the hill, but I remained within my limit of exertion.

Gail cheered when I reached the top. I pulled over next to her. My stopwatch read 6 minutes, 37 seconds. Satisfaction flooded through my veins. Maybe the hills were my friends after all. We celebrated my first ascent with a high-five.

The one thing I hadn't allowed for in my weekly training schedule was that real life refused to be boxed into its allotted slot of Saturdays. Skiing trips displaced the long ride on four winter weekends. A bad cold and flu took me out of action for nearly two weeks. Breakfast meetings and evening events pushed aside several morning runs, swims and even the occasional spin class. No matter how fast I spun the plates, one of them always seemed to wobble and fall off when I wasn't looking.

I had to find a way to protect the remaining sessions in my schedule. Ten minutes before I was due at the gym, Alternate Persona would remind me how much it hated training and would beg to be let off, just this once. But one missed training session was the start of the slippery slope. I would only find more reasons to miss the next and the next. Then I'd end up unprepared for San Jose.

I made a deal with myself. I wouldn't think about weights or spin or swim at all. I would focus on walking into the locker room and getting changed. If I still wanted to stop when I had changed, I gave myself permission to go home. But once I was in my cycling shorts, swimsuit or gym clothes, I would march off and spin, swim or lift weights. In two months of intense workouts, I went home only once after getting changed.

But despite two whole months of intense workouts, I saw zero progress. Time to dig deep. I had no immediate results to motivate me. I had to grit my teeth and keep the faith. Sometime, something would change. In the first week of March, everything did change.

At Gail's spin class that week, I powered through the hill exercises. I was on fire, chasing Lance Armstrong up the Pyrenees, driven on by fluttering Union Jacks and the cheering crowd. Two days later, I ran down to Cristina's house instead of driving, did our weekly run together and ran all the way back. I toughed it out up the huge climb back to my house, stopped just twice and ran for fifty-eight minutes. I was flying. I only broke off because I would be late for work if I carried on. The hours of training had paid off. I had broken through to a new level of fitness.

Now that I could run for fifty-eight minutes, I aimed to run for 1 hour, 10 minutes every time. I changed my route to walk down Gail Hill, do circuits on the flat and force myself to run back up again. Forget its previous incarnation as Hell Hill. My willpower needed toughening up to drive me through hard spells in the race.

Three runs later, Cristina joined me at the bottom of Gail Hill. We set off on our weekly catch-up and jog. Within twelve minutes, my right knee seized up. I was reduced to a limping walk. The tightness was so bad that Cristina had to give me a ride back up the hill. But within ten minutes of reaching home, the pain disappeared. The same thing happened next time out. Twelve-minute run, seized knee, walk home. On my third run, the seizing began even earlier, as I was walking down the hill.

What was the difference between a pain you should ignore and one that told you something was seriously wrong? Ten minutes after I finished running, my seized knee would return to normal, so it couldn't be that serious. But when I tried to run, the pain reduced me to a limp. Should I consider going to the doctor?

I had missed one of Gail's classes through work commitments and she had arranged a substitute for another. When we finally caught up, two weeks after the start of the knee problem, she asked me to describe my symptoms and my training.

"So you went from running thirty-five minutes to an hour and ten?" she said. "When we reviewed your training program, it had nothing about running an hour and ten. Why didn't you tell me?"

I thought she'd be pleased with my leap of progress.

"Training is about being patient," she went on. "It's about building up gradually and not stressing your body with huge changes in distance. Your knee is letting you know that you pushed too far. If it gets worse, you should definitely see a doctor. But it sounds to me like you have a tight IT Band."

"I have a what?"

My eyebrows pulled together.

"Your Ilio Tibial Band is a ligament that connects the outside of your knee with your hip, right here." Gail put her thumb on the pivot point on the outside of her hip. "If you're not that flexible, you'll aggravate it when you run and then the band tightens up. That's why you get that pulling feeling in your knee."

"So what should I do about it?"

"First, I want you to stretch every night. You need to improve your flexibility in your legs and hips."

Gail had repeated over and over that stretching was important. But stretching was boring. There was no immediate result, a bit like lifting weights. Except that the result of not stretching was a problem like this. And this wasn't the first time I had ignored Gail's advice and done my own thing with my training plan. I sighed. What was the point of paying someone to give me advice and then ignoring it?

"OK," I said. "Stretching. I'll do it."

"For the next two weeks, I want you to try water walking," Gail said, getting into her stride. "Wear a buoyancy belt, tread water in the deep end of the pool and practice running in the water. It strengthens your knee without the strain. There's a class Tuesdays and Thursdays."

"If that's what it takes, I'll do it. I promise."

"On the third week, start each run by stretching and then walking to warm up. Do gentle running only. And twenty minutes tops for your first week. Build up five minutes a week from there. That's five minutes, not twenty because you're feeling good."

I hung my head. My stubborn inexperience had caused havoc with my training plan.

"Don't worry." Gail smiled and put an arm round my shoulder. "We all learn from our mistakes. And don't neglect that stretching. Got that?"

Yes, ma'am. Time for me to do as I was told.

I joined sixteen ladies of generous proportions and nicely coiffed, dry hair at my first water-walking class. I wore my swimcap and goggles. They all bobbed round slowly to music in a large pinwheel formation. The instructor at the central pivot point shouted commands like "Cossacks!" and "Can Cans!" On the surface, nothing changed. The Coiffed Hairdos continued chatting, laughing and circling. I ducked down. Underwater, the sixteen ladies all kicked their legs in unison in a different direction with each command. I never did get the hang of Cossacks and Can Cans. I just bobbed up and down, furiously running on the spot and getting nowhere. They all smiled in encouragement and waved as they can-canned past me.

I stretched every day over the next two weeks, including a special stretch that Gail showed me for my Ilio Tibial Band. I had to squat down almost to a sitting position, then rest one ankle on my other knee and sit back even farther. The stretch reminded me of that casual way guys often sit with one ankle on the knee. Mrs. Kershaw, my fifth-grade teacher, had groomed all the girls in our class that we should sit gracefully and never adopt such an unladylike pose. I wondered what she would have made of Casual Seated Guy stretch.

I returned to gentle running on week three. I went through my warmup routine as I had been instructed. I ran. I stopped the moment I felt the slightest twinge and did my IT Band stretch. The knee tightness eased off and I could continue running.

My knee problems had wiped out most of my March training. I had managed only two spin classes, one swim and a bike ride each week. Water walking had replaced weights and swimming on Tuesdays and Thursdays. I had only just returned to running a short distance. My schedule was in tatters. I needed something to fire me up. I needed an event.

Photo: David King

Photo: David King

LEFT: Cycling by the Big River, near Mendocino, CA, my first time back on a bike in thirty-one years. **RIGHT:** I learned never to combine wine with cycling again after this lunchtime break at Geyser Peak Winery, Healdsburg.

Photo: Jane Booth

Photo: David King

Our first road trip with our new bikes. Outside Quivira Winery, Healdsburg, CA.

Photo: David King

Photo: David King

LEFT: Apprehension before my first ever endurance event—the Bethel Island one-mile swim. Note I'm still wearing my wedding ring. **RIGHT:** A steward helps me out of the water, seconds before I stubbed my toe.

Photo: David King

Where has everyone gone? Water, reeds, me.

LEFT: Yes, I really did it! Joy after the swim (without wedding ring). **RIGHT:** Pulling on a brave face prior to my first multisport race, the Salmon Duathlon.

T1 (first transition) in the duathlon. I'm not last, but not far off.

Photo courtesy of Photocrazy.com

Outward leg of the duathlon ride. Note this ride was still in my toe clip phase.

Photo: Scott Giese

Photo: David King

LEFT: Celebrating David's victory in the Human Race. **RIGHT:** So you want me to smile now? This was the best I could manage, after returning from the far side of weird on the bike leg at my first Uvas Tri.

Photo: David King

LEFT: Determined stride through T2 (second transition) at my first San Jose Tri. **RIGHT:** Where are my socks? I NEED those socks… T2 at my first San Jose Tri.

Photo: David King

The only shot I have, shared with an anonymous cardboard box, of me finishing my first San Jose Tri. Still not yet learned to cross the line and smile at the same time.

Photo: David King

Photo: Scott Giese

LEFT: Celebrating the San Jose Tri with (l. to r.) Gail DeCamp, Mike Popa and me. Gail finished so early, she had time to change. **RIGHT:** I was all smiles on the bike leg of the Olympic-distance TriOne in Alameda, CA, but I fell apart on the run.

Photo: Louise Smith

September 11. A big date in history. Our twentieth wedding anniversary. We always celebrate, no matter what.

Photo courtesy of Brightroom.com

Coleman Road bridge during my second San Jose Tri. I spotted the photographer just in time, hid the half-empty Gu packet in my right hand and put on my confident face. I rode the rest of the way with Gu dribbles over my fingers and handlebars.

Photo courtesy of Brightroom.com

A rare photo of me running. I tried to smile–not bad, considering I was just finishing the five-mile run at my second Uvas Tri.

Photo courtesy of Brightroom.com

David's running career took off after I took up triathlon. Running the San Francisco Bridge to Bridge race.

17-Mile Drive in Carmel, CA. Cycling is still one of our favorite recreational pursuits.

Photo: Nicole Lazzaro

Finish of my first half marathon, San Francisco. Note to self: learn to smile when crossing line. David had already finished his race and came back to run in with me.

Photo: Nicole Lazzaro

A celebration of the half marathon, my best ever race to date: (l. to. r.) David, me, Kevin Kennedy.

Final Preparations

Temperature of water in Aquatic Park on practice swim: 49°

Reaction of Alternate Persona to 49°: unprintable

I enrolled in my first triathlon on the last day of March. I chose a "sprint" distance triathlon at Millerton Lake, near Fresno, about four hours' drive from home. Any event short of the Olympic standard of one-mile swim, twenty-five-mile bike and 6.2-mile run was known as a sprint distance, although I doubted whether I'd be doing any sprinting.

The Millerton Lake race was a four-hundred-yard swim, twelve-mile bike and three-mile run. I reckoned I had done enough training to get round. But I still needed to do three things to prepare for the event.

First, I wanted clipless shoes. This was the proper name for bike shoes with cleats on the soles. I wanted to look the part of an experienced athlete. Toe clips would give the game away.

I dug out my notes on Michelle Cleere's talk at Sports Basement. She had discussed clipless versions of regular bike shoes and mountain bike shoes. Regular bike shoes had smooth soles and a bulky cleat, which created the sensation of walking around on stilettos that had lost their heel. Mountain bike shoes had a deeper tread and a built-up heel that made walking with cleats easier. Triathlon regulations insisted that athletes walk their bikes through the transition area. Michelle advised beginner athletes to start with mountain bike shoes because they were easier to walk in. The last thing I wanted to do was to slip and slide like a beginner through the transition area in my stilettos that had lost their heel.

David and I visited three shops that weekend before I found a pair of mountain bike shoes that seemed to fit. I insisted on a pair that had velcro strips instead of laces, so that I could fasten and unfasten them quickly in transition. But when I tried out the shoes at spin class and on the road, the right heel chafed my ankle. I just hoped that I could break them in before the Millerton Lake Tri. As consolation, I was surprised that I had no difficulty in twisting my foot sideways to release the shoe from the pedal. I must have worked out all my angst about pedals when I first got the toe clips.

My second task was to reacquaint myself with open water swimming. I hadn't swum in open water since the Bethel Island race six months ago. Would I still have navigation problems or could I now swim in a straight line?

I arranged to swim at Aquatic Park with Mike Popa. Mike and I had met a couple of months earlier at our church. We discovered that we were near neighbors and new triathletes. Mike had done his first triathlon the previous year, and we had checked in regularly about how our training was going.

The day we had chosen to swim at Aquatic Park was not an ideal day for swimming. I drove us up to San Francisco through near-horizontal sheets of rain. Legions of thunderous gray clouds marched across the sky. The outside temperature registered 46°. Mike and I exchanged glances. Today was my only free day before Millerton Lake. Swim now, or rely on my meager experience from six months ago.

We drove along Embarcadero. Six-foot waves charged in over the low wall and onto the sidewalk. Should we continue?

Mike had arranged for us to meet up with his friend Steve at the Dolphin Club, a private and very select members-only swimming and rowing club situated next to the pier. Steve wouldn't be swimming today. He had traveled over thirty miles just to sign us in, so that we could enjoy the luxury of the locker rooms. We didn't want to let Steve down. We agreed to check what the conditions were like at Aquatic Park before making a final decision.

I parked in one of several free spots right in front of the Dolphin Club. How different from my first wetsuit dip at this very spot, when I had ended up at a parking meter miles from the water. We looked out across Aquatic Park. The breakwater sheltered small boats tied up to buoys. The harbor remained untouched by the chaos out in the Bay. A handful of swimmers already plowed through the water, strung out along the line of buoys marking the swim course from the wooden pier on the eastern side to the large white buoy on the western side. Some of them didn't even wear wetsuits. I shivered.

Steve stood by the entrance, bundled up in his ski jacket, his hands thrust deep in his pockets. He signed us in and showed us to the locker rooms. I unpacked my wetsuit and changed. When I pulled on my hothead swimcap, I paused. I had less than two miles' open water swimming experience. Now I was poised to swim a mile in unfriendly water. How would I cope with the cold? Could I swim if I turned numb?

I mustn't worry. Mike would swim nearby. He was a powerful swimmer. He would rescue me if need arose. But his prescription swim goggles hadn't arrived in time and he was very short-sighted without his contact lenses. He would be relying on me to navigate. Would he even see me, camouflaged from head to toe in black neoprene in cloudy water? What a team. A drowning woman and a myopic man.

I locked up my belongings, walked out to the pier behind the clubhouse and looked out once more across the harbor. The rain had eased off to a drizzle. Steel-gray water with a slight chop, but no six-footers like those we had seen at Embarcadero. Maybe, just maybe, we would cope.

Mike and I tiptoed down to the water's edge. We agreed a plan. Swim one lap from the pier out to the farthest white buoy and back, then decide if we were capable of a second. I would swim on his right and call out if he drifted too far over. He would call out if he needed help sighting the next buoy.

Steve shouted out the latest water temperature reading. 49°. I took four steps into the water and stopped. Stinging cold water attacked my skin the moment the first innocent waves brushed across my feet. The icy shock nailed me to the shore, threatening that if I took one step farther, that frigid water would unleash a glacial torrent that would numb me to my core.

I stood on the brink, me versus the biting cold. I took another step. My feet stung. I kept walking. Ripples of dread spread out from my stomach as I anticipated the inevitable moment when caustic water would seep down the neck of the wetsuit and hit raw skin. When the water reached my chest, I could no longer hold my balance. I plunged forward.

An iron band of arctic cold strapped itself round my chest and tightened round my ribs. I inhaled sharply. I couldn't breathe. I forced air out of my lungs. The cold punched back. My lungs snatched another frightened, gulping breath, holding fast as though it were my last.

Go back! Go back! Go back! Alternate Persona screamed at ear-piercing pitch.

Nothing had prepared me for submersion in biting cold. But I couldn't go back. This was my only free day to swim before Millerton Lake. Steve was here to let us in and Mike was here to swim with me. I couldn't let them down. And I certainly couldn't let me down.

I held my head up and pulled a few feeble breaststrokes while I fought to release myself from the grip of the cold. I wouldn't be able to swim freestyle until I could put my face in the water and breathe more deeply. I would focus on breaststroke and dip my head down now and then to acclimatize to the cold. Kick. Pull. Kick. Pull. I struggled round the end of the pier.

Six minutes later, I reached the first buoy. My body had grown numb, except for my arms and the stinging of my red face. I had lost contact with my feet long ago. My breathing relaxed enough to put my face in the water. I settled into my three-strokes-and-breathe rhythm of freestyle, looking over every fourth breath to see that Mike was still on track. Yes, there he was—two chalk-white arms attached to his sleeveless wetsuit, plowing through unforgiving water.

By the second buoy, I was numb all over. Good. Numbness eliminated the shrieking cold. No feeling, no pain. Numbness also permeated time. I had no idea how long I had been in the water. I rounded the end buoy and headed back for the pier. So numb now I could no longer feel the water rushing past my face. How fast was I moving? I couldn't tell. Instead, I was suspended in deep-frozen animation.

"Say, Jane, where are we headed?" Mike called out.

The dark brown posts of the wooden pier had blended into the muddy, gray-brown background of the breakwater wall.

"Mike, we'll sight on that tall mast on the sailing ship." A sailing schooner moored in the historic ships collection along the breakwater wall provided a beacon to guide us home. "We'll adjust when we get closer to the pier."

When we reached the pier, I checked in with Mike. We had no feeling in our limbs, so another lap wouldn't hurt. He agreed. I swam the second lap on autopilot. Maybe this was what cryogenics felt like.

Mike and I rounded the pier after the second lap and scrambled for the shore. I checked my stopwatch. We had stayed in the water for thirty-six minutes. Probably not quite one mile, but far enough for today. I stood up and stumbled up the beach, my waxy-white feet immune to the sharp edges of broken shells that were scattered on the beach.

I stood on the clubhouse deck, my frozen fingers searching for the zipper cord. Once I yanked the zipper down, limbs that had lost their sense of direction refused to remove the wetsuit. I yanked, pulled, struggled and fought, my hands repeatedly grabbing and slipping on smooth black neoprene that refused to budge. My wetsuit finally gave up the fight after six freezing minutes. I was oblivious to the fact that I was standing outside, wearing a clammy wet swimsuit in the middle of winter.

Mike and I shuffled like zombies into our locker rooms. I read the instructions posted by the shower on how to identify someone with hypothermia symptoms. Shivering, loss of coordination, confusion, pale skin. I would own up to loss of coordination and pale skin. Methods to revive victims were hot drinks and a hot shower. I thawed out for a long time under torrents of steamy water, each defrosted muscle sounding off like kids at roll call. Blotches of corpse-like skin turned pink, then to tingly, prickly red as the blood rushed to the surface.

I dried off, dressed and went to wait outside the men's locker room for Mike. When he finally emerged, he couldn't stop shivering. His sleeveless wetsuit had offered only moderate insulation. I marched him straight out and into my car, turned the heater up high and found a deli nearby. I put a twenty-ounce hot coffee into his hands and drove him home.

My third and final preparation for the Millerton Lake Triathlon was to practice the transition from wetsuit to bike. That was how David came home one night to find me rushing down the hallway into the living room in my dry wetsuit, yanking the zipper cord down as I ran. He stared, open-mouthed, as I prized my way out of the suit. He remained speechless as I stood in the middle of the multi-colored area rug wearing my swimsuit, bike helmet and shoes, with triumphant outstretched arms. The suit would have been easier to remove when wet, but I drew the line at running up to the bathroom and diving under the shower, then peeling off a wet wetsuit. I could only cope with so much surrealism in one evening.

A few days before the Millerton Lake Tri, Gail emailed to say that she wanted to compete as well. What great news. I would be sharing my first tri with my coach. I was ready. I couldn't wait to race.

Swim, Bike, Run

Accident history so far: 0

Accidents waiting to happen: 1

Friday. The day before my first triathlon. I had been looking forward to the race all week. Then, this morning, I ate hardly any breakfast and walked around on jelly legs. What had changed from yesterday? Did the day before a race always feel like this?

Emergency email to Kevin. Emergency reply eight minutes later.

> **All normal feelings, and they still happen to me before just about every race. But once the gun goes off, everything will be fine.**

I hope so, Kevin, I hope so. If Kevin still experienced race nerves after years of competing, then I shouldn't worry. I smiled. What reassurance to have a friend who always supported me with immediate, dependable advice, no matter how small the perceived crisis.

I spent the entire day packing my bag, re-packing my bag, checking that everything on my gear list was in my bag and re-checking my list to make sure I hadn't missed anything. Although if I hadn't noticed something was missing by now, it couldn't be that important. A complete waste of time.

Five o'clock. Time to pick up Gail from her new part-time physical therapy job in Mountain View, and drive to Fresno. I pulled up in my SUV. She was waiting outside the office. Taut, pale skin framed by wavy, auburn hair. Pinched, sleep-deprived face, dark circles round her eyes. She walked, shoulders down, across the car park, wheeling her black Kestrel racing bike next to her. A changed woman. We loaded up her bike and gear. Thank goodness I'd offered to drive.

We drove in near silence southwards down Highway 101. I was worried about her. But if she wanted to tell me what was up, she would do so in her own time. Rush hour traffic was heavy, with no respite even in the car pool lane. One hour later, I pulled off at Morgan Hill to look for somewhere to eat. Gail was beyond decision-making. I found Betsy's, a local diner, four hundred yards off the freeway. The menu promised basic carbs rather than a classic dining experience, but at least we would avoid fast food.

We both ordered pasta and chicken. As we munched through our salad appetizer, Gail unwound enough to manage some small talk. Then the entrée arrived. Gail put down her utensils and leaned back.

"So I had some surprising news three weeks ago," Gail said. "My husband told me that he was fed up with our marriage and wanted out. No counseling. Just out."

Ouch.

"So he's filing for divorce."

From then until the end of dinner we had a long, deep conversation about her feelings and her options. The part-time job was a first step to pursuing her dream of becoming a physical therapist. Learning new skills on top of divorce turmoil had been a struggle. At the end of the meal, I double-checked the cash we had left in payment and found that she'd left an extra twenty-dollar bill above the generous tip. Then I stopped her wandering into the men's restroom by mistake. When she nodded off in the car, I let her sleep undisturbed for the three-hour drive to Fresno.

We arrived in darkness at our motel on the outskirts of town. Typical city neighborhood, main road, gas stations, Dennys, IHOP, 7/11 shops, traffic. I woke Gail up and checked us both in, making sure our rooms were round the back, away from traffic noise. I helped her unload all her gear into her room, including her prized bike. She had talked over dinner about mocking up my transition spot in the hotel room to show me the fastest and most logical way to transition from swim to bike to run. But she was in no state to conduct a training session now.

"Shaving a few seconds off my transitions isn't top of my priorities for this race," I said. I put my arm round her shoulder. "Don't worry about it. You're still a great coach. Now get some sleep."

6:00 a.m. Straight out of bed, on with my brand new triathlon gear of fast-drying black bike shorts, maroon sports bra and top, followed by my sweats. This was the first time I had ever worn triathlon gear. I had decided against wearing my gear under the shower at home and then taking a quick ride, just to try cycling in wet clothes. That experience could wait until today.

I wandered into the bathroom and poured water into the empty coffee maker. Gail had advised me to bring instant oatmeal and make it up with water heated up through the coffee maker. Lukewarm liquid dribbled over anemic powder and turned it into a glutinous, pale gray sludge in the bottom of a polystyrene cup. This was indeed my breakfast, not some gut-churning concoction fed to hapless contestants on a reality TV show. I forced down the gluey mess. I needed the carbs to race. This might work for you, Gail, but I would make alternative plans in future.

I checked my tire pressure, then went next door to see how Gail was shaping up. Her face had more color and she looked rested. She had abandoned her pre-race ritual of cleaning her bike and lubing her chain, but otherwise, she was having a much better morning than evening. We loaded up the car and headed off on the twenty-mile drive to Millerton Lake.

Within ten minutes, city neighborhoods melted into rolling hills bathed in pale April sunshine. The land was still coated in bright winter green. Summer sun had yet to scorch the Central Valley into uniform bleached straw. I found the State Park entrance and drove along a narrow pavement. Several cars in front and behind, all heading in the same direction. Orange cones sprouted at the side of the road. This must be the cycle route. Large California oaks, a view of the lake nestled between long sweeping hills, car park, open spot close to the registration area.

Gail and I unloaded our bikes and tri bags. I leaned my bike against the side of the car. Had I got everything? Yes. Had Gail got everything? Yes. I locked the car. Gail, why do you want me to unlock the car again? What have you forgotten? Didn't you check first? We're going to be late. Can I lock the car now? Are you sure? We really will be late now.

All I could feel was the stress of the moment. I slammed the rear door shut and stepped sideways, knocking into my bike. Gail grabbed and steadied it.

"Let's go find the transition area," she said with a smile.

This morning she was calm, focused and relaxed. She took my stress overload in her stride. Time for her to guide me.

Gail led the way. About half of the two hundred bike spots were still available. She picked out two places next to each other near the end of a row, and we racked our bikes. I laid out a peach-colored towel and placed my running and bike shoes on it, then balanced my bike helmet and sunglasses on the bike handlebars. My wetsuit lay draped over the crossbar.

We collected our race numbers and event swimcaps from

the registration table, then headed off to the restrooms. A long line stretched outside a small concrete building. We waited twelve minutes to reach the front of the loo queue. That left only twenty-six minutes before the start of the event.

"Just time for a ten-minute warm up," Gail said, glancing at her stopwatch. "Let's do a loop down the road and scope out part of the run course."

"Are you sure we have time for that, Gail?"

I stood with my hands on my hips. Wriggling into that wetsuit would take ages. How could she propose a warmup run now?

"Yes, Jane," she said, with another smile. "It's a coach thing. There's always time to warm up."

We jogged out along the empty road. Soft breeze, about 60°. Perfect conditions for racing. A red truck with two latecomers breezed past us and disappeared into the car park. Two women runners in navy sweats ambled back. Six minutes out. We turned round. A guy on a bike painted in the Bianchi brand color of pale mint green rode past us.

I checked my watch. Eleven-minute warmup so far. Fifteen minutes to race start. Were we ever going to reach the transition area? Last night, Gail had suggested we set off at 6:15 a.m. to allow enough set-up time. I had insisted that 6:45 a.m. would be early enough, based on a quick calculation of driving distance and my preference for sleeping in instead of getting up in the dark. She had been too tired to argue. I should have heeded her advice.

We reached the transition area and came to a halt by our bikes. Our row was almost deserted, except for a couple of wet-suited competitors rearranging their gear. Gail grabbed her wetsuit. I reached for mine. Only then did I notice that my wetsuit was still inside out, the way I had left it after the living room dry-run exercise. I groaned. More lost time.

I thrust my arm down the left leg and wrenched the neoprene halfway out, then the same for the right leg. The suit objected to rough treatment, and I ended up with a tangle of arms and legs pulled through the zipper opening. I slowed down, backtracked and right-sided the suit. I smeared *Bodyglide* round my neck, wrists and ankles, then inched the suit up my legs. Gail was already into her suit. Forget the protocol of pinching the suit between fingers and thumbs to avoid ripping it with my fingernails. I gripped the neoprene with both hands and yanked upwards as fast as I could. It was a miracle the legs didn't rip.

Gail zipped up the back of my suit and tucked the cord under the velcro fastener round my neck. Then she sprayed cooking oil on the arms and legs of my suit so that it would slip off more easily at the end of the swim. I pulled on the fluorescent orange race swimcap with event logo of pine tree and mountains printed on the side. We ran in bare feet to the boat slipway and into the lake. Cool water seeped inside my suit. This was almost Mediterranean after last week's arctic Bay swim.

We caught the end of the race director's briefing. We found out that the swim course was a clockwise triangle round two buoys. The bike and run courses would have to take care of themselves. I couldn't get lost over such a short distance.

I wished Gail good luck. The starting gun sounded. Kevin was right. The gun was a catalyst that turned stress into adrenaline. I had a race to compete in.

I put my face in the water. For a brief moment I tasted a hint of boat fuel. My head jerked back on contact with cold water and I snatched a breath. But this time I knew what to expect. I pulled my first freestyle strokes. I concentrated on breathing deeply to acclimatize to the cold on my face. Within a couple of minutes, I was into my regular three-strokes-and-breathe rhythm.

Churning water, windmill arms, a sea of bobbing orange

caps. Limbs thrashed all round me. Tiny bubbles glittered as they swept by beneath me, catching the light like strings of iridescent glass beads.

I looked up every ten breaths to sight on the orange buoy. Passed a couple of swimmers. Rounded the buoy. The field had thinned out. Sighted again on the second buoy. I swam more or less in a straight line. No zigzagging this time. Fixing a sight point on a bright orange buoy was a lot easier than on a bank of reeds.

I rounded the second buoy. Legs and arms strong. Overtook two more swimmers. Pulled for the shore. The ribbed pattern on the concrete slipway emerged from the gloom of cloudy water. I remembered Gail's advice. Swim right in until your fingers brush the bottom. You can swim faster than you can wade. When the water became too shallow to swim, I stood up and strode through calf-high water up the slipway.

I eased my goggles up my forehead. Experienced athletes pull their wetsuits down to their waists and run to their bikes at the same time. I had practiced this in the dry run at home. Time to run and unzip. I ran up the slipway. Unzip the wetsuit, Jane! I stopped running and stood still. I forced my arms behind my back. What have you stopped for? Start running! You're supposed to run and unzip at the same time. I started running, then couldn't remember what to do next with the wetsuit.

What was wrong? My thinking was disoriented, not exactly dizzy, but confused why I couldn't handle both actions at the same time. Whatever my problem, I couldn't continue with these stop/start antics up the slipway. Ignore the wetsuit. Run back to my spot.

When I reached my gear, I clicked the stopwatch on my heart rate monitor to check my laptime. Swim and run had taken 11 minutes, 27 seconds. Not bad. Now I just had to lose the suit. I pulled, prized, yanked and complained at that suit. It put up a brave fight and relinquished me nearly four minutes later. So much for the dry run.

I cast a glance over the remaining bikes. Gail's bike was gone, of course. About thirty others left. Not even close to last yet. I slid my feet into my clipless bike shoes, fastened my helmet, grabbed my sunglasses and bike, and strode through the transition area.

Orange cones led the way from the exit out along the bike course. I set off. A sheriff held back two cars and a bunch of spectators at an intersection on my right. I cut through the still morning air at seventeen miles an hour, creating a breeze that chilled my damp clothes and made them cling to my body. Water trickled down into my shoes and found my sockless feet. Great. Less than half a mile out, and I was coated in a layer of clammy fabric from my thighs to my neck, with a bucket of cold water tacked on each foot for good measure.

I sped along the road that Gail and I had driven along less than an hour before. But I could remember little about it. What gradients lay ahead of me? A blink-and-you'll-miss-it slope in a car could translate into a mountain for a bike. With no forward planning, I had to rely on the amount of effort I plowed into the pedals to pick the best gear for the moment. At least the road was well-paved and empty of traffic.

The lake receded and the road took off over gentle hills dotted with California oaks. I overtook a couple of lone riders. Nearest rider behind me was over a hundred yards back. End of mile two. The next hill reared up and buried me in a long-haul climb in my lowest gear. Panic stirred in my stomach. Would I have enough strength in my legs to push me to the top?

The updated James Bond theme, the one from *Goldeneye*, began to play in my head. One of Gail's "tough hill" tracks from spin class. My spin class buddies surrounded me: Angelo on my left, Kelly on my right and Moira behind my wheel. I'd paid my

dues with all those hours of grueling hill exercises. My investment in my leg muscles would get me to the top of this hill. I
pedaled in time to the music. My spin buddies pedaled with me.
They cheered when I crested the hill, then melted away.

A long fast run down the other side meant only one thing.
Another gut-wrenching climb on the way back. At least this time
I would know to pace myself. I hunkered down for another hill.
Just as I reached the crest, a bunch of eight or nine race leaders
shot past in the opposite direction. I spotted Gail on her Kestrel
bike. She was right up there with the leaders, about the sixth or
seventh rider and third woman. Her face was fixed in determination. I wanted to cheer her on but I didn't want to disturb her
concentration. Seeing her up with the leaders energized me. I attacked the descent and hit thirty-one miles an hour, the fastest I
have ever cycled. I was having a great bike leg.

Fluorescent yellow flashed in the distance. Race stewards.
My speedometer showed that I had cycled 5.2 miles when it
should have registered six to the turnaround. But who cared?
Race stewards meant that I was halfway round already.

I slowed down as I approached the turnaround. I would have
to execute a sharp left turn round the steward standing in the
middle of the narrow road. A car approached from the opposite
direction. The roads hadn't been closed for the event, although
the course was clearly marked for drivers to avoid. I unclipped
my foot and prepared to stop. But the steward held the car back
and waved me round. What to do next? I don't turn sharp corners
well. And if I ride too slowly, I fall off. Now I would have to turn
slowly with an audience. I somehow clipped back in, wobbled
counterclockwise round the steward and set off back up the road.
No fall, no embarrassment, no one the wiser. I exhaled a quick
sigh of relief.

But within ten feet of the turnaround, the pedals stiffened

up so much that I could hardly turn them over. I stamped down hard on them. No impact. I looked down at my chain ring. I was still on my biggest ring and fastest rear cog, the perfect choice for flying downhill and gaining ground on competitors. The worst choice for climbing my way back up. With all the distraction of car and turnaround, I had failed to prepare my gears.

I switched down to my middle ring. Clanking noises. The pedals spun round under my feet. No resistance. The chain must be stranded somewhere between the rings. I clicked my gear lever again. Still nothing. And with no chain to connect the pedals to the wheels, I was going nowhere.

Within seconds, my bike keeled over to the right. I unclipped my right foot on reflex, but not in time to break my fall. The bike slid out left from under me. My right leg and hip hit the ground. The end of the handlebar pinned my right knee to the pavement. Pain shot up my thigh and filled my eyes with tears.

I knelt awkwardly on my right knee, half wrapped round my bike with my left foot still clipped into the pedal. I twisted my foot out and rolled sideways until I was kneeling on all fours. Pain seeped into every limb and blotted out my ability to think. The bike was a blur through my tears.

After half a lifetime, I stood up. I bit my lip to bring the tears under control. I had to get back in this race. Several riders had overtaken me, but I wasn't sure how many. I picked up the bike and inspected it. The chain had jumped off the ring. I had no idea how to fix it. What was I supposed to do now?

Yesterday I had mulled over the all things that might slow me down. Never once had I considered anything that could end my race completely. How could I have been so stupid as to ride a bike for eight months without learning how to fix the wretched chain? Worse than that, I'm mechanically inept. No matter how hard I try, I can't convert my creative/expressive thinking skills into logical/analytical problem solving. My chances of fixing this hovered around zero.

My knee throbbed. The logo from the end of the handlebar started to form a red and purple imprint on my skin. Focus, Jane. You have to work out how to slide this chain back over the rings. Otherwise your race is over.

"What's the problem?" a man's voice called out to me.

I had been so consumed with pain and confusion that I hadn't noticed that a race steward had wandered over to find out what was going on.

"I fluffed the gear change," I replied. "I dropped my chain, and I don't know how to put it back again."

The steward knelt down. Within seconds, he slipped the chain back onto the smallest ring and whirled the pedals round.

"You're good to go," he said. "You OK otherwise?"

"Nothing broken." I forced a smile. "Thanks for getting me moving again."

I climbed gingerly back on the bike. I didn't care how many riders had just overtaken me. I just wanted to regain my equilibrium.

I worked my way up the long hill, soothed by familiar pedaling action and deep breathing. My immediate problem was to climb this hill. Head down, pedal hard, crest the hill. Not as bad as I was expecting. The nightmare turnaround had put these hills in perspective. They were no longer tough, just long.

But I couldn't stay on my smallest ring for the rest of the race. I would need a higher gear to match my leg speed and effort on the flat and downhills. Or else I'd be stuck pedaling very fast and getting nowhere. I was terrified of dropping the chain again, especially as I hadn't seen what the steward had done to fix it. But I had to switch rings. I took a deep breath and clicked. The chain clanked and switched to the middle ring. Relief. I was going to stay on my middle ring for the rest of the race, come what may.

I coasted down the last hill. The sheriff still stood at the first intersection in the distance. I took an inventory of my race readiness. My knee had stopped throbbing and was now numb. Five miles of cycling after the shake-up had calmed me down. My clothes had dried off when I wasn't looking. My shoes had settled down and no longer rubbed my heel. Even my feet were warm from exertion. And I was still in the race.

What's more, I wasn't last. I had ridden past riders still on their outbound bike leg. What was I waiting for? I pushed up my leg speed and clicked up a couple of gears, wringing every scrap of advantage out of this last swooping hill and flat. I halted by the transition area entrance, dismounted and checked my stopwatch. My bike lap, including unscheduled stops, had taken 52 minutes, 16 seconds.

The transition area was empty of people and full of bikes. I racked my bike next to Gail's. I heard cheers and turned round to see a couple of young guys, the first finishers, cross the line. Gail must still be out on the run course somewhere. I changed my bike shoes and helmet for running shoes, socks and hat. I was back out on the run course in only forty-three seconds.

Before the race, I had secretly hoped for a 1 hour, 30 minute time. I was now 1 hour, 2 minutes into the race. I could only run ten-minute miles at the best of times. Even if I ran a personal best time, my chances of finishing within my goal were dashed. But I could aim to finish as close to 1 hour, 30 minutes as possible.

I ran round the corner and back along the road. Gail's pale green race top jumped out at me from a group of three men and a woman racing to the finish.

"Go, Gail!" I yelled.

"Hey, Jane! Great job!"

She was way up with the leaders and eighty yards off the

finish. I was thrilled that she was having such a good race.

Five hundred yards. Empty road. Just me and the cones. My lower calves tightened. I had expected this. Gail had warned me that bike-to-run was one of the hardest stages of a triathlon. Everyone goes through misery. But all that practice of running straight after spin class and bike rides had done me good.

I paced myself to the aid station at the one-mile point. The tightness loosened. I rewarded myself with a cup of Gatorade. Footsteps. A woman overtook me. Damn. Why hadn't I checked before the Gatorade to see who was waiting to pounce? I hated to lose advantage, especially over an optional activity like a drink.

Cones led the way to a gap in the wooden fence behind the aid station table. Maybe this was a discreet open-air comfort stop? Surely the course couldn't go off-road? But the runner who had overtaken me had just hared off like a jackrabbit up the winding path.

"Yes, that way!" a woman with short brown hair, T-shirt and jeans called out as she poured Gatorade into cups.

My puzzled face must have demanded a response.

I dropped my cup in the trash and set off after the jackrabbit. The track led uphill through a steep, twisting gully full of potholes and stones. How do people run over this stuff? My weak left ankle was a reminder of my fall on the Champs Elysees ten years ago. One pothole could twist my ankle again and leave me stranded.

The path snaked first up and then downhill, past straggly bushes and rocky outcrops that threw sharp shadows across the pockmarked dirt. I pushed on, running a few steps on smooth ground and slowing to pick my way over rough terrain. I was going to finish this race somehow. But forget the finish time. I wasn't designed to be a mountain goat.

The course made one more sharp turn and deposited me

back on the road, right by the two-mile marker. One mile to go. That should take about ten minutes. OK, Jane. Let's see what you're made of. I channeled my mountain-goat frustration into my legs and picked up the pace.

Six minutes later, the finish line came into view. I kicked for home. Fast feet, fast feet! Gail's instruction to quicken my pace rather than lengthen my stride when I wanted to sprint rang in my ears. I surged forward, eating up the ground.

A park ranger held back departing traffic. I rounded the last bend. Spectators cheered, some applauded, others rang cowbells. That noise was all for me. I glowed with pride and put in a final spurt to the finish. I crossed the line in 1 hour, 32 minutes, 27 seconds.

Gail was waiting at the finish line with a bottle of water. Her skin glowed from the achievement of racing, so different from last night.

"You were awesome!" she said. "Great job on your first tri!"

Her congratulations meant a lot to me. I had someone to share my elation with, someone who knew how hard I had worked to get here. We talked over my race, checked on the progress of the ugly bruise spreading out across my knee, and picked out lessons to learn for next time. All surrounded by the satisfied contentment of my first tri.

"So how did you do in your race?" I asked. "You were right up there with the leaders."

"I think I've just won my age group."

"You mean you've waited till now to tell me? Great job!"

I gave her a hug.

We went over to the results board. I had posted fourth out of six in the 40-44 age group. Gail was first in the 30-34 age group and fourth overall amongst the women. I cheered like mad at

Gail's podium moment. I told everyone I bumped into that my friend had just placed first in her age group.

We made our way back to the hotel, showered and set off on the four-hour drive home. We had a contented, winding-down time to mull over the race, our plans and our lives. This race had meant a lot to me. This was my first tri. But the race turned out to mean a lot more to Gail. She had taken up triathlon after she was married. Somehow, triathlon belonged to the married part of her life. She worried that her dedication to training might even have been the cause of the split. Although she was awash with uncertainties, she had attacked the race and had won through. Triathlon had been there for her when she needed to reinforce her self-belief.

"My mojo has returned," she said, her face illuminated once again by that wide smile I had come to recognize.

I smiled too. I was happy for her. Gail was my coach and my friend.

She had also been there for my first tri. And today, for the first time, I called myself a triathlete.

An Unlikely Opponent

Number of triathletes in our household: 1

Number of spouses who would prefer never to hear another word about triathlon: 1

Congratulations! Good on ya for getting back up, shaking it off and soldiering on. Enjoy the accomplishment!

From the day after my first triathlon at Millerton Lake, I had Kevin's email taped to the bottom of my computer screen. His encouragement reminded me how proud I felt at the finish, especially when I carried on after falling off my bike. My first tri was a great start to the countdown. Only nine weeks to go from the Millerton Lake Tri to the San Jose Tri on the last weekend in June.

My objective for May was to take part in a couple more events. I wanted to experience transitions from swim to bike to run and practice some more open water swimming in a race setting. Those races would also give me a yardstick as to how I was shaping up for San Jose.

I enrolled for two events in May. One was the South Bay Triathlon at the Uvas Reservoir in Morgan Hill on the third weekend in May. Like the Millerton Lake race, this was another short-distance or "sprint" triathlon; that is, any event that is shorter than the Olympic distance of one-mile swim, twenty-five-mile ride and 6.2-mile run. The Uvas Tri had a five-mile run, close to the 6.2 miles I would run at San Jose. The bike ride was only sixteen miles instead of twenty-five miles. But like the San Jose course, the ride was mainly flat with one killer hill in the middle.

I also signed up for the Human Race, a 6.2-mile charity run scheduled for the second weekend in May, a week before the Uvas Triathlon. This was the exact distance I would run at San Jose, albeit without the swim or bike. I still hadn't run 6.2 miles in training, reaching five miles at the most. But I was confident I could keep going for the extra mile or so. I was aiming for a finish time of fifty-six minutes, the equivalent of nine-minute miles, which I calculated would translate to around one hour on tired legs. That would keep me on pace for a three-hour total finish time in the San Jose Tri.

I took the opportunity with the charity race to raise sponsorship dollars for Masterworks Chorale, a local nonprofit where I sat on the Board of Directors. My email solicitation to friends and family raised $350 in just one week. And by going public, I put more pressure on myself to finish in a decent time.

Five days before the race, a friend forwarded me a surprise email.

> My wife, Jane, is training for a triathlon in June. This is not her only topic of conversation, but it's close. Would you sponsor me to beat her in the Human Race? I've never run farther than five miles in my life, so finishing for me is not a foregone conclusion. If Jane finishes ahead of me, I will repay all the money I collect, plus put up with endless chatter about triathlon training without complaint. But if I win, my life at home will be so much more peaceful!

Well, well, well. Wasn't my beloved husband full of surprises?

I had been encouraging David to race with me for the last few days. After all, he had been running three times a week for the last two years. Surely a 6.2-mile run was within his capabilities. And it would swell the monies raised for Masterworks Chorale. But what was with the "sponsor me to beat her" bit? That wasn't in the plan at all.

When David walked through the door that evening, he had an impish grin on his face.

"Hello, darling," I said.

Darling in our household is a code word for mild irritation.

"Hello, dear," he said.

Dear in our household is a code word for "yes, I know you're mildly irritated." His grin widened.

"Since when did you say you were going to race?" I said, strumming my fingers on the kitchen counter and trying to look stern. I gritted my teeth to stop the infectious spread of his grin. "And since when did I agree to shut up about triathlon if you win?"

"You do get a bit wrapped up in yourself now and then," he said, with classic British understatement. "But I've got used to it by now. Anyway, my ploy raised more money than you."

"Like, how much more?"

"Like, $470 in eight hours. Beats $350 in a week. Just shows you that people like a bit of competition. I think for an extra $470, you'd gladly shut up if I beat you."

I burst out laughing and flung my arms round his neck. I knew David was having a joke at my expense. And he had most definitely outmaneuvered me on this one.

Now that David had thrown down the gauntlet in a public challenge, I wanted to check out the competition to see just how fast he ran these days. We had run together a couple of times in my early days of running. But that had only proved to me that I didn't enjoy running with him. First, he ran faster than I did. Second, he had this endearing habit of throwing out comments that he thought would encourage me.

"Not much farther," he would shout. "Keep it up!"

Out loud, I said nothing. Inside, my grumpy voice would chunter on in sullen mode. Does he think I don't know how much longer I have to keep up this punishment? Does he think I'm enjoying this so much I've lost all track of distance? I'm barely keeping up and he knows it. I'd rather be grumpy in silence than hear condescending comments, thank you. Deep down, I knew I was being ungrateful. He was only trying to help. But to avoid bringing out this unpleasant side of me, I chose to run on my own.

The day after the surprise email, I did a three-mile run with David. He wouldn't admit it, but I could tell from the glances he shot in my direction that he also wanted to see how I was doing and whether he had misjudged his challenge entirely. We drew up a ground rule that he wasn't allowed to speak to me while running. He grinned instead. I could handle grinning. He still ran a little faster than I did, or maybe he ran a lot faster and was slowing down to fool me. But neither of us knew what would happen over 6.2 miles.

On Wednesday before race day, I visited the dental office. Our dentist, Brett Hofmann, had taken an interest in my triathlon training ever since we went to watch him finish the San Jose Tri last year. He had recommended training programs, useful websites and checked on my progress. I told him about the Human Race and the husband/wife challenge. He put some money into my sponsorship pot and decided he too would sign up for the race. He was competing in the Newport Beach Sprint Triathlon one week later, so this would be a good training run for him.

The three of us met up at the Human Race just before eight o'clock. on Saturday at Coyote Point County Park in San Mateo. Bright sunshine, mid-60s, a warm but not too hot temperature for running. The finish area was packed with nearly a thousand runners. Walkers and spectators milled round the nonprofit expo booths and stood in line to collect race numbers. Others took part in the group warmup exercises and sang the national anthem.

The Human Race had four events in total: a 6.2-mile run and walk plus a 3.1-mile run and walk. The 6.2-mile route would take us from the start by the flat park playing fields, southwards along the path beside the Bay for about three miles, then back again. An extra loop wound up one short, wooded hill just before the finish, but otherwise the route was flat and scenic.

At eight o'clock, the announcer called all runners to the start line. Brett, David and I lined up in the middle of the pack of around two hundred 6.2-mile runners. Some of them were in costume. I admired the chutzpah of the girls from the women's cancer nonprofit who wore cardboard signs on their heads reading "Fallopian Tubes" and "Ovaries." I was secretly thankful that I represented a music nonprofit, so my dressing-up options were limited.

I looked down the tunnel of spectators packed three deep, waiting to cheer us off. Last year I had done the 3.1-mile walk with my Masterworks Chorale colleagues. We had stood in that throng, cheering the runners off as they started the 6.2-mile race. This year I relished being right in the thick of the action.

The gun sounded. The pack of runners burst off the start line along the tree-shaded road, then turned right onto the Bay path. Tranquil bay water lapped against the rocky shore. The wide, paved path stood proud on a sun-bleached levee, edged on the left by water and on the right by flat, open land reaching across to the road and ranch-style houses. The early morning sunshine dissolved the panoramic vista of the East Bay into soft focus.

The coil of runners unwound into the haze of straw-colored headland and powder-blue sky. I lost sight of Brett within a minute. After three minutes, David had pulled ahead by about ten yards. Should I let him go or stick with him? I let him go. I had to run my own race. I didn't want to fall apart at the end by running too fast early on.

Runners ahead, runners behind. All settled into a regular tempo. All overtaking had happened within the first ten minutes. Now the lead runners approached in the opposite direction. Still no sign of the turnaround point.

Alternate Persona started up its needling, whining complaint. How can you pace yourself when you don't know how far you have left to run? You might not make it. Uncertainty tightened my breathing. I forced myself to remain calm. Just when I wondered if I were racing to San Diego and back, I spotted Brett approaching on the return leg.

"Go, Jane!" he called out and waved. "David isn't far ahead."

I had no energy to smile back. I still had a long way to go. I stared at the pavement and retreated into my shell.

"Not much farther to the turnaround!"

I recognized that voice. I looked up. My grinning husband breezed past in the other direction. He was doing the encouragement thing again. Except this time, I welcomed it.

The aid station at the turnaround was about fifty yards ahead. That meant that David was only one hundred yards in front of me. Maybe I could catch him after all. I slowed to a walk at the aid station table, grabbed one of the white plastic cups filled with cold water, drank it within a few seconds and started running back.

I ran the next ten minutes on winged feet. Maybe the return

stretch tipped slightly downhill, enough to require no effort to run. That would account for the struggle to reach the turnaround. I held my head up and ratcheted up the pace. I still couldn't single out David from the string of runners ahead, but he couldn't be that far in front.

The wide bay path welcomed me. Waves lapped the shore on my right. Just this flat stretch, then over the hill and across the finish line. I approached the wooded hill. Someone stepped forward onto the path with a camera and took my photo.

"Hey, Jane!" the photographer called out. "Way to go! David's not far in front."

I turned to look at him. I recognized the tall, lean figure and blonde hair of Scott Giese, a marathon runner and work colleague of David's. He had turned out to witness the epic marital duel and record it for posterity.

Scott's news was not good. David might be "not far in front" but he was still out of sight. I hadn't caught him on the flat. And wouldn't catch him now.

I plowed on up the hill, my hamstrings and gluts down the backs of my legs working like pistons to push me one step closer to the brow. Large redwoods held an umbrella of cool shade over me. The sun was a long way off throwing its mid-morning heat blanket over the exposed path, but mid-60s heat was still enough to coat my body in sweat.

Not far now. My legs tumbled down the other side of the hill, pushed along by that final, expectant flood of energy that would carry me over the finish line. I reached the point from which David, Brett and I had departed fifty minutes earlier. The finish banner was where I remembered it, on my left. But the route to the finish was blocked off with orange tape. An arrow pointed me straight ahead. The anguish of realization spread over me. This wasn't the route to the finish at all.

How had that happened? I hadn't consulted the map before the race. I had just assumed that we would turn left after the hill and through the finish. How stupid could I be? Of course, now it was obvious that this couldn't be the finish. I had only run for fifty minutes. No way could I have run 6.2 miles in fifty minutes. I must still have about one mile left to run.

The motivation that had carried me up and over this hill hit dead air and collapsed in on itself. My limbs turned to concrete and began to sink in the bottomless ocean of the unknown route. Orange cones led me forward along an uncharted path. Where were my private markers that told me I'd reached the quarter-, the half-, the three-quarter-mile points? How would I know how far I had left to run? Where was my lifeline to the finish?

I forced myself to run. Running was faster than walking. And David was still ahead of me. I pushed on with five minutes of dig-deep running round a pancake-flat field. Employees wearing Franklin Templeton T-shirts handed out orange quarters to the first of the 3.1-mile walkers. I wasn't a walker. I hadn't earned orange quarters. I hadn't even finished my race. David would have won by now. I fell back to a walk but didn't take an orange quarter.

"Hey, don't stop!" a woman's voice called out to me over my right shoulder. "I've been pacing you all the way round. You kept me going."

A slender woman, about my height and in her late forties, ran past me. She had caught me by surprise. I had no idea she was there. But I couldn't do any more. I had nothing left to give. I watched the back of her bright blue top pull ahead by ten, then twenty, then thirty yards.

Enough. Snap out of it. You have to finish this thing. You're certainly not going to do all the work and let her finish ahead of you. Stop whining and start running.

My motivation found its second wind. Forget tired and dejected. My legs itched to race. I kicked into action and raced after her. I blasted down the last two hundred yards as though I were at a track and field meet. I pipped her just as I reached the chute channeling the runners to the finish. I heard Brett cheer me on. I saw David waiting at the end with Scott. I crossed the line in 60 minutes, 23 seconds.

Scott took some photos of the happy couple at the finish. We met up again with Brett. He had had a good race, finishing well up the field in around forty-seven minutes. David had finished in fifty-seven minutes. He was thrilled with his win. Not so much in beating me, just that he had acquitted himself well in his first-ever race. I was so proud of him. He didn't need to say how proud he was of me. A squeeze of my shoulder, a look in his eye, his body language said it all.

"So that means I'm not allowed to mention the T-word at home from now on?" I asked, my defiant look softened by the stifling of a grin.

"You can," he said. "But I get breakfast in bed as a forfeit every time you do."

"But if talking was an Olympic sport, I'd be on the England team," I said, mock dismay puckering my face. "You'll have breakfast in bed till you're ninety at that rate."

"All right then. Breakfast in bed tomorrow and we'll call it quits. And no ban on the T-word."

I hugged him.

"Anyway," he added, "after nineteen years of marriage, I couldn't cope with the silence."

"That's all right, dearest," I said. "We play to our strengths. I do the talking and you do the thinking."

"Good job it's not the other way round, then."

I pummeled him with fake punches.

I didn't want to spoil the mood by moping, but my day was tinged with disappointment about my miserable performance. Not that David had beaten me. I had secretly expected that he would. More that I had finished in such a poor time. How did I hope to complete the run at the end of the San Jose Tri in one hour flat, when I could barely manage that time over the same distance on fresh legs?

I emailed Kevin when I got home. I needed a pep talk from my motivational coach. Reliable as ever, he got back to me in less than two hours.

> **Congrats on the 10k finish! You've come a long way to accomplish that. As we "Type A" personalities progress in anything, we set higher and higher bars for what we should be able to do. The trick is to balance the challenge of the higher bar with appreciating and savoring the progress that you've already made. Everything is on track.**

Kevin's email reminded me that in last year's Human Race, I had walked 3.1 miles in the same time as I ran 6.2 miles this year. I should ease up on myself and savor the accomplishment.

Thinking back over the race, my problems were caused by my unfamiliarity with the course. Uncertainty had gnawed away at my fragile confidence, leaving me unable to concentrate on running. Learning the route made a huge difference to my mental state. I told David I had to scope out the bike and run course for next week's Uvas Triathlon, and do it soon.

The next day, we took our bikes down to the Uvas Reservoir. We followed the bike route printed out from the event website. Ten miles of gentle undulation round the reservoir. All along empty country roads with the odd house dotted about. At mile eleven, we rounded a right hand bend. And there it was. The killer hill.

I turned round and rode one mile back down the course. I needed a marker. I identified a white-walled house with a shingle roof and a single tree on the run-in to the bend. Those would be my markers that the hill was almost upon me.

Back to the bend. Straight up a steep slope lined with trees, followed by a slight leveling off by a farm gate, then a viciously steep stretch of about one hundred yards. I dropped down my gears and hauled myself all the way up without stopping. I waited at the top under a tree canopy for David. He was walking the vicious bit. That made up for him beating me the day before.

We cycled the last five miles back to the car park that was marked as the transition area. No surprises en route. We loaded our bikes into our SUV, then drove out and back along the five-mile run course. We identified trees and gates as intermediate checkpoints to remind me how far I had to go. Now I was properly prepared for the race.

I took things easy over the next week. One gentle spin class and a couple of runs, just enough to keep myself moving without wearing out my legs. On Saturday afternoon, the day before the race, I set off with my buddy Mike Popa on my first-ever experience of another pre-race race ritual—the packet pickup.

There were too many competitors at big events like Uvas to check everyone in on the day. Instead, competitors had to turn up the day before and sign in, show USA Triathlon Association membership cards to confirm that we had paid for race insurance, and collect our goody bag. The bag contained race numbers for the run and bike, color-coded swimcap, T-shirt and timing chip.

In my previous four races, a race official had recorded overall finish times by writing my race number on a clipboard as I passed under the finish banner. A low-key, low-tech method. At

Uvas, I would fasten a black fabric band containing a timing chip round my ankle. When I ran over a special mat at the end of the swim, the bike and the run, the chip would automatically record my split times and total time. The Uvas Tri was in a different league of racing altogether.

Packet pickup for Uvas was held at Lake Almaden, site of the San Jose Tri. Mike and I would both race at Uvas tomorrow. We checked in and collected our packets. Then we wandered around in the bright afternoon sunshine with scores of other triathletes, soaking up the pre-race excitement and browsing through some of the race gear stalls near the check-in tent.

I spotted a red, white and black race top in my size. When I bought my tri gear for Millerton Lake, I'd had to settle for a dull shade of maroon because that was all that was available in my size. I had always imagined myself running in red, my favorite color. I bought it. Two triathlons, two race tops, who was counting? I looked forward to racing in my new colors the next day.

My last piece of pre-race preparation was to find out how to put my chain back on my bike. Mike had said he'd show me how to fix the chain after packet pick-up. I didn't want to find myself helpless at the killer hill with a dropped chain. Stranded Woman was not my style.

We drove home. After I had shown David my new purchase, I got my bike out and coasted the mile downhill to Mike's house. We spent all of three minutes learning how to put the chain back on and a geeky twenty minutes comparing notes on our bikes. He had a Trek bike too but his was several notches up the pecking order from my workaday Trek 1200. I couldn't speak bike mechanic, but whatever he was talking about sounded great. And his bike looked cool in its white paint job.

I rode back home, curious to ride my bike up hills that I had only ever run up before. But I was confident that I could tackle the gradients. My taste buds prickled as I rode through wafts of barbecue smoke tinged with char grilled meat aromas. The soft, late-afternoon sunshine mingled with the shadows of California oaks. I clicked down a couple more gears by a bunch of birthday balloons tied to a gatepost and stepped up the pedaling a fraction. Excited children's voices squealed behind a garden hedge. The air was warm and heavy with the scent of eucalyptus trees that dropped long strips of peeling bark over the road. I breathed in lungfuls of contentment. I had covered the last bit of prep for this race. I was as ready as I'd ever be for tomorrow.

I hit the ground hard when my bike tipped over. No warning. I had forgotten about Hell Hill. The monster lurked round a blind corner, its ugly gradient rearing up like a brick wall.

My pedaling hit standstill. Then my bike did what all bikes do with no forward movement. They fall over with the rider attached. Panic surged through me, an uncontrollable electric jolt that set every nerve on edge. My right hip and shoulder hit the pavement so hard I almost bounced.

I unclipped my shoes from the pedals and dragged my bike next to me at the side of the road. I sat on the curb, my head resting on my hunched-up knees. My heart raced. Pain radiated out from my hip to fill my whole body. My God, this hurts. This was Millerton Lake all over again. How would I get home? And what about tomorrow? I can't do this. I-can't-I-can't-I-can't.

Tears flowed down my face, but only in part because my hip hurt so much. Pain had opened my eyes to what was really going on. To what I had refused to admit to myself for the last four weeks since Millerton Lake. I was terrified of that surge of panic that erupted the moment I realized something dreadful was about to happen.

I had been kidding myself that the problem lay in not knowing how to deal with a dropped bike chain. But the dropped chain had been an easy fix. What I couldn't fix was my fear of falling off the bike, of sharp pain, of hurting myself badly. That split second when my body jolts with a shot of adrenaline rushing through my veins, when my inner voice cries out to do something, anything, to stop this fall and all I hear back is silence. No answers. Just the certainty that I'm about to crash, that the pain will really, really hurt. And that I can't do a thing about it.

It wasn't in my game plan to confront fear when I first started riding a bike. Challenge, yes. Fear, no. I always intended to stop well short of fear. Now, twelve hours away from a big race, I faced one significant problem. I was afraid of my bike.

The Far Side of Fear

Personal bests so far: 1.2-mile swim, 35.8-mile ride, 6.2-mile run (but not all at the same time)

Personal worst so far: about to happen

I dried my eyes and stood up. Checked over my bike. It hadn't been damaged in the fall. I was only two hundred yards from home. I had to get back. But a barrier of fear had wedged itself between me and the bike. I couldn't even contemplate swinging my leg over the crossbar and pedaling those few strokes.

I walked my bike home. The garage was open. David was inside, sorting empty cartons and newspapers into recycling boxes. He stopped when he heard bike shoe cleats tapping on the concrete driveway. He turned round, took one look at my drooping shoulders and tear-stained face and strode over to me.

"What on earth happened to you?" he said.

He grabbed my bike, leaned the wretched thing against the wall, then rushed back and wrapped his arms around me.

"I fell off, that's what happened."

"Did you hurt yourself badly?"

"No," I said. The pain in my hip had now subsided to the level of a grumble. My voice trembled. Tears flowed again. "But I'm scared to go and race tomorrow."

He listened while I poured out the whole sorry story. The nasty bend on Hell Hill. The fall. The awful truth that I was afraid of my bike.

"You know, that's why they call it 'getting back on the bike,'" he said. "Everyone feels a bit shaken up when they fall off. You simply get back on."

"It's more than that," I snapped back. "I just don't think I can ride my bike up that hill tomorrow. End of story."

"Hey, it's not that bad," he said, massaging my shoulders and neck to release tension. "Think of the practice ride last week. You left me standing on that hill. I had to walk it. You've done enough training to get you round the course. Just believe in yourself and go out and do it."

Mindset, Jane, mindset. Michelle Cleere's words about positive self-talk rang in my ears. If I believed I couldn't do this, I wouldn't. I had to tell myself I could ride my bike up the Uvas hill. What's more, I had to believe it. And David was right. I had ridden my bike up the Uvas hill without stopping last week.

I spent the evening packing my triathlon bag with everything on my gear list. I imagined myself out on the bike course, shooting past the house and tree with one mile to go to the hill, charging up the hill to the slight plateau by the gate, then toughing it out to crest the ridge.

"I'm strong," I said out loud. "I've done this before. I can do it again." Out loud sounded more convincing. "I WILL do this. I WILL," I shouted as I rammed each bike shoe into my bag.

4:14 a.m. I was already awake, ready for the signal that the wait was over. My hand reached over to switch off the alarm before it sounded. No point disturbing David. He wasn't coming to the race this time. I crept into the bathroom, switched on the light and stood in front of the sink. A puzzled, dazed face stared back at me from the mirror. Did you really fall off your bike last night?

I washed my face in cold water and toweled off. I plastered my face, arms and legs with suntan cream. Its coconut scent transported me back to the secluded, tropical beach on Kauai, where I had last used this cream. I never expected to apply it in pitch black of night in my bathroom.

I brushed my teeth and took one last look in the mirror. The person who was going down to the Uvas Tri today stared back. I took a deep breath and pulled on my determined face. The determined person who would nail that hill and cross that finish line and have a great race today stared back. The droplets of fear that had risen to the surface after yesterday's fall evaporated. I refused to let a bike spill derail me now. I'd ridden the Uvas hill. I'd ridden lots of other hills over the last six months. I wouldn't give in to stuff and nonsense.

I pulled on my race clothes and sweats, gave David a quick peck on the cheek and tiptoed out of the bedroom. I went downstairs and heated up the oatmeal I'd prepared the evening before. I rarely ate oatmeal and syrup at any other time, but it was about the only thing I could face when my stomach would prefer not to be force fed.

I collected my tri bag and bike from the garage and walked to the end of our driveway to wait for Mike Popa.

I wondered again why David had chosen not to come to the race. Especially as the Uvas Tri would be a tough test for me. David and I are usually so in tune that we instinctively know when something is important for the other person. We always support each other. But something didn't feel right about the nonchalant way he had said he was going to give this one a miss. My thoughts were interrupted by the sound of Mike's truck. We loaded up my bike. I looked back. David stood in his dressing gown, silhouetted in bright light from the garage. I walked back.

"Good luck in your race," he said and gave me a hug. "You'll do fine on that hill. Just believe you can do it."

I was pleased David had come downstairs to wish me luck.

I debated one last time about asking him why he wasn't coming. In the end, I chose not to. He must have had his reasons, and I wasn't about to lay a guilt trip on him about it.

Mike and I set off on the one-hour drive down the empty freeway to the Uvas Reservoir. At 5:26 a.m. the stars disappeared and the first glimmer of dawn crept across the sky. Eighteen minutes later, the landscape was plunged into daylight. The speed of sunrise at this 37° latitude always caught me unawares. I was still conditioned to the languorous, hour-long dawn in England that creeps round houses and nudges people out of their dreams.

I thought about all the training I'd done to get me here. About the difference in my life between now and this time last year, before I'd even watched the San Jose Tri. About how much fitter I was, about how often I'd stepped outside my comfort zone during training. I remembered Kevin's encouragement after the Human Race, that I should savor accomplishments as they happen rather than raise the bar ahead of time and see each event merely as a stepping stone. I resolved that whatever happened in this race, I would celebrate it as an achievement. Taking part was achievement in itself. Finishing was a high-five.

We reached the Uvas Reservoir, a slender finger of water hidden deep in the South Bay countryside, encircled by undulating hills sweeping down to the water's edge. Mike followed the line of traffic into a field that had been allocated for parking. We stepped out of the truck. Around two hundred hushed athletes unloaded gear, checked tire pressures and walked down to the transition area. Like them, I didn't feel that chatty at six o'clock. I just wanted to focus on my race.

Mike and I unloaded our bikes and gear and walked three hundred yards back along the road to the transition area. I rehearsed the race in my head. In two hours' time, I would begin my three-quarter-mile swim, then tackle the sixteen-mile bike ride and nail that killer hill. Then head back up the road we had just driven down for a five-mile run.

Mike and I scoped out the transition area, picked our spot and racked our bikes next to each other. I checked out where I would enter and exit the water, what route I would take back to my bike, where the bike exit and entrance were and where I would leave for the run route.

I set off in my sweats for a fifteen-minute jog. I'd come a long way since the duathlon, when I didn't trust myself not to wear out my legs by warming up. I looked out over the reservoir on my left, tinged with pristine, early-morning light. A spur of headland jutted into the water. The swim course started on the eastern side, then took off out of sight round the spur and finished at the boat jetty on the western side. Triangular orange buoys pointed swimmers round the headland. The water lay unruffled and serene, waiting for the assault of eight hundred pairs of thrashing arms that would soon rupture its surface.

When I finished my warmup, I went to get bodymarked. This triathlon started in waves five minutes apart, based on age group. I would be in the "women over 35" wave that departed second to last. I removed my sweats. A race volunteer wrote my race number of 80 on top of each arm in waterproof ink. I was no longer an anonymous body. Then she added a number 4 on my left calf and 2 on my right calf. I wouldn't turn 43 until next week.

The transition area was now chock-full of bikes. Competitors changed into wetsuits. Others wandered over to the loo queue. I walked towards my bike. Something glinted on my wheel. It was the reflector clipped onto the front spokes. I looked round, expecting the sun's low angle on the horizon to light up everyone else's reflectors. Why did the sun catch only my bike's reflector?

I realized with slow horror that every other bike had had its reflectors removed, except for one lonely mountain bike that stood as odd one out in the cascade of road bikes. So it must be totally uncool to have reflectors and nobody told me? The full weight of the social faux pas descended on me. If I'd had a multi-tool in my saddlebag, I'd have removed the reflectors immediately. Still, no point fretting about niceties. They were there, and they'd have to stay.

7:21 a.m. Time to squeeze into my wetsuit. I coated my ankles, wrists and neck with *Bodyglide* lubricant. Then I edged myself into the suit—first my ankles, roll it up over my knees, now gently edge folds of neoprene up my thighs. I took my time to get the fit just right.

"Everyone out of the Transition Area!" I jumped at the surprise instructions over the loudspeakers. "NO exceptions. We can't start this race until you move. It's race rules. All competitors to the water immediately. Stewards will MOVE YOU OUT NOW."

A human dragnet of race stewards walked through the transition area towards me, sweeping up the last few stragglers ahead of them. I'd not planned on moving for at least another fifteen minutes. My wave didn't leave until 8:05 a.m. Why did they want me out of the transition area by 7:30 a.m.?

I yanked the suit up to my waist, thrust my arms down the sleeves, grabbed the can of cooking spray and shot a jet of oil on the calves and forearms of my suit. I snatched up my timing chip, heart rate monitor, goggles and dark red swimcap with race logo on the side. I took a last, hurried look round my gear layout next to my bike and rushed out of the transition area.

My bare feet tiptoed over a scattering of road chips and pebbles down to the reservoir edge. I spent a few minutes adjusting the upper part of my wetsuit, then asked another competitor to zip it up for me. I spotted Mike, his muscular frame standing tall amidst competitors clad in uniform black neoprene. Mike was 6 foot 3 inches and weighed in at 205 lbs. He had entered the race in a special category known as Clydesdales, reserved for heavier-built male athletes. This category would leave last, directly after my wave, along with relay teams, mountain bikers and Athenas, the category for heavier-built female athletes.

The elite athletes, the first two Men's waves and the Women Under 35 wave were already underway. A few minutes later the announcer called out names of the first elite competitors to emerge from the water.

"And a big thank you to everyone for freeing up the transition area so our elites have a clear run through," the announcer added. "We don't want them tripping over you folks."

So that explained the rush to clear the transition area. At least I would know for next time.

The horn sounded, launching the blue-capped Men Over 40 wave forward in a flurry of spray and arms. Fifteen minutes to my wave. I pulled on my swim cap and goggles.

"Have a good race, Mike!" I called out and waved to him from about twelve yards away.

"You too, Jane," he called back and waved. "See you at the finish!"

Time to get in the water. I walked in up to knee height. Mud oozed up between my toes. I strode in quickly. Better to reach swimming depth as soon as possible than imagine what bottom-dwelling creatures I might be disturbing. I swam a few minutes of gentle freestyle in the warmup area. Plenty of time to accustom my face to the water temperature.

The wave before mine of Men Over 50 set off. I made my way over to the start line, part of the swarm of red-capped Women Over 35. Just us and the lime green caps left. I positioned myself in the middle of about forty swimmers. I was ready for this. I was about to race.

The crowd chanted the ten-second countdown. I pictured pulling those first few strokes of freestyle. Five. Four. I hit the stopwatch button on my heart rate monitor. Three. Two. A blast of the horn, a cheer from the crowd, a churning of arms.

I soon settled into my three-strokes-and-breathe pattern. Time to work through my proper warmup and aim for the first buoy at the end of the headland. The crowd of swimmers thinned out. A couple of women about twenty yards ahead, several about twenty yards behind me. None of us gained on each other.

How far was that buoy? Just me and the cloudy green water. I looked up every ten breaths to sight on the flash of fluorescent orange. Still swimming in a straight line, thank goodness. I took forever to reach the buoy. Rounded the headland. Forever plus eternity to reach the next buoy. Fatigue in my arms. And soreness at the back of my neck, as though someone had been pulling my hair. What could have caused that? Switched to breaststroke. The headland blocked out sound from the loudspeakers. Peaceful water. Back to freestyle. Nothing to remind me I was in a race except for a scattering of red caps and the occasional lime green cap. The sore patch on my neck began to throb. I plowed on.

I rounded the next buoy. The twelve-foot high, dark blue inflatable arch with the word FINISH across the top rose above the boat slipway. Adrenaline tingled in my limbs. End of the swim in sight. I put in one last aching spurt. The arch moved closer. The ribbed slipway emerged from the gloom beneath me. When my fingers brushed concrete, I stood up and walked out of the water. The timing chip machine beeped as I walked over the mat. My stopwatch showed 32 minutes, 43 seconds.

Surely not? How could I have swum that slowly? Based on last year's one-mile open water swim time of thirty-four minutes, this three-quarter-mile course should only have taken me about twenty-six minutes. No time to think about that now. Focus on transition to the bike leg.

I walked to my bike. Mike's bike was gone. So were most of the other bikes. Mike must have overtaken me in the water somewhere. I yanked the suit off in one giant swoop. First time I had managed a smooth suit removal. But what was that stuck to the plastic velcro strip round the neck? A thick wad of matted hair, my hair, covered half the plastic strip. That sore sensation of having my hair pulled out was for real. The two parts of velcro strip had not overlapped completely. The exposed part had latched onto wisps of hair escaping from my swim cap and pulled them out. A lot of them.

I rubbed the sore, bald patch on the back of my neck. Forget it. Move on. I slid my feet into my bike shoes, slapped down the velcro straps, pulled on my helmet and made double-sure I'd strapped it up. I didn't want to risk being disqualified for riding my bike without fastening my helmet. I walked my bike to the exit, clicked my stopwatch button to record a laptime and set off up the road.

The run course ran parallel with the bike course for a couple of miles. I cycled past a string of a dozen runners. They had already finished their bike leg by the time I got out of the water. I passed the tree and bend that David and I had identified as the 1.5-mile mark on the run course. I would be back here myself in an hour or so. The run course turnaround marker sailed by on my right. Fourteen miles of the bike course lay ahead. I imagined myself powering to the tops of the hills and flying along the flat by the reservoir.

The road curved round and over a switchback of gentle slopes, through clumps of California oaks, a dip in the road leading me back to the lazy shores of the reservoir. I had tackled easy rollers like these dozens of times. But I held my breath each time I clicked up or down a gear. I didn't trust my bike to end up in the gear I intended. My mental picture had changed. Instead of cresting the hill and swooping down the other side, I heard the clank-twang of a dropped chain and felt the jolt of an abrupt stop.

A sheriff waved me round a sharp right-hand corner that marked the start of a five-mile flat stretch. The nearest rider was about two hundred yards ahead of me. No one behind me. For now, I had my own space to settle down. I didn't need to change gear on the flat. Come on, Jane. Get a grip. Breathe deeply. Banish the image of that dropped chain. Your bike won't let you down, not after all you've been through together.

I focused on the wide, smooth road that swept round the reservoir on my right. A vista of shallow hills folding into water shimmered through the early-morning heat haze. Ancient oaks on my left threw shade over the road. The steady rhythm of pedaling and whirring of spokes soothed my nerves.

A strange, cool sensation crept up through my ankles. My feet were cold. Worse than cold. My feet had turned into dull, pewter-gray metal. They were welded to the pedals. I'd wrench my feet sideways, I'd fight to get out of those pedals and when my bike slowed to a stop, I'd fall over and hit the ground. What had happened to my feet?

Calm down, Jane. Be sensible. Feet don't turn into metal and get welded to pedals, ever. Your mind is playing tricks with you. Why, I don't know, but it's a trick. You could unclip your feet any time you like, you're in control, you just don't choose to unclip for the fun of it in the middle of a race. Rational Me coated me in soothing, sensible reassurance.

I hadn't seen a single car since I rode past the sheriffs who were holding back traffic to favor riders. I looked behind me. Still no one there. The rider ahead had pulled out of sight. I was alone. Harsh sunshine hardened the road to a smooth ribbon of steel and bleached the trees to a matte, murky green. A bubble of silence enveloped me and followed me along, trapping within it the sound of my anxious breathing and the insistent whirr of my spokes. The race melted away. The world shifted a couple of degrees askew from normal. I was in a universe of one, where welded pedals were standard issue.

I'm losing it. No one to help me. Everything looks normal but isn't. And soon I'll have to do battle with my bike on that Hill. My bike, the Enemy. It won't want to change gear and I'll fall off. I hate my bike. I hate it.

Come on, stop tormenting yourself with this welding nonsense, the parallel universe and the evil bike. The bike isn't your enemy, it's an inanimate object. The bike does what you tell it to do. A bike doesn't have a mind of its own. It certainly doesn't have feelings. It's only my feelings about the bike that aren't very charitable right now.

An insistent breeze chilled my skin. Rational Me weakened to a feeble squeak. My breathing grew faster and shallower. I clung to the one certainty that this had to end some time. Normal life would be resumed when I reached the safe haven of the transition area.

I passed the house and tree. One mile to The Hill. Time to dig deep. Breathe slowly. Change gear. Do it now.

I dropped right back to the lowest cog on my back wheel. But I didn't dare risk switching from the middle to smallest ring. The big-middle-small ring switches were the ones most likely to cause the dropped chain. I had cycled up here last week on the middle ring. I could do it again. I cranked the speed on the run-up to The Hill. It was here. I was on The Hill.

The gradient began to bite. I slowed down. I fought to keep the pedals turning over. How far to the plateau by the gate? My quads strained under the pressure, yelling at me to stop. I looked up. In that instant, a bolt of lightning shot up through the pedals and blasted my feet out of the clips. My bike tipped over and my right foot hit the ground. I stopped abruptly.

I was stunned. Alternate Persona had staged a ruthless take-over of my decision-making function. I wasn't allowed to cycle any farther up this hill. And this decision wasn't up for negotia-tion. How could I not be in control of my actions? My heart beat way too fast. I almost shook, fearful of what may happen next in the parallel universe. I had reached the far end of weird.

No point trying to get back on the bike and pedal the rest of the hill. The gradient was too steep. I'd never be able to push off, get my other foot clipped in and start pedaling before I fell over. I swung my leg over the crossbar and began to walk. The Hill was littered with people who were walking. Just look at all the competitors I could have overtaken if only I could have held myself together.

One hundred yards later, I reached the top. I took a deep breath. Relief percolated through my body, its warmth seeping to the ends of my fingers and toes. I was cushioned by shouts of encouragement from spectators. Mellow sun returned the trees to a rich, dark green and threw dappled light across the road. The level ground released me from the scary world of welded pedals.

I reached an uneasy truce with my bike. I persuaded myself to get back on and set off. Five more miles to cycle back to real-ity. I took several deep breaths. On each exhalation, I chanted the word "relaaaax" out loud. I would deal with what had just hap-pened after the race. Open roads, easy downhill cycling, two right turns. A cyclist dressed in black top and shorts riding a metallic blue bike overtook me. I let her go. I wasn't up for racing. I had to pull myself together to tackle the run when I got off the bike.

The last two uneventful miles led me back to the refuge of

the transition area. I dismounted and walked my bike back to my spot. Had I really visited a solitary world of welded pedals on the other side of that hill? I pinged my stopwatch. The bike leg had taken 1 hour, 13 minutes. I was hoping for closer to one hour. But considering what I had been through, I would take a time of 1 hour, 13 and be grateful.

I removed my bike shoes and pulled on my running shoes, all the while going over my run rhythm of breathing two steps in, four steps out. Breathe steady, settle into the groove. I forced my mind to shed the skin of the bike nightmare. I was no longer a cyclist. I was now a runner.

My hands located my hat, hidden under my wetsuit where I had dropped it on the ground. I pulled on the hat, yanking my pony tail through the gap at the back. I clipped my race belt with my number 80 attached round my waist. Ready to run. I threaded my way out of the busy transition area through bikes and gear and turned right by a giant inflatable Nantucket Nectar bottle. My feet connected with solid road. I took my first steps on the run course.

I prepared myself for what lay ahead. I would have to fight my way through the pain barrier of the bike-to-run transition. And Gail had warned me of an optical illusion that made the first half mile look flat when it was uphill. That would make the switch double-tough.

Two hundred yards later, right on cue, the bike-run switch caused my calf muscles to tighten. And the intensity of running uphill made my body feel like it was dragging twice its weight around. Why hadn't I done more practice of running after each bike ride? I had shied away from the agony that awaited me every time I ran straight off the bike. My own personal gravity field weighed me down in direct proportion to the gradient. I could barely drag myself up this hill. My ankles to midcalves tightened up, forcing me to shorten my stride. I stared at the road five feet ahead of me, concentrating on keeping my legs turning over.

Just a long, empty road marked by telegraph poles that disappeared round a bend. Had the road flattened out? I wasn't sure. Run to the telegraph pole. Now the next. The one-mile aid station appeared when I rounded the corner. I took a cup of water from a volunteer's outstretched hand. Permission to walk for half a minute. I threw the empty cup in the trash and ran. Twelve minutes since I left the transition area. Four more miles to get through. A glut of runners streamed towards me. Probably the main bunch of Men Over 35.

"Go, Jane!"

Mike appeared almost at my elbow, running strong, heading back to the finish.

"Go, Mike!"

I waved. He waved back. I was pleased he was having a great race.

Right on the nineteen-minute mark, the tightness eased off, leaving my legs feeling spent but mobile. The main bunch of runners heading back had thinned. I counted six runners up ahead of me—two running together and four on their own. The two-mile aid station appeared ahead. I grabbed more water, walked and then pushed on.

A change in gradient. Please, not a long hill. I didn't remember a long hill from my scouting trip. But cars have such contempt for slopes that runners call hills, I may have overlooked it. Remember that Kevin calls hills friends. I smiled. The hill is my friend – the hill is my friend, I chanted in time to each step. My weary quad muscles took a breather and my gluts took over. Maybe this was what Kevin had meant all along about the hill being my friend. Hill-running used different muscle groups.

The turnaround marker sprang up on me by surprise. Large

chalk arrows guided me counterclockwise round the marker and slung me back down the course. My scouting trip was correct. Hardly a hill at all. More a short slope. I headed back, energized that I had run over half the course already. I overtook the couple running together, plus three solo runners.

Then my energy spurt ran out. I dragged myself past the tree that served as my 1.5-mile marker. Past the aid station. Couldn't be bothered to stop for water. Must get home. The row of telegraph poles pulled me forward. Just one more mile. I forced my legs forward in a shuffling run.

I rounded the last corner. The Nantucket Nectar bottle stood sentry by the entrance to the finish line, about three hundred yards ahead. My legs told me what Gail had assured me; that this was now a downhill slope, payback for the uphill push at the start of the run. My pace speeded up. No point holding anything back. My legs propelled me downhill. Overtook the sixth runner. The bottle grew ten feet tall. Five yards to go. Turn left by the bottle. Past the transition area. Sweep right across the finish.

I pinged my stopwatch. I finished the run in fifty-five minutes, for a total event time of 2 hours, 46 minutes, 39 seconds. A race volunteer removed the strap with the timing chip from my ankle and handed me a bottle of water. I stood still, disoriented, my legs not knowing where to take me next.

"Smile!"

I heard a familiar voice and looked up, just as David took a photo of me.

"Where did you spring from?" I said, a smile breaking out across my face.

My instincts had been right. David's cover story about staying home hadn't rung true. I had suspected he might come down for the finish. I just didn't allow myself to believe it in case I turned out to be wrong.

David put his arm round my shoulder and steered me through dozens of finishers milling around the gear stalls. Mike and his wife, Nancy, sat on the grass near the reservoir, their two young daughters playing with their Barbie dolls next to them.

"We couldn't let you both race without coming to cheer you on," David said.

"So we hatched a plan when you and Mike were at packet pickup," Nancy continued. "We had to be here to see you guys finish."

"I'm so glad you did," I said. "It's good to have the Supporters' Club here."

I caught sight of my stopwatch, fixed at my finish time of 2 hours 46 minutes. I ought to congratulate myself, especially considering the nightmare bike leg. Remember, finishing was an achievement in itself. I wandered over to the athletes-only food tent. Long rows of tables held empty fruit, burrito and bagel boxes. Abandoned plastic knives pointed to the presence of cream cheese, long since consumed. At the end of the last table, someone had left a box with a couple of plain bagels and a handful of orange wedges. Never mind. I had finished too slowly to get a full plate of food, that was all.

I walked over to the results table that listed all the finishers and their official times. I checked the list. My name wasn't on there yet.

The six of us sat down in the sunshine to watch the medal presentations in each age group. The top woman in my 40-44 age group had finished in 1 hour, 47 minutes. After the presentations were over, I headed back to the results table. The list hadn't been updated since I checked twenty-five minutes before. The volunteers had started to pack up, so the list wouldn't change now.

David came over to see what I was looking at. I told him that the preliminary results were in, but the latecomers would be on the website. No big deal. We said goodbye to Mike, Nancy and the girls, collected my gear and walked back to our car in silence.

Remember, finishing was an achievement in itself. Forget that I finished too late to get any food. Never mind that I was missed off the organizers' results page. I wasn't too slow to count on the official listings. The omission was an oversight, not a judgment call. I tried desperately to stick with Kevin's advice of celebrating accomplishment. But I had a hard time believing it.

I didn't say much on the drive home. I phoned Kevin and Gail. I left them both a voicemail about my result, mentioning I had passed six people on the run, but leaving out the weird bike stuff. David and I stopped off for a late brunch. I ordered mushroom and spinach omelet, hash browns and toast. As I sipped my English Breakfast tea, I reminded myself I was supposed to hold onto the good stuff, of somehow finishing the bike leg and passing people on the run. This race was meant to be a confidence-builder for next month's San Jose Tri. Instead, I had learned that positive self-talk was no help at all when deep down, I no longer believed in myself.

Picking Up the Pieces

Number of physical mountains to climb: one killer hill in the race

Number of mental mountains to climb: don't even go there

What would you do if you discovered that the real you, the one buried far beneath your daily routine, your decisions, your hopes, your relationships, your ego, doesn't give you a snowball's chance in the desert of succeeding at your goal? The day of the Uvas Tri, I found out exactly what I would do. I went into shock.

I had lied to myself in the Uvas Tri. I was terrified of falling off my bike, yet I had refused to admit it, even to myself. On the surface, I had been going through the motions of positive self-talk. Deep down, I didn't believe a word of it. Somehow, I knew all along that I was paying lip service, that I would never quell the fear of falling with trite words. Ignoring my fear would not make it disappear.

Furthermore, I had reached the age of 42 without fully understanding the power of my subconscious mind. When my feet shot out of the pedals at Uvas, an uncontrollable part of me had made that decision. As far as I was concerned, the only part allowed to make decisions was the conscious, Rational Me. I was in complete control of everything. Might I fail because my subconscious decided it was time to put away the toys and go home?

After all my physical preparation for the race, the last thing

I expected was for my subconscious to sabotage my plans. But what could I do? Surface babble about "sure, you can do the hill" was simply not enough to reach deep down and touch the real me. My subconscious stared back at me with folded arms and pursed lips, a tough, cynical boss that refused to be convinced by fancy rhetoric. My subconscious sought only hard facts. I would have to find a better way than wishy-washy catchphrases to persuade this tough nut to cooperate.

I remembered a presentation given at work by an occupational psychologist about twelve years ago. We had been discussing the use of psychometric profiles for recruitment. Partway through, the group wandered onto the subject of the subconscious mind. The psychologist told us that the subconscious was where emotions reside. Most of us have a hard time communicating with our subconscious because it doesn't respond to words. Instead, it communicates through images. But you could train yourself to communicate through images with your subconscious. This was what the essence of hypnosis was all about.

We immediately dropped the boring stuff about recruitment in favor of a group hypnosis exercise. We switched off the overhead office lights and closed our eyes. The psychologist painted a word picture of a beach, a visual metaphor for a calm, safe place to which we could return any time we needed to relax. My coworkers and I relaxed on that beach for well over an hour, yet we all swore we had spent less than ten minutes there.

I can still summon up my beach whenever I need to escape. I lie in a secluded spot, eyes closed, bathed in late afternoon sun, trickling warm, silky sand through my fingers, breathing in the heavy scent of jasmine bushes, a gentle breeze caressing my skin, the soothing ebb of waves playing in my ears. A sense of profound calm settles over me. That oasis of peace gives me strength to overcome the worst obstacles that the day can throw at me.

Apart from the beach-calming trick, I had never bothered to reach out to my subconscious. And certainly not through something as off-the-wall as hypnosis. But my subconscious had definitely reached out to me. That image of welded pedals in the Uvas Triathlon was a last-ditch attempt to alert me to my true level of fear.

I wandered around in shock for three days. How could I deal with an obstinate subconscious? On day four, I formed an action plan. I would call on my coaching buddies and friends to help me find a way through this.

First, I turned to Cristina, my running buddy and only other member of the exclusive Running and Chatting Club. We'd built a friendship through our weekly runs together and our shared battle to run on winter mornings. Cristina had a psychology doctorate. Surely she could shed light on whether my subconscious had the power to scupper my race.

"Ready to run, Cristina?"

I steadied myself with one hand against my SUV while doing my warmup quad stretches before our Thursday run.

"Sure," she said, removing her navy and pale blue sweats. "Usual route along the Bayshore or somewhere different?"

"Usual route," I said. "I need to concentrate on our conversation today."

"Hey, are you OK?"

Cristina turned to me with a worried look.

"Yes, I'm fine," I said. "There's something I want your advice on, that's all."

We set off along the creekside path, the day still gray with marine layer fog. A woman walking towards us in a pink track suit pulled her black lab dog closer on its leash to give us space to run past. I pulled ahead to run single file, then dropped back alongside Cristina.

"So what's up?" Cristina asked, once we had the path to ourselves.

I spent the next five minutes spilling out all my concerns about my subconscious hijacking my decisions.

"Sounds like you pushed yourself beyond where your subconscious was prepared to go in your last race," said Cristina. "It did what it did to protect you."

Our footsteps pounded over the wooden footbridge across the creek, right opposite the five imposing dark blue glass towers of the Oracle headquarters. We turned left to run along the other bank. The tide was out, leaving behind an expanse of dull brown mud flats dotted with white, stick-legged egrets foraging for food.

"You know, few people ever have a chance to interact with their subconscious the way you have," Cristina continued. "You've been doing it without realizing since the beach hypnosis exercise. Don't worry. You've been training your mind to go with you as you push to each new level of endurance. You're not starting from scratch."

She suggested I should visualize reaching the top of the hill on the San Jose course, just as I had done on the actual rides with Gail. I needed to communicate that particular achievement to my subconscious in an image. She also advised practicing the thing that scared me most in a safe environment, then building up from there. So I should practice changing gear on hills of increasing steepness. I could reassure my subconscious with the image of a gear change, repeated time after time, with no dropped chain, until I was confident I could nail the hill.

We reached the end of the inlet and ran past picnic tables in a small park. Local office workers would gather here for lunch, but for now we had the place to ourselves. We paused at Marine Parkway and waited for the lights to turn. Then we crossed all six lanes and began our clockwise circuit of the lake, past the smart outdoor patio of the Mistral Restaurant.

There was something else that troubled me, something that I only wanted to share with Cristina.

"So do you think it was my subconscious that made the decision to take up triathlon?" I blurted out. "And that I can't work out what's driving me on because my subconscious hasn't sent me an image to let me know yet?"

After all this time, I still hadn't worked out why I was doing the triathlon. I had spent months, off and on, trying to understand why I was being dragged towards something so out of character for me. The best I could come up with was that I needed to test myself with a huge challenge after a couple of years' wait for my green card. But that was simply too weak a reason to drive me on through all this. It didn't feel right. It wasn't enough.

"Sounds like it probably has made this decision for you," she said. "Your subconscious is also the site of your beliefs and aspirations. Something is compelling you to do this. Maybe in time you'll find out, or maybe you'll never find out. Just go with it and see where it takes you."

I didn't much like the idea of my subconscious deciding something without consulting Rational Me, but I didn't exactly have a choice in the matter. Our conversation eased down a gear. We looped round the lake through the Sofitel Hotel grounds, chatting about the rest of my training schedule and her plans for the summer. We headed back to our cars and said our goodbyes.

Next, I emailed Kevin. He gave me lots of advice on mental issues. Then some tips on coordinating the rear wheel cog switches with the middle ring-small ring switch to avoid the dropped chain. He also suspected that the front derailleur, part of the gear-changing mechanism, might be slightly out of alignment. I should have the bike checked out to rule out anything mechanical.

Three days later, I took my bike into Chain Reaction Bicycles. Greg, the friendly mechanic who had sold me the bike nearly a year ago, performed a thorough check on the bike. He adjusted the front derailleur to make the middle ring-small ring switch easier.

Next I phoned Gail. I hadn't seen much of her over the last month. She had stopped teaching spin class in favor of more hours at the physical therapy practice. She was upbeat, having resolved to take a Physical Therapy doctorate as soon as she could get into her chosen grad school on the East Coast. I was pleased for her that her life was moving on. It compensated for my disappointment that she would shortly be moving out of mine.

I poured out my tale of woe in one long, uninterruptible stream of words.

"Hey, easy there," she said, when it was all over. "We've got time to build your confidence. Here's what we'll do. We'll ride Bailey Hill over and over together until you're absolutely convinced you'll get to the top. And we'll devise a gear strategy. By the time race day comes, you'll blast that hill to pieces."

Gail and I met the next week at Lake Almaden, site of the San Jose Tri. I spotted her unloading her bike, wearing her favorite yellow cycle jersey with the weird red and orange squiggles. I smiled. I had been forced to stare for way too long at those garish squiggles on our first bike ride down the Foothill Expressway. She told me that day that she had chosen the pattern on purpose. If it had that effect on me, then she would stand a better chance of getting car drivers to give her a wide berth, too. I would miss Gail a lot, but I wouldn't miss that jersey.

Apart from our two SUVs, the car park had only seven other vehicles scattered round the edge. A handful of dog-walkers and moms with toddlers were dotted along the lakeside path that would form the run course of the Tri. A flock of Canada geese grazed on the grass by the waterfront. I could scarcely imagine the park filled with two thousand competitors and spectators in four weeks' time.

We set off along Coleman. A right turn on Santa Teresa, then a leisurely spin along wide suburban roads, pausing now and then for traffic lights. Just how I remembered the terrain from our winter ride of this course. We reached the edge of town and built up speed along the straight, flat road through artichoke fields. Waves of panic turned my knees weak as I thought of the impending hill. No matter that I'd cycled it before with no problems. I would just have to trust Gail and her gear strategy, forgive my subconscious if it sent me a lightning bolt attack, go back down and start over.

We turned right onto Bailey Avenue. Quiet, innocuous road. Past the IBM Research Center sign on our right. Across the little bridge over the creek.

"So the bridge is your first trigger on the gear strategy," Gail said.

I checked my gears. Middle ring, sixth rear cog out of nine.

"Change down a cog by this boulder."

I changed. Another change by the road sign. Past the tree. Time for the big change. Click of the little black lever. Smooth drop down to my small ring.

"It doesn't matter if you're on the small ring sooner than other people," Gail said. "You want to switch on the flat, before the gradient of the hill puts too much strain on the chain. You'll go slower, but your objective is to stay on the bike and not be forced to stop. Now let's do that hill!"

I rounded the left-hand bend in the lowest of my gear options. Three-foot-high roadside reflective markers were positioned every hundred yards up the hill. They reminded me of the mailboxes that had marked my run at the duathlon. Each one a lasso, waiting to pull me up that section of the hill and fling me on to the next waiting marker. Within ten seconds, my legs stepped up to ninety-five percent effort. I rode past the first marker. My stomach fluttered with apprehension. How soon till the effort turned into pain? I kept my head down. Past the second marker. My legs pushed their hardest against the pedals. I could only keep this up for a few minutes at most.

Gail, my guardian angel, pulled me along by riding inches off my front wheel. I breathed in some of Gail's energy in her slipstream. I'm on – my way – I'm on – my way, I chanted to myself with each tough pedal stroke. Third reflective marker. Shouldn't the gradient ease round about here? That's what I remembered from our last visit. Right on cue, my legs communicated a slight easing in the slope, just before the hairpin bend. The halfway point. My subconscious unfolded its arms and nodded. Ease of gradient, slope manageable, enough energy to reach the top. Yes, those were hard facts.

The instant my body received the nod, a beam of confidence radiated out from just above my stomach. Remember this feeling, Jane. This is what a true positive mindset feels like. Your mind believes you will succeed. Every fiber in your body believes you will succeed. Your mind and body are in sync. So don't fool yourself with lip service ever again.

Confidence carried me to the top. Gail and I pulled off the road at the entrance to the field on our right. The world spread out before us. We shared a high-five.

"Ready to do it again?" said Gail.

"That's what we're here for," I replied with a grin.

We freewheeled back down the hill and cycled up again. This time, Gail pulled about fifty yards ahead. I had to prove to myself that I could do this hill on my own. I stuck to the gear plan, kept my head down and put in maximum effort. That warm glow of self-belief filled every nook and cranny of my body. I powered past the third marker, round the hairpin and surged to the top. I pulled up alongside Gail. I leaned on my handlebars and took a mental snapshot of the road curving back down and out of sight. If I had doubts over the next few weeks, I would email that snapshot to my subconscious to remind me of today.

One week to go before the San Jose Tri. Time to set my expectations. Back in January, I had planned for a finish time of three hours flat. Based on my time for the one-mile Open Water Swim last September, I had expected to clock around twenty-six minutes for the three-quarter-mile swim. Allow five minutes for the first transition. Then an hour and a half for the bike leg, including the second transition, and one hour for the run.

But my swim over the same distance at the Uvas Tri had taken me thirty-three minutes, a long way off twenty-six minutes. As ever, Kevin had the answer. If I concentrated on two disciplines and ignored the third, my performance would fall off in the one I ignored. I had to keep all the plates spinning at once, even if it meant sacrificing speed. I'd just spent the last four months ignoring the swim, with barely two swims every three weeks, thinking that my race speed wouldn't suffer. I wasn't going to make up that speed with one week to go. I had to accept that I would have a slow swim.

I still felt I would ride close to one and a half hours on the bike. So that left the run. After my disappointing outing at the Human Race, the best I could hope for was 1 hour, 5 minutes. Which, when added to the transitions, came to a slow 3 hours, 15 minutes.

On Saturday, Gail emailed me a detailed race plan. She gave me sound advice about the swim start and finish, plus the gears, nutrition and pacing on the bike. She finished off with the run.

> The run is flat. It can be very hot. Take Gu
> carbohydrate gel with you. Drink water or en-
> ergy drink at the aid stations. You can also put
> ice in your hat or splash yourself with water.
> You'll see people come apart in the late stage
> of the race because they get tired and lose
> focus. You can catch them here.

I wasn't sure if I would catch anyone at all. And what if it was me getting tired and losing focus? Still, if I had somehow pushed myself with a start/stop/start technique up and down five hilly miles at the Uvas Tri, I should get myself round 6.2 flat miles at San Jose, even if I had to walk part of it.

I phoned Gail that evening.

"Thanks for the race plan," I said. "But I can't see myself coming anywhere near my race goal time."

"So what are you aiming for?" Gail said.

"I really wanted three hours flat. I thought back in January that I'd do it. But now the best I can hope for is three fifteen."

"Hey, slow down a minute!" she said. "Can you guess what my time was for my first Olympic-distance tri?"

I hadn't a clue.

"It was 3 hours, 18 minutes", she replied. "So don't beat up on yourself. You've done great to get yourself in shape to even attempt this. Three fifteen would be outta sight! I suggest you give yourself three goals—that way, you'll hit at least one of them. And don't let it all hinge around three fifteen or bust."

After Gail's phone call, I sat on our front veranda with a glass of Pinot Noir and watched the sunset. I mulled over what she had just said. Why was the goal of simply finishing not good enough for me any more? What had happened to my enjoyment of becoming a triathlete?

I knew the answer. I had just refused to admit it to myself

until now. Spoiling the enjoyment was exactly what I did in real life. I would set a goal, exceed it and then bypass the celebration because I'd already set a new goal. You would think that working in sales, I would have had lots of achievements to celebrate. Instead, I moved the goalposts just as I approached my target. So I always fell short of my own standards. I was never good enough.

How did I end up like this? I recalled my first steps in selling, when I worked for a high-profile headhunting practice in the UK. I moved into recruitment two months before the start of a brutal, four-year recession. I had had to build a client base from scratch when companies were shedding more employees than they hired.

I had been at least ten years younger than anyone else, and one of only nine women out of eighty-six consultants. Not exactly a great fit. Even though I'd been promised a mentor, it had never happened. The only way to survive had been through self-help. After each sales call, I'd sit in my car, write down what went well and what I could have improved upon. Over time, I didn't bother writing down the good stuff, just the things to improve upon. At the end of four years, I was a top-ten performer out of twenty-seven consultants still left in the company.

I went on to run a branch of a different search firm in London for six years. Then I came to the US. Here I learned how to sell in a different cultural environment and business sector. I'd never lost that mental critique of what I could have done better on every call. But in the process, I'd eliminated the ability to praise myself. When American colleagues congratulated me, I'd thank them. Inwardly, I'd brush it off as that gushy, over-the-top American praise that I couldn't quite get myself to believe was genuine. The result was that I'd killed a lot of the reward for doing the job —recognition from others and from myself of my achievement.

Time to give myself a break. I would celebrate the triathlon, no matter what the outcome. Getting myself in shape to compete was a huge achievement. Just finishing would be a result. Not finishing but trying my best would be a result.

And I would learn a lesson from triathlon. From now on, I resolved to give myself a break in the rest of my life. I would celebrate each goal before I allowed myself to reset the bar. I couldn't kid myself that everything I did was an achievement. But when I met my standards of the moment, success was going to count. I may not be able to believe my American colleagues wholeheartedly when they surged into overdrive on the praise and encouragement thing, but I would at least give them the benefit of the doubt.

That night, I wrote down my three goals for the triathlon. My first goal was to finish. My second goal was to finish above last in my age group. Considering I finished forty-fifth out of forty-seven in my age group at the Uvas Tri, that was not as simple as it sounded. Finally, I wanted to finish in 3 hours, 20 minutes, although my secret goal was 3 hours, 15.

The week before the Tri, I did a couple of gentle runs so that I would start the event with rested muscles. But I still had one more round of practical preparation. Race rules stated that competitors would be disqualified if they received outside help. I could deal with a dropped chain on my own. I could change a flat on the front wheel. But I still had no idea how to extricate the back wheel from the derailleur if I had a rear wheel puncture. And I had to learn to change a tire faster than my twelve-minute record.

On Friday morning, forty-eight hours before the race, I went down to the garage and wheeled David's bike out from the utility room. I spent nearly two hours grappling with the front wheel, letting out air, sliding tire levers round the rim, yanking out the inner tube, putting it back and pumping up the tire. I didn't want to practice on my wheel in case I wrecked it before the race. But I could sacrifice his wheel without him knowing.

Then I took his bike into Chain Reaction Bicycles. Greg wasn't in, so I asked another mechanic to give me a lesson in removing the back wheel. Daniel was patience personified. He showed me step by step how to move the rear derailleur out of the way and jiggle the wheel out of its socket. He gave me tips on changing the inner tube, when to use brute force and when not to. He supervised me making four rear wheel removals and replacements in a row. When I returned home, David's bike was still in one piece and he was none the wiser.

Throughout the rest of the afternoon, my body began to tense up in anticipation of race day. 362 days after I first started training, I was about to race the San Jose Triathlon. Would my subconscious throw a wrench in the works and dump me out of the race? Had I done enough training? I walked around in my own personal time warp, my mind working on double speed while the traffic, the people, the clocks were stuck in slo-mo. I wanted Sunday to arrive yesterday.

I took a deep breath. Enough already. No point worrying about my subconscious. Or about how much training I'd done or not done. Whatever I'd done would be good enough. Barring a complete mechanical breakdown on the bike, way beyond flat tires or dropped chains, I'd get round. Even if I walked most of the run, I'd get round. And I would savor the finish. I had put hundreds of hours into training. This race was my reward. I thought about my calm, safe beach. I trickled sand through my fingers and breathed in the scent of the jasmine bushes. I was ready.

On the Saturday morning before the race, I phoned my mum for our regular weekly catch-up call.

"So tomorrow's your big race day!" Mum's excitement

tingled over the phone. "I've had that date on my calendar for weeks."

"Yes, the big day," I said. "What will be, will be."

"I'll be cheering you on from three o'clock until you say stop," she said. She had already adjusted in real time for the eight-hour time difference. "And whatever you do, wherever you finish, I'll be so proud of my triathlete daughter."

I wished that she could be here on Sunday to see me finish. At times like this, even the power of phone and internet couldn't bridge six thousand miles.

On Saturday afternoon, Mike and I drove down to Lake Almaden in San Jose. We repeated our packet pickup routine and collected our race numbers, timing chips and T-shirts for the race. When I returned home, David was in the garage, holding a screwdriver.

"There's one last piece of bike maintenance you need," he said. "Would you like me to do it for you?"

What could I have forgotten? David smiled and knelt down by my bike. In a couple of deft moves, he removed the reflectors from my front and back wheel spokes. Now I was well and truly ready.

The San Jose Triathlon

Number of hours spent training for this day: approx. 350

Number of hours about to be spent competing: approx. 3.5

I was never meant to do this at all. I was never meant to push myself through a year of intense training, challenge willpower, extend beyond my threshold and fight the fear that lies on the other side. I was meant to coast through my comfortable life, soaking up life's pleasures and choosing only those projects where I was guaranteed to succeed.

Instead, I lie awake in bed at four o'clock on a Sunday morning, rubbing my neck to relieve tension. I am about to tackle three of the most grueling hours of my life. Alternate Persona reminds me that I've volunteered to do this. I'm about to endure pain for a reason I don't fully understand when I could just as easily sleep in and nobody would mind either way. No, I am most definitely not coasting.

I switch the alarm off at 4:14 a.m., one minute before it is due to go off. I shelve the self-analysis and get straight out of bed.

I rehearsed this pre-race routine when I did the Uvas Tri last month. No need to think. Wash face with cold water, brush teeth, apply suntan cream, pull on tri outfit and sweats, slurp down hot oatmeal with golden syrup, check tire pressure on bike, wait for Mike. He arrives at 4:50 a.m. No husband to wave me off this time. We've agreed ahead of time that he'll catch some sleep and will come down to watch later.

I also know what to expect at the race venue. Mike and I rack up our bikes next to each other on row nineteen out of thirty-four. I leave myself plenty of time for my routine of loo queue, warmup jog and bodymarking. Competitor number 330 is stamped on my arms and age 4 and 3 on my calves. Then on with the wetsuit. I reach the artificial beach by the lake at 6:51 a.m.

"Welcome today to the eleven hundred athletes competing in this year's San Jose Triathlon, the premier event in the Bay Area!"

A torrent of announcements streams from the loudspeakers, squeezed in between adrenaline-pumping music. The noise crushes the soft, still air around me.

"All competitors make your way to the beach now!"

"Elite wave leaves in five minutes!"

Spectators, race officials, stallholders and volunteers mingle on the green turf lining the beach. Nearly fifteen hundred people. Almost all the competitors are wedged onto a tiny strip of sand by the water's edge, a huge, hovering swarm of black neoprene covered with a rash of color-coded swimcaps. The outer flank spills into the water and skims in every direction across the surface of the warmup area, filling it with short bursts of windmill arms. A colony of silver swimcaps peels away and coalesces round the start buoy, ready for the first wave.

I catch my breath. I'm part of the swarm, the collective body of tension that will unleash a coil of energy as each wave bursts from the starting line. Even the clean, pale daylight holds its breath, waiting for the race start.

I burrow my toes into cool sand and breathe in the anticipation. Fifteen months ago, I'd have treated the prediction of me doing a triathlon with as much ridicule as a palm reading. Now

I'm locked onto the target of the finish line. A tiny part of me is still bewildered, wondering how I ended up here. Maybe my subconscious will deign to let me know at some point. Or maybe it won't. It always did have a stubborn streak.

The explosion of the starting gun sends a shock wave through the air. Spectators cheer. The elite wave surges forward from the start buoy. Silver caps propelled by powerful arms shoot across the surface.

I stand on the lakeshore and watch the next wave of blue-capped Men Under 30 line up. My wave of Women Over 35 will not leave for another forty-eight minutes. If I enter the water too soon, I'll get cold. I rehearse the race plan that Gail drew up for me. First, a steady swim of around thirty-five minutes to settle my nerves. Three minutes for the transition, then the bike leg of one and a half hours. Allow a couple of minutes for the second transition. Then out for a run of around seventy minutes, for an overall time of 3 hours, 20 minutes. And if I trim a couple of minutes off the bike and run, I may even hit my secret time of 3 hours, 15.

Colored strings of caps bob their way counterclockwise round the perimeter of the lake. The blue-capped Men Under 30 finish their swim. The yellow caps of the Men Under 35 and the orange-capped leaders of the Women Under 35 wave approach the shore. Gail should be finishing around now, but she's so well camouflaged in her wetsuit and orange cap that I can't make her out. Seventh wave leaves. I wade into the water and swim some easy laps in the warmup area.

My wave of white-capped Women Over 40 and the lime green wave of Clydesdales, Athenas and relay teams merge on the water's edge. Mike is again registered in the Clydesdale class and will leave in the last wave. Six minutes left before my start. I make my way over to the start buoy with the other white caps.

One minute to go. I run on the spot in the water. How long

can one minute be? I just want to swim, bike and run and get this whole race over with. After a year's wait, all that training and effort has come down to this moment. Three hours plus from now, I'll cross the finish line. Ten-second countdown. I hit the stopwatch button on my wrist. The starting gun explodes and releases me from the purgatory of waiting.

Cheers from the bank. A surge of white caps. Head down. Three strokes and breathe. Relief at being underway shoots a current of energy down my arms and legs and pushes me on at an unsustainable pace. I resist the urge to keep up with the leaders and settle into a moderate tempo.

Fronds of tiny bubbles drift by underneath me in the opaque, brown-green water. I remember the Canada geese I saw here on my ride with Gail. Don't even think about what those geese have deposited in the lake. I retreat into my cocoon of concentration. Water fills my ears and insulates me from all but the sound of my own breathing.

Round the second buoy. Fifteen minutes and counting. My arms turn to lead. I curse my wetsuit, convinced it's responsible for slowing me down. But it's an excuse. My arms follow a pattern. Ache, complain, then turn numb to the ache and recover. I have to be strong now. Six minutes later, right on cue, my arms turn numb. I pick up the pace.

Five hundred yards to go. I swim on my own in open water. The nearest white cap is thirty yards ahead of me. I breathe to my left. A lime green cap passes me. Wait a minute, a green cap? I roll onto my back and glance behind me. Four or five white caps and about twenty green caps. I roll back and look ahead. More green caps. So I've already been overtaken by the final wave?

The people left in the water now, including me, are the very last people out on the course. Once we're done, the organizers will start collecting the buoys and cones. The awful truth about setting off in the penultimate wave punches me in my ribs. The slower I swim, the closer I come to the back of the pack.

I do the math as I swim. If a competitor sets off in Gail's wave, thirty minutes ahead of me, and finishes in 3 hours 40 minutes, twenty minutes slower than my goal time of 3 hours 20 minutes, then she'll finish after me in the overall placements. But she will have crossed the finish line ahead of me. Why couldn't I have taken this sport up fifteen years ago and finished in 3 hours, 40 minutes and hidden myself in a bunch of later finishers? I jettison all of my planned objectives. Forget all those things other people say about the noble achievement of just finishing. The one thing I will turn myself inside out to avoid is to cross that finish line last, trailing the cone collectors behind me.

I push on towards the beach. I swim right up to the shore until my fingertips brush the sandy bottom, then stand up and walk out of the water. I ping my stopwatch button to record the split time. Laptime is 33 minutes, 40 seconds, well within my thirty-five-minute goal. And most important is that I'm not last.

I pull hard on the zipper cord dangling down my back. The suit unpeels behind me. I grab the collar, yank the suit downwards and wrench my arms out, turning the sleeves inside out. Result. First time I've got my suit down to my waist when I exit the water. I half-walk, half-run to the transition area, my tender feet tiptoeing across the cold, gritty surface of the pavement.

I find row nineteen. Empty of bikes, except for mine and one other. Mike's bike is already gone. He must have been one of those lime green caps who overtook me.

I prize my suit down from my waist. The neoprene bunches up at my knees and refuses to budge. The more I pull, the more it tightens its grip. Great. My knees are locked together by a recalcitrant wetsuit and all I can do is wobble and hop round my transition spot.

I move to my next line of attack. A wetsuit is easier to re-move when it's wet. I grab my spare bottle of water and splash it over my thighs and knees. I peel and wrench again. Surplus water runs in rivulets down my legs and forms a patch of dark tarmac round me, marking the exact spot where a jubilant wetsuit has gained the upper hand on a luckless competitor.

The suit remains glued to my knees.

Thank goodness I didn't take up this sport fifteen years ago. I'd be surrounded by Women Under 35 and Men Under 40 all watching the wetsuit get the better of me. It's not as though I can stand around nonchalantly, pretending to do something else while my knees are bound together by a wetsuit. Everyone knows I'm stuck.

The sight of an approaching green cap galvanizes me into action. I smooth the bunched neoprene back up my thighs and then peel down in one long, sweeping action. The suit gives up on my knees and makes a bid to hang onto my calves. But I've won the decisive skirmish. I stand on the inside of the suit with my left foot and yank my right leg upwards, hanging onto the bike rack to steady myself. The suit peels off my right ankle. Re-peat action for the left ankle. I stomp on the wretched suit and dump it next to my bike.

Fasten helmet and bike shoes, grab bike and sunglasses, shoot final stare at telltale wet patch, walk bike to transition exit. Nearly five minutes in transition. I've blown the precious seconds I gained through the remove-suit-on-the-beach maneuver and clocked up more besides. Get on the bike and put it behind you.

I ride out onto The Almaden at a gentle pace, enough to warm my legs up slowly and regroup. My black tri shorts, red top and sports bra are wet from the swim. Water droplets trickle down my legs into my bike shoes. The breeze chills my skin and my feet squelch in damp shoes.

I swing right on Coleman and cross the bridge spanning the lake. I ride over a sparkling confetti of empty Gu carbohydrate gel packets. If more experienced athletes than me consume Gu here, I may as well do the same. I rip off the first of three packets I've taped to my crossbar with electrical tape, leaving the tab fastened to the crossbar. I squeeze the sticky, clear gel into my mouth and take a swig of water. The instant sugar high generates a rush of energy. I plan to eat one more Gu at the end of the bike run. The third is a spare in case I drop a packet by mistake.

I turn right onto Santa Teresa. Three riders come into view up ahead, the nearest about two hundred yards in front. Last time I rode this route with Gail, we had to stop for most of the dozen sets of traffic lights. This time, local police officers are stationed at the intersections, holding back traffic to give priority to cyclists. As I approach each junction, a traffic cop halts every single car in all eight lanes. I can't stop myself grinning but I resist the urge to wave.

Five miles out from the start. Six miles to Bailey Hill. My average speed on the bike speedometer reads 13.7 miles per hour. Is that all? I calculate that I will take 1 hour, 50 minutes to complete the twenty-five-mile course if I ride at 13.7 miles per hour. Unacceptable. I'm aiming for an hour and a half maximum. I push my leg speed and turn the pedals over faster.

The houses thin out. I'm only about forty yards behind the rider in front of me, a woman in a purple tri suit. We have both gained on the slower guy in front of her. Just one short hill, about two hundred yards, and I'll be out of the suburbs and into open farmland. I drop down a couple of gears and maintain a good speed. Halfway up the hill I slow down. I could drop down another gear. Instead, I stand up on the pedals and climb out of the saddle.

Back in the early days, I had so many problems with this

maneuver. Then Gail taught me how to do it. Now I stand up automatically. I give Gail a mental high five. Energy floods into the pedals and I eat up the remaining yards. I pass the woman in purple.

Out on the flat, straight road through farmland planted with artichokes. A sharp gust of wind blasts me sideways with such force that I'm pushed a couple of yards to my left. I grip the handlebars and hang on. The wind changes to a strong headwind. I'm riding the wrong way down a wind tunnel. No shelter anywhere on this road. I pound the pedals and hang on, just to keep riding forward in a straight line. My speed drops to 9.1 miles an hour. The specter of Last Finisher crosses my path, laughs at me and dances across the fields.

My inexperience on the bike has found me out. I don't know what to do except hang on and keep pedaling. I'm in the worst position for a strong headwind. Should I reach down to the bottom curve of the drop handlebars to maintain a lower profile and reduce wind resistance? Gail told me that a race is not the time to try something new. But this is an emergency. I reach down.

Bad move. It throws my posture off. I can't transmit the same level of energy through my legs to the pedals. When will I ever learn to listen to Gail? Purple Woman passes me. I sit up.

My tri suit has dried off and my upper body is warm with effort. But this fierce wind rips through the fabric air-vents on my shoes and turns my toes numb. I dig into my reserves of determination. Focus on finishing the bike leg. Maybe the wind will be calmer on the other side of Bailey Hill.

I keep my handlebars steady in the wind. I stare no more than ten yards ahead, concentrating on fighting the cold, gripping wind. Slower Guy moves into my line of sight and I overtake him. Head down again. I wait for the IBM Research Center on Bailey Avenue to trigger Gail's ascent plan of The Hill.

It's here. The Research Center. The little bridge. Check the gears. I'm right where I should be, on the middle ring, sixth rear cog. Where's that hill? Don't look up. You might panic. I said DON'T look up. There's the boulder. Drop down a cog. Another switch by the road sign. Next switch is the small ring when I reach the tree. Do-it-now-do-it-now-do-it-now. Clunk. Feet spin faster. Feel the road tilt upwards. Small boulder, drop down another cog. Two more to go. The moment the road curves round the left-hand bend, the gradient will bite hard and I have to be on my lowest gear. But I'm only riding at seven miles an hour and I haven't hit The Hill yet. Have I miscounted and switched too soon? Too late to worry. Large tree, another cog. Thirty yards to the bend. Change now. Lowest gear.

I settle in for the long haul. My feet are so cold I can barely feel them. Breathe in two pedal strokes, breathe out three. Count my breathing. No words. Only numbers. Breathing hard, five miles an hour.

My Self-Doubt Icon jumps on my shoulder and whispers in my ear. If your speed drops below four miles an hour, you won't have enough forward momentum to keep the bike upright. Then you'll fall off.

Why are you telling me that now? You want me fall off, is that it? After all I've done to coax my subconscious into believing I can do The Hill? Self-Doubt Icon hops gleefully from one foot to the other. Four miles an hour and you're history.

A painful image of me toppling over and crashing to the ground, feet still attached to the pedals, detonates a burst of adrenaline that electrifies my legs and sweeps me forward. Self-Doubt Icon loses its footing, tumbles backwards off my shoulder and splats onto the road.

I pass the third reflective marker. My legs spin so fast I have to click up a cog to find some resistance. I power round the right-hand hairpin bend and head for the top. A thirtysomething dark-haired guy in white top and black shorts is walking his bike up the hill. I know what he's going through. I want to shout out something encouraging. But what? Nearly there? No he isn't, he's got half a hill yet. Good job? But the poor guy's walking. Way to go? I've never quite understood this American phrase. He knows the way to go and that's to the top. I say nothing.

My hard-working leg muscles register the pressure melting away under the pedals. I look up. I've reached the crest of the hill. A release of tension floods over me. I allow myself to coast down the short, steep descent, rewarding myself with one whole welcome minute of time out before the homeward stretch.

At the bottom of the hill, a sheriff holds back traffic and points the way round the sharp right turn onto McKean Road. My scouting trip told me what to expect here. A smooth, country road of gentle, part-wooded rolling hills that winds its way past the broad open water of the Calero Reservoir on my left. I click up to my middle ring, ready for the switchback of rollers. No wind, thank goodness.

I refocus on Gail's race plan. She's seen a lot of people take a mental vacation after tackling Bailey Hill in previous races. I can make up time by pushing the pace on the downhills and pass those who are coasting. Purple Woman rides fifty yards ahead. I haven't let her out of my sight since she overtook me on the windy stretch. I'll either match her pace or pass her. Pass her is best. I pour effort into my pedals and click up the gears to maintain resistance. I overtake her on the downhill. My legs turn over as fast as they can. I glance round. Purple Woman is fifty yards behind with the gap still widening.

Bright sun throws sharp shadows of fences and trees across the road. Two teenagers stand by an awning over a roadside stall stacked with dark red cherries and bright apricots. I fly along, energy flowing from my core to the bike, wheels whirring in sync with my legs. Three lone riders ahead of me, strung out over the next two hundred yards. I sail past them all. That's three more between me and the very back of the pack. I pick off two more. I have to build as much of a buffer as I can before the run.

A right turn at the end of McKean, another traffic cop holding back cars. The turn marks the boundary between rural ranches and suburban houses. Five hundred yards later, a left onto Camden. I ride past parked cars and kids playing in the side streets. Two families sit on folding chairs in their front gardens, cheering on riders.

My speedometer shows I've ridden 23.7 miles. Not far to the finish. I take an inventory of my body. I've survived The Hill and the wind. But my feet have disappeared. All feeling ends just below my ankles. Traffic lights up ahead mark the turn onto The Almaden. As long as my feet are clipped in to the pedals and my ankles are connected to my shins, I'll keep moving forward if my knees go up and down. Concentrate on those knees. They're the pistons in the engine house that will drive you home in one piece. Barely half a mile and you'll be home and dry.

The orange cones lining the route thicken until they form a fluorescent funnel that leads me into the transition area. Bunches of spectators sprout on either side of the path. I halt by the three-foot-tall "BIKE DISMOUNT" sign, written in chalk dust on the pavement, then walk my bike back to my transition spot.

I hit my stopwatch button. Laptime is 1 hour, 33 minutes, 57 seconds. I must have made up a big chunk of time on the route back from Bailey Hill to put me within shouting distance of my overall target time. Way to go! Or something like that.

Gone is the telltale wet patch by rack nineteen. Now it's chock-full of bikes. Several competitors are packing up their stuff. Others wander with tri bags over their shoulders towards the parking lot. More reminders that I'm right at the tail end of the race.

I wedge my bike into the last remaining space in the crowd of wheels, handlebars, wetsuits, helmets, towels, shoes and other detritus. I still have the run ahead of me. Focus. Remove helmet, unstrap bike shoes. My feet are waxy white. I planned to run without socks but my feet cry out for warmth. I need my socks. Where are those socks?

I fumble in my tri bag, grab my socks and pull them over my uncooperative feet. Then on with my running shoes. I pull on my hat, clip my race number 330 on its belt round my waist and stuff a couple of Gu packets in the side pocket of my race top. With all the distraction of my freezing feet, I had forgotten to eat the second packet on the bike. David stands a few feet away from me, leaning on the barrier round the transition area perimeter.

"Keep going!" he shouts. "You're doing really well!"

"Thanks!" I wave. My body registers a blip of reassurance somewhere above my midriff. My partner through life is here to see me finish my special race. "See you in an hour!"

I rush to the end of row nineteen and head for the exit. I tear past the children's play area, the gear stalls, the finish arch and the crowds who are cheering home a tumultuous stream of athletes. I imagine myself crossing that finish line in an hour.

I fly along the edge of the lake and pound across the wooden footbridge. Orange cones and big chalk arrows on the pavement direct me along the creekside path to the right. I haven't run the course before, but I have studied the map in detail. The course is a Y-shape with the footbridge at the junction of the three spurs. A spur to the right along the creek and back to the footbridge, then a spur left to the percolation ponds at the Santa Clara Water Board. Then back across the footbridge and down the stem of the Y to the finish.

My calves should be aching like thunder right now, as they have every time I've run straight off my bike in training. But they don't feel too bad, just tired and tweaky. The path narrows. Competitors run towards me in ones and twos on the return loop. I glance behind as each woman runs past me to check what age is written on her calves. All except two are women in my age group who are faster than I am.

The route quietens down. No one heading back. Just me and the lonely slap-slap-slap of running shoes on pavement. Overhanging trees throw large pools of shade over the path. A gray squirrel darts in front of me and up a tree five yards ahead.

I can no longer hear the announcer at the finish line. I pass a couple of families out for a stroll in the park. How far to the turnaround? My lower calves ache. The last drops of adrenaline that fueled my euphoria dry up. The backs of my ankles cramp and tighten. And I haven't even reached the one-mile marker yet.

Why didn't I scope out the run course, as I had done with the Uvas Tri? Why did I think I could rely on a map when I know how much a new course unsettles me? Wisps of self-doubt circle round my head. It's not enough to see the mile markers. I need my own private markers in between, the trees and gates and bends in the path that tell me I'm at the quarter-, the half-, the three-quarter mile marks. Instead, I'm on an unknown course in my Race of Races. And this is my own stupid fault for not checking out the full route beforehand.

The tendons down the back of my ankles cramp so tightly that they almost seize up. I approach the one-mile marker, positioned facing the other way on the return route. Each step becomes more labored. Bad news. I haven't made it to one mile yet and I'm already in trouble.

The path makes a slight turn, bringing the turnaround into view. I shuffle round the marker in the middle of the path and head back. Arrows of pain shoot up from my heels and force me to stop.

Keep calm. Walk for a while to ease the tension, then run the remaining five miles in reasonable shape when I loosen up. I stumble forward. Walking always cured the pain whenever my calves tightened in training. Not this time. Knives cut into the back of my ankles with each step. My calves are as taut when I walk as when I run.

I reach the one-mile marker. Five and a quarter miles left to go. No way can I walk round the course when I'm in this much pain, let alone run. Walking was my worst-case fallback to complete the race. Now I won't even be able to do that.

Panic grabs my throat. I snatch a few shallow breaths. My throat closes up. My eyes prickle with hot tears. I stop walking, rest my hands on my knees and take a deep breath. I can't drop out. Not now. Not after one year of busting a gut with spin class, treadmill, weight machines, bike, running and swimming. I can't limp back to the finish and tell David and Gail and Kevin and Mike and the whole world that I've given up.

I pull off to the side of the path under a large California oak and do some upper and lower calf stretches. Stretching gives me mental space to regroup, but doesn't do much for the burning sensation above my ankles.

I stand up and put my hands on my hips. Another deep breath. I am not going to quit. I'll fight through this pain. If walking hurts as much as running, then I may as well run. The agony will be the same and running will be quicker. I force myself into a shuffling, almost-walking-pace gait that stretches my tendons to snapping point with every step.

I default to my tactic of last resort. I count my breathing. Breathe two paces in, four paces out. Ten breaths equals sixty paces. Ten breaths times ten fingers equals six hundred paces.

Fourteen fingers equals half a mile. I know this one by heart.

The beauty of counting is that I have no room in my head for words. My body tells me it's in astonishing pain. But I can't acknowledge or sympathize or give in to its desperate pleas to stop because I'm on breath number four on my ring finger. Numbers are not commands. Numbers are logical and beautiful, devoid of pain and emotion but above all, devoid of any ability to tell my body what to do.

Purple Woman and a dark-haired guy with a black top run towards me on the outward loop. I'm not last yet. Count my breaths. Two. Three. Four. There's every chance that they will overtake me. Five. Six. Past the wooden footbridge on my left. Seven. Eight. What will I have to go through before I'm back here again? Don't even think about it. Nine. Ten. Second finger, right hand. This isn't getting easier. One. Two. OK, I'll cut you a deal. You can walk when you reach ten fingers.

The path widens out after the footbridge and follows the line of the lakeshore. No trees here, just picnic tables and an open play area filled with families out to watch the race. I fall back to a walk. A glut of competitors heads back towards me. They pound down the path, driven on by the sight of the dark blue finish arch waiting across the footbridge.

I glance at my stopwatch. Total time so far is 2 hours, 32 minutes. Mike must still be out on the course somewhere. I have to look in good shape when he passes me. I can't have him report back to base that I'm falling apart. Or that I'm walking. He's bound to turn up within another ten fingers. I must run.

I spot a white and gray shirt in the distance and recognize Mike's tall, muscular frame. I grit my teeth through the counting. Whatever you do, keep running. Don't let him see you walk. When Mike is twenty yards away, I adjust my game face so that it reads effort and enthusiasm.

"Hi Mike! Good job!"

I wave and smile.

"Hey, Jane! Way to go!"

Mike rounds the corner out of sight. I stop running.

The two-mile board calls out to me from four hundred yards away. Run to the board. You can go through the flames of hell by running quickly or walking slowly. But there's only one way out of hell and that's past the two-mile board. Run to the board.

My legs creak into action. I occupy my mind by calculating how many blocks of four hundred yards lie between me and the finish.

Once past the board, I reward myself with a ten-breath walk. I check in with my ankles and lower calves. The cramp is not as severe. I pounce on this shred of good news as though I've found water in the desert. New game plan. No matter how much it still hurts, I have to run. But the three-mile board might as well be on the other side of the planet. I have no mental markers to encourage me.

I'll make my own markers. If fourteen fingers is half a mile, then I'll count up to fourteen fingers, walk, repeat and reach mile three in two chunks. Then repeat three times. The last quarter mile will have to take care of itself.

I settle in for the long haul. Count. Ignore the screeching ache in my legs. I stare at the ground, taking in only the next ten feet of pavement. Count. Fourteen fingers. Permission to walk for ten breaths. That was twelve. Quit arguing. Start running. Numbers only, no words. I reach the aid station at mile three. I rip open a Gu packet, reward myself with an instant sugar boost and wash it down with water.

Now for the percolation pond. A boring path round a very large, boring hole in the ground. Nothing to distract me from pain. My legs ache from top to bottom but I run twenty-one fingers without a break. I'm in better shape than I thought. I stop again at the aid station for more water, then kick-start my legs into a run. A scattering of competitors heads towards me on their way to the pond. I'm still not last. No one has overtaken me. A few of them are having as hard a time as I am.

"Not far now to the turnaround!" I call out.

"Thanks!" a couple of girlfriends shout in matching blue tops. "Great news!"

I press on past the four-mile board. I still have over two miles to go. Please no, not four entire sets of fourteen fingers and a bit more besides? I can't go on.

My sugar-fueled high expires and my determination evaporates with it. My creaking legs tremble and break down to a walk. Dusty brown path. Dusty brown scrub. Dusty fence. Dusty sunlight. I'm stranded far from home in the middle of featureless nothing.

Sweat trickles down my cheek and leaves a salty taste in my mouth. A volunteer's fluorescent yellow vest glows through the heat haze way off in the distance. And the vest isn't even at the five-mile board.

What's the point? Nobody's making you do this. You were an idiot to start this triathlon nonsense. You should have stuck to life's game plan of playing to your strengths and avoiding your weaknesses. And you should have stayed in your comfort zone where you never, ever finish last. I mean, why half-kill yourself with this stuff? Can you tell me that? Alternate Persona taunts me with relentless questions to which I have no answer.

I won't listen to defeat. One last-gasp run will bring this misery to a close sooner rather than later. But Alternate Persona hears rumors of my running plan and jams the communication channel to my legs. No way can I run. A repeating loop pleads with me not to jump-start the agony of running, reassures me that no one cares if I'm last, soothes me with the temptation of walking the last two miles.

Temptation. That's what this is. Temptation was never about an external force. It isn't about double chocolate cheesecake waiting to ambush me in the fridge. How could I ever have thought that? Temptation is the voice within, pleading, begging, imploring me to stop, give in, back out. Fighting temptation is the fight to conquer Alternate Persona.

I know what I have to do now. I have to run. I have to prove that I won't give in. Start running with just ten steps. Don't think of the burning that will ignite in my calves. Just count. My only purpose in life is to run the next ten steps.

I stagger on. My exhausted legs are almost spent but they will keep going as long as my brain tells them to. Running becomes a mind game of intense concentration. One slip in the counting and Alternate Persona will nip past the defenses and sabotage my legs.

The outside world melts away. I'm in a huge, dark cavern. I can't touch the sides when I reach out. My lifeline to the surface is a string of numbers. I pass the five-mile board. Don't disturb your concentration. Keep counting.

Way off in the darkness, at the farthest reach of my fingertips, a tiny trapdoor opens just enough to let a stream of shimmering, incandescent light escape round its edges. I catch the briefest glimpse of what's on the other side. The trapdoor closes.

In that split second, the reason that has forced me into this, the elusive reason I have spent the entire year searching for, unveils itself. Now I understand. Life has been too easy for too long. I've spent too many years playing to my strengths, avoiding my weaknesses, always sidestepping uncertainty or fear. But life won't always let me hide in my comfort zone. It may send catastrophe my way.

I have to prove to myself that if I faced the unthinkable, I would have the steel within to stand firm and fight back. If I were paralyzed in a horrific accident, would I have the guts to rebuild my life as a paraplegic? If I lost the person dearest to me, would I have the courage to carry on?

I still don't know. But the closest I can come to knowing is to push myself against pain, for no other reason than to test how much I can withstand. For that fleeting moment, my inner core revealed its gleaming, dependable resilience.

I emerge from the cavern. I pass the six-mile marker. The announcer's voice floats across the water. I can't make out the words but I'm within striking distance of the finish. Across the wooden bridge. Only three hundred yards left now. Push the pace. Turn the corner. The finish arch beckons. Adrenaline ignites my legs. Spectators applaud. David and Gail wave and cheer. I sprint home. I cross the line in 3 hours, 26 minutes and 19 seconds. I punch the air. Now I know what this has all been about.

Is the Triathlon Done with Me Yet?

What I expected to get out of completing a tri: physical fitness and kudos

What I actually got out of completing a tri: a lot more than I bargained for

I lay on my stomach and burrowed my fingers and toes into the warm, silky sand. The sound of languorous waves trickling over the beach whispered in my ear. A gentle breeze stroked my back. I took a deep, relaxing breath. This could be the beach of my hypnotic safe place. Instead, I was lying under a palm tree on Grand Cayman, five days after completing the triathlon. Reward for David as well as for me.

My world had tilted a fraction on its axis since the triathlon. Everything was still where I had left it, yet somehow rearranged. I now looked at the world through a prism of self-belief. I felt more secure and confident in myself, even though I'd never considered that I had been particularly lacking in either quality.

Running to the center of myself in the triathlon had taught me that I had a chance of surviving the very worst that life could throw at me. And I could stand up to fear. Not that I wished to confront either with a spot of bungee jumping or whitewater rafting. My approach to life was more like my skiing. I'd rather stick to a cautious descent of the intermediate blue category slopes and deal with a super-advanced, almost vertical, double-black diamond category run if I took a wrong turn. Except now I knew that I could deal with a double-black diamond ski run if I had to. Just as I could deal with life's double-black diamonds.

I lay on the beach, taking stock of where I had reached and where I was going. I'd been living in the US for four years. I was getting the hang of the people, the language and the culture. David and I were making plans to celebrate our twentieth wedding anniversary later in the year. I enjoyed my job selling business services to hi-tech startups, but I was ready for something more. I would start planning ahead. And then, of course, there was my next triathlon.

I hadn't given much thought before the San Jose Tri as to what would happen afterwards. I knew better than to wrest the decision away from Rogue Code. Would Rogue Code let me close this chapter of my life and move on? Or would I do another event? I found out soon enough. I knew with absolute certainty on the first aching, creaking, groaning day after the San Jose Tri that it was not a question of "whether" but "when."

I wasn't surprised by the decision. I wanted to continue to tackle a discipline that made me work on my weaknesses. Not primarily to test myself by pushing against pain, although I was ready for that. But more that the discipline of regular training would improve personal qualities I needed to work on, such as patience and steadfastness. And it would do me good to work consistently at something without the motivation of instant results.

Then there was the whole issue of "doing things my way." Doing things my way had gained me a finish in the bottom four percent of the field at San Jose. I placed 43rd out of 46 in my age group, 950th out of 983 finishers. Why did I deceive myself that I was learning from other people when I simply selected the bits of training I liked and ignored the rest? That was exactly what I had done with Gail. I had turned to her for practical instruction in cycling and running and asked her to comment on the training plans I had devised. She advised me when I hit a roadblock of injury and had given me race plans for specific events. But I hadn't let her devise my training plan. I retained full control on accepting or discarding her advice. This was my plan and my life.

Triathlon had taught me that I would be more successful if I adjusted my attitude to doing things my way. Starting with Gail.

Allowing Gail to devise my training plan wasn't ceding control of doing things my way, it was learning from someone more experienced. And I should learn to recognize the difference between rejecting advice based on sound judgment and rejecting advice because I didn't like what I heard. I would follow Gail's plan, ask questions for sure, but do as I was told. And greater involvement meant that I would pay her more money. I would raise the stakes for not doing as I was told.

I phoned Gail the first day back from Grand Cayman. Although she had applied for graduate school, we would still have one year together before she left. I asked if she would be willing to have more involvement in my training.

"Great!" she replied. "We'll start with endurance. Most other athletes do their base training in the winter. You do yours in July. Never mind. You're doing it and that's what matters."

We both chuckled.

To build endurance, I was to run twice a week for thirty minutes and once for fifty minutes, using my heart rate monitor to make sure I stayed at or below 150 beats a minute. Ignore how fast I ran. If my heart rate went over 150, I was to walk. After a while, my fitness would improve. Then I would be able to run faster at the same heart rate. And I should build up my long run by five minutes a week. I did as I was told. Within three weeks, I could run at a heart rate of 150 or less without stopping.

We added hill repeats to build muscle-specific strength in

my legs. Gail required me to run short, repeated bursts up Kevin Hill at Water Dog Lake in Belmont, that eleven-minute blinder of a hill that almost brought me to my knees when I was training for the duathlon. To add speed, we went to De Anza College at Cupertino where I ran structured workouts under Gail's supervision round the athletics track.

David had started to run longer distances on his morning runs over the past couple of months. When he heard about my visits to De Anza, he wanted to join in. So Gail planned some workouts for him too. Track workouts were something David and I could do together but separately, without getting into the grinning/encouraging thing that I so disliked when we ran together. I also noted how strong his running had become since the Human Race three months earlier.

Gail's greater involvement meant that I enjoyed my training a whole lot more. Her structure gave me a goal to push against and a better yardstick to measure my progress. I had to find the extra ounce of strength to finish the last lap or run the last hill repeat because I couldn't alter Gail's goals as flippantly as I could my own. After five weeks, I could run nonstop on Sawyer Camp Trail at Crystal Springs Reservoir for 1 hour, 15 minutes, which was longer than I had ever run before. I even had a dribble of energy left over at the end.

Gail then suggested I join a women's cycling group. If I swam with master swimmers, ran with pure runners and cycled with specialist cyclists, rather than purely with triathletes who are good but not expert at all three, then the single-discipline group I joined would drag me along with them until I achieved a higher standard. Triathlon would now help me address another weakness—dislike of women-only groups.

I had persevered with women's networking groups when I arrived in the US. But I never did see the point of excluding over half the business population from a networking event. I had no patience for topics of conversation about how women did things differently from men, or how women relied on the sisterhood for moral support and self-affirmation. Three of the most supportive people on my triathlon quest were men—my husband David, Kevin Kennedy and Mike Popa. So what did that tell me?

But Gail had recommended that I try a women's cycling group. I did as I was told. I met the Velobella group outside Summit Bicycles in Los Gatos, near San Jose, for their weekly Thursday evening summer ride. On our first outing, they stretched me with twenty-one miles of hills, plus a face-the-fear moment when my road bike slithered but remained upright down a steep, gravelly, off-road hill.

The Velobellas wanted to encourage more women to take up cycling. So they always assigned at least one woman to wait for the last cyclist, which on every occasion was me. Never once did they leave me behind. They trained me in cycling techniques. And towards the end of each ride, they would all bunch up to "pull" me home. I learned to ride inches off the back wheel of the woman in front. In return, I would be "pulled" along by drafting off her slipstream.

I also enjoyed the social anthropology of this women's group. Not just that these women were dynamic and fun to be around. They also weren't that bothered with a "women only" rule. The couple of guys who occasionally rode with us—the Velo Fellas—turned out to be very smart indeed, for where else do you increase your chances of meeting young, unattached, incredibly fit women who more often than not reach the top of the hills first? From my vantage point at the back of the pack, I observed some interesting flirting on four wheels. I had an added incentive to keep within striking distance of the main group if I wanted to watch the next episode.

My summer rides with the Velobellas turned into some of the most fun, challenging and satisfying rides of my cycling to date. Never mind that I was the slowest rider every time. The Velobellas helped me learn to deal with last place with their support and congratulations. And I solved my women-only group problem; it had just been a matter of finding the right group.

I decided to put my newfound skills together with another triathlon in the third week of August. The TriOne Triathlon was a local event across the Bay in Alameda, organized by the ALS Association to raise funds to fight Lou Gehrig's Disease. This event had same-day registration. I shuffled forward in line that morning, rehearsing the sprint course in my head—a half-mile swim in the Bay directly off the Alameda ferry pier, an eight-mile, pancake-flat bike ride and a three-mile scenic Bayshore run. But when I reached the front of the queue to register, an eight-mile flat ride and a three-mile run no longer sounded far enough to measure all the effort I'd put into training. I signed up on the spur of the moment for the Olympic distance event.

The one-mile Bay swim was calm. The twenty-five-mile ride was fast and flat. I set out on the 6.2-mile Bayshore run. After five minutes my calves cramped in exactly the same way as they had at San Jose. Plus a particular sort of headache, the sort that was my body's signal that I was dehydrating rapidly, started to pulse in my temples. The sun beat down on the bare, treeless path. I grabbed water at every stop. The scenic Bayshore route mocked my attempts to run.

"Congratulations, number 362, you're goin' home!" a cheery volunteer called out as I staggered round the halfway turnaround point.

A weak smile crept across my face.

"Copy that, Houston!" I called back.

I was a lot farther away than he thought.

Along the return route, a construction crew hammered away in my head. No amount of water at the aid stations could dilute the pounding. I could hardly focus on the path in front. I ran towards the last aid station. It was deserted, except for a forlorn pile of plastic cups half-filled with Gatorade. The cone collectors passed me on their way back down the course on golf buggies, removing all trace of the run route and returning the path to the care of the Bayshore. The fear of the cone collectors gaining ground on me and trailing me to the finish spurred me on. I struggled home alongside a couple of tail-ender guys who had teamed up to encourage each other to the finish.

The TriOne Triathlon taught me an important lesson. I needed to treat endurance sport with a lot more respect. Triathlon was the grand master. I was the first-grade pupil. I couldn't spend a few weeks training and then think I could treat an Olympic-distance event like a cakewalk. There were no short cuts to skills and fitness.

In September, David and I celebrated one of the most important days in our lives so far—our twentieth wedding anniversary. We invited sixty-five of our friends to Sunday lunch in our favorite restaurant. David and I toasted the strength we derive from our commitment to each other, the fun we have together and the joy of sharing our lives.

We also decided that our anniversary lunch was the perfect time to set the record straight. When we were first married, we told people that we had dated for six months at college before we got engaged. As time went on, we changed that down to five weeks. We had just used the six-month story at the beginning to avoid any incredulity that we could make a marriage work based on just five weeks of dating.

At the twenty-year mark, we decided our friends finally deserved the truth. We hadn't dated for six months. Or for five weeks. It was ten days before we got engaged. And that truly was our final answer.

The week after our wedding anniversary, David made a surprise announcement. He had signed up for the US Half Marathon in San Francisco in October. David's style was the opposite of mine. He had to be absolutely sure he was going to succeed at something before he went public. He had increased his running distance and done track workouts over the summer, all without explanation. Now he was ready.

I drove him to Aquatic Park in San Francisco one Sunday in October, ready for a 7 a.m. race start. The role reversal was not lost on me. I recognized and sympathized with his nervous tension. I waved him off proudly at the start. Tears welled in my eyes when I saw him run down the home stretch by the Maritime Museum, 2 hours, 7 minutes later, a full eight minutes faster than his best estimate. He grinned the whole time during the journey home. I grinned too. We basked in his personal victory.

The half marathon marked the start of David's own endurance sport career. My miserable relationship with running would prevent me from ever running a half marathon. He could never see himself doing a triathlon because of his aversion to swimming. So the chances of us competing in the same event were minimal. Yet we could share the buzz and achievement of endurance events as participant and supporter and share the reward for the intense but separate training we both undertook. And triathlon had been the catalyst.

In November, Gail had some surprising news. Her chosen graduate school on the East Coast had offered her early acceptance into the doctorate program. She would be leaving within the month.

"What a fantastic finish to such a rocky year for you," I said. "I'm thrilled things have come good. You deserve it."

We reminisced over all that had happened for both of us this year. I thanked her for all that she had done for me and for sticking with one of her less-than-compliant trainees.

"Don't be too hard on yourself," she said. "I've never worked with anyone with the tremendous determination you have to work at something that's alien to you. I got a huge buzz out of seeing you achieve an incredible goal. I've seen you transform yourself into an athlete."

I remembered sitting on my veranda before the San Jose Tri, where I committed to the lesson of celebrating achievements as they happened instead of merely identifying areas of improvement. Gail was right. I had had a great year. I had transformed into an athlete.

But I had achieved more than that. My approach to life had been transformed. I had rediscovered the desire to improve myself and to learn new things, rather than stick with things I was good at. I threw myself into projects that lay well outside my comfort zone, brimming over with confidence that no matter what I encountered, my steely inner core would see me through.

What a great year. Gail was on her way to grad school. My running buddy Cristina had secured a postgraduate place at Tufts University and loved her new life on the East Coast. David had completed his first half marathon. Kevin had had an awesome year, qualifying for the International Triathlon Union World Championships in New Zealand. As we rushed towards December, I overflowed with optimism that the time was right for new horizons in my professional life.

I wanted more flexibility in my work schedule to include time to write. Working self-employed from home would give me that. Within ten days, I had found two clients who were perfect for me. David encouraged me to quit my job sooner rather than later, so I would have time to set everything up for a New

Year start. And I would be doing something I had a passion for. Next year would be a year full of possibilities. I handed in my resignation.

The morning after I quit my job, at 9:47 a.m., one phone call turned all those possibilities into uncertainties. My mum had been diagnosed with esophageal cancer.

Triathlon to the Rescue

Number of times I call on my inner core to pull me through: lost count

Number of times it let me down: wait and see

The moment I heard the devastating news about Mum's diagnosis, I joined the millions of people who are engulfed by the tumult of emotion over a loved one's serious illness. First, the tidal wave of questions. Will she pull through? What if she doesn't? How long have we got? Then the helplessness that I couldn't make it better for her. And then emptiness. All the things that were urgent yesterday were meaningless today. A big rock in my world had just dissolved into sand and left the landscape forever altered. After such a groundbreaking year, I never expected that I would be calling on my steely inner core so soon.

The family was plunged into waiting. Waiting for endoscopy results, waiting for the prognosis, waiting for the treatment course, but above all, waiting. Waiting became a never-ending haul up a relentless hill. Waiting turned seconds into hours and days into years.

Distance added to the cruelty. I wanted to be there next to Mum but flights to the UK in December were heavily overbooked. An eight-hour time difference meant fewer overlapping hours when we were both available to talk on the phone.

Nine days before Christmas, we had good news. The tumor was localized. Mum would receive chemo to shrink it, then surgery to remove it. Lucky I had already quit my job. I put my startup plans on hold and spent January in England.

Those few weeks in England were uncharted territory for both of us. Mundane tasks, such as a shopping visit to Marks & Spencer in the southern county town of Guildford, or making hearty winter lamb casserole on her cast-iron Rayburn cooking range, became special moments. Laughter, reminiscences, imparted wisdom of her favorite recipes, anticipation of the surgery, optimism for the future. She began the first of her chemo treatments in the second week of January, with surgery scheduled for late March.

When I returned to the US, I received a daily update from my family on her progress. But not much change. More waiting. We were all in limbo, waiting for Mum's chemo sessions, waiting for her surgery. But real life couldn't wait. I had a business to set up. I embarked on a major sales effort for my two new clients. I had to think confident thoughts and fix the smile on my face, regardless of the chaos under the surface. After all, no one buys from a desperate salesperson.

As if my business challenges weren't enough, my annual health checkup revealed a small breast lump. How much more could I endure before the smile muscles refuse to work? I had to stay strong and optimistic for Mum as well as me. Remain calm. Wait. Mammogram. Wait. Specialist visit. Wait. I remembered that fleeting glimpse of my steely inner core in the San Jose Tri. I reached inwards for strength.

The breast lump turned out to be benign.

Relief over the breast lump reduced the stress one notch in my frantic, uncertain world. But I needed something more to center myself. I found my center in swimming and cycling. For the hour or two of every session, I could concentrate on physical activity and clear my head of the what-if's. Alongside tiredness, a therapeutic sense of calm and order settled over me whenever I tackled a tough bike ride or a long-haul swim. Training became my touchstone.

I decided to work towards two repeat events—the Uvas Tri in April and the San Jose Tri in June. I was cutting it fine with only seven weeks left until my first race. My training would have to focus on essentials.

At the beginning of those seven weeks, I went to a seminar at Sports Basement by elite triathlete Wendy Ingraham, winner of Ironman Brazil and a top-ten finisher at the world Ironman championships on eleven occasions.

"If you remember only one thing today, then remember this," Wendy said. "Your brain is your most important training tool."

The phrase rang a bell. Michelle Cleere had said something similar in her introductory triathlon seminar.

"When you think you've reached your limit, force yourself to do an extra mile or an extra hill," Wendy said. "Your mind will push you on to a level you never knew you had. It's out there. Push through the barrier and you'll find it."

I resolved to ratchet up the intensity of my training.

Two days later, I found a spin teacher who could fill Gail's shoes. Julie Sweeney taught a Thursday lunchtime spin class at the San Mateo Y. She would burst into the room, a bubble of dark-haired, bouncy energy, arms full of gear and the CD of special music she cut for us each week. Julie gave us tough, cycling-specific workouts to build endurance and strength. She mixed in technical exercises to promote good technique. And she added a fun commentary with her themed music—anything from the Lion King, picked by her three preschool kids, to Riverdance, in honor of Saint Patrick's Day.

I poured every last ounce of effort into Julie's class. When

I reached exhaustion point I gritted my teeth, cranked up the resistance meter just one more turn and set a goal to cycle for another ninety seconds. My body screamed out to stop and my quads radiated pain. But after sixty seconds, the pain fell back to a manageable ache, as though my brain had sent out an anesthetic. I found I could continue every time for ninety seconds and beyond.

Physically I was hardly any different from one training session to the next. Certainly not different enough to account for my performance improvement. The difference was mental. My mind pushed my body through to the next level—the level that Wendy Ingraham had promised was there. And pushing to the limits exercised and strengthened my inner core. Physical endurance became more than a way to keep fit; it was a way to sharpen my mental determination at the time I needed it most.

I approached the Uvas Tri with a lot more confidence than the previous year. Uneventful swim, not that fast. On the cycle route, I hunkered down in my very bottom gear at the foot of Nemesis Hill, reached the plateau and forced myself to the crest with each pedal stroke. I ran slower than last year but I ran within myself the whole distance.

The San Jose Tri followed a similar pattern. I came out of the water in about the same time, although the swim course had been set a few yards longer than the previous year. I finished the bike leg nearly five minutes faster. Even the run was not quite such a hate-hate relationship. I never approached last year's valleys of desperation.

Maybe my races were so satisfying because I had set no expectations. After only seven weeks of training, I had set no standard by which I could fall short. My achievement was to finish. I was learning to celebrate each victory and take the pressure off myself.

However, I had momentary lapses when I would revert to type and bypass the celebration stage. One of those moments happened when the national triathlon rankings for the previous year were published in *Triathlon Times* magazine.

I looked up Kevin's ranking. He had had a stupendous year, finishing thirteenth out of 1,246 in his age group and gaining All-American status. I looked at the qualifying requirements. Athletes had to participate in three races recognized by USAT, the USA Triathlon Association. Each finisher received points based on length of race and final placements. Maybe I had done three USAT-sanctioned races by accident? I had. I looked through all 864 names in the Women's 40-44 age group. I was 863rd. Rather than celebrate that I had made it onto the list at all, I spent two days lamenting the fact that 862 women of my age were a lot better than I was.

Mum's surgery at the end of March had gone well. But four days later, she endured painful and unforeseen complications, a further surgery and a ten-week stay in hospital. I went back to the UK in May and spent time with her every day. I returned again in July, shortly after she had been released from hospital.

England laid on an idyllic summer, with warm, fragrant days hidden like verdant jewels amidst the grayness of rain. Mum and I delighted in the small joys of life. I pushed her in her wheelchair through the medieval market town of Midhurst, Sussex, to search out silk threads for her cross-stitch pattern. She savored every mouthful of cannelloni in the Italian restaurant after her hospital liquid diet. We meandered through acres of abundant, cottage-garden blooms in the Horticultural College Gardens, where Mum gathered ideas for her flower bed project next to her greenhouse. We parked at the top of Harting Hill near Winchester, Hampshire and gazed out over ancient mosaics of fields, hedges and coppices. Chestnut-brown roofs clustered round the skirts of protective church towers, marking the centers of villages that reached back before the Domesday Book. In the distance, swathes of gentle rain washed over the bright green South Downs hills.

David came over to join me later that month. We went on holiday to Devon, a picturesque rural county in southwest England. We stayed in the ancient country hamlet of Dittisham, close to the homes of Sir Walter Raleigh and Agatha Christie, on the banks of the River Dart. The second day, we planned to take the passenger ferry downstream to the port of Dartmouth. Rather than drive to the pier, we chose to walk the mile or so down twisting, narrow lanes. We took time to appreciate the Norman architecture of the thousand-year-old church and rows of compact, centuries-old thatched stone cottages with climbing roses framing wooden front doors.

We reached the top of the steep hill down to the river. A small, open dinghy without so much as a wheelhouse chugged towards the jetty. The Dittisham Ferry. David and I legged it down the hill, to the amusement of two retired gentlemen trimming lavender and pink hollyhocks in their front gardens. We should have known better. The ferry is used to picking up tourists who misjudge the distance to the river. The ferry waits. This is Devon Local Time, not Pacific Daylight Time.

The next day, my right knee ached whenever I walked up or down stairs. It continued to ache for the entire holiday. My running gear stayed in my suitcase. Four days after returning home, my knee calmed down. I ran. Same ache. Repeat performance. Rest. Run. Ache.

Three weeks later, I read an article about knee problems in David's copy of *Runner's World*. My symptoms corresponded exactly to patellar tendonitis, an inflammation of the tendon that runs from the thigh, down over the kneecap and into the shin. The cure was exercises to strengthen my quad muscles, lower-impact cross training such as cycling, and cease running for now. For the next three weeks, I stopped running, stepped up the cycling and did a few exercises in the gym to strengthen my quads. By September, I had seen zero improvement. Time to visit the doctor.

"Good news," she said. "There's no physical damage. No tear in the meniscus membrane. But you need to do some specific strengthening exercises."

She gave me a booklet of exercises to do every day.

I hunkered down for the long haul. I persevered with daily exercises for seven weeks. All that relentless training had built up my resistance to giving up when there was no visible progress. But my knee did not improve. I returned to the doctor.

This time, she recommended physical therapy. I chose a practice that said they dealt with sports injuries. I visited the office twice a week. On each visit, I did a circuit of exercises, along with eighteen or so other patients, with a PT Assistant checking in now and then. Then some ultrasound and ice. I also followed orders to take nine ibuprofen a day to reduce swelling around the knee joint.

Christmas, the biggest holiday of the year in the UK, crept nearer. A time for turkey and all the trimmings, for putting real life on hold for Christmas Day and for recovering from celebrations on Boxing Day. But above all, a time for loved ones. David and I spent Christmas in England, a joyful family reunion celebrating the final round of Mum's additional chemo after her surgery. Just after the holiday, she had a CT scan. No sign of the tumor. Our release from waiting was over. Mum and I spent gleeful hours discussing her visit out to see me in April, a trip she had delayed exactly one year to the day due to her illness.

I returned home and continued with physical therapy. But I rarely saw the therapist. Whenever I did see him, I asked what else

I could do to speed my recovery. What about some home exercises? They probably wouldn't help much. What about swimming? Yes, I could go swimming. How much swimming? About half my usual amount. Would that exercise my knee? Yes, it would. I went swimming. I exercised half my usual distance and included ten laps of leg kick with fins on my feet to strengthen my quads. The next day I could barely climb in and out of the car.

Seven months since Dittisham and my knee was worse than ever. Lots of people had shared their stories with me about how their knee injuries had forced them to give up running entirely. Maybe my knee was damaged permanently. Maybe I too would be forced to give up running.

A shudder ran through me. I couldn't give up running. It would leave a hole in my life that had previously been filled with the challenge of working at something relentlessly, of beating something that always had the upper hand. Running held out the elusive prospect that somehow, one day, it might reveal that runner's high that I had heard so much about but could only imagine. Running had welded itself to my psyche when I wasn't looking.

My concern grew that the physical therapist was more interested in pushing patients through the practice than in supervising my recovery. But I was nervous about questioning the competence of a healthcare professional. The threat that I might never be able to run again forced me into action. I emailed Gail, explained the sort of treatment I was receiving and asked her what I should do next. She emailed back the same day.

Watch out for a clinic where you see several different PTs and your program mostly consists of unsupervised exercise and ice. If you're not getting one-on-one attention and rehab, get out of there.

This time I made sure I followed Gail's advice.

I interviewed the therapist at Carrola Physical Therapy for fifteen minutes on the phone before I considered making an appointment. Jeff Jaramillo reassured me I would receive one-on-one therapy. He talked in detail about his approach to treatment and his extensive experience with a range of pro athletes. His calendar had hardly a spare slot all week, with a waiting list to secure prime appointment times. He must be good. But I booked only one appointment. I wanted to see what he was like before I believed the hype.

These PT treatments had to work. My entire running career was on the line. Instead of the cursory, five-minute discussion and quick prod of my knee I'd received before, Jeff spent one hour taking a detailed history and performing a thorough examination of all the muscle groups in my lower body. He watched me run on the treadmill. And then he gave his diagnosis.

Yes, he could fix my knee. But fixing my knee was no simple matter. My running style would have to change. Several weak muscle groups that were causing my knee problems in the first place would need strengthening. I was to stop all running, swimming and cycling at once. We would start with exercises to loosen up my Achilles tendons and strengthen my quads and hamstrings. I would have to work hard at home on a structured set of exercises he would give me. And I should stop the ibuprofen immediately. Six weeks of nine tablets a day was not good.

Jeff passed the test. He treated my knee twice a week. He supervised my exercise schedule. He made sure I didn't cause further damage by doing things that I didn't know were bad for me, like swimming with fins. In between visits, I threw myself into a stretching and strengthening program. I iced my knee several times a day to reduce internal swelling. Jeff added more into the program on every visit, including exercises to change my running style. After four weeks, I could run on the treadmill with my new style for ten minutes.

We then addressed other problems. My weak abductors and IT bands, the muscles and ligaments down the outside of my hips, needed work because they weren't strong enough to support running for long spells. And I had to strengthen my ankles, especially my left ankle which had been weakened by the Champs Elysees episode. To help with ankle problems, Jeff had me stand on a board set atop what looked like half a soccer ball. Once I had reached a wobbly state of precarious equilibrium, he had me squat down and up.

"So how exactly does this help me, Jeff?" I asked in mid-wobble, forever curious to know every last annoying detail about my treatment.

"Beats me," he replied. "But it sure is fun watching."

I laughed so hard I almost fell off.

In March, I received an urgent phone call from my youngest sister, Louise. She would undergo a minor foot operation the next day that would leave her unable to walk for two weeks. Mum was ill with a tummy bug. My middle sister Sue's son was hospitalized in London. Louise begged me to go back to England to help look after her and her children. There was no one but me. I dropped everything and flew back immediately.

I threw myself into being a full-time, stand-in mom. I dropped off and collected her kids, cooked, cleaned, did laundry and found time to catch up with Louise. I visited Mum every day at home. We all shared Sue's relief when her son was released from Intensive Care.

But Mum's stomach bug was getting worse. The doctor wanted to run more tests and give her stronger drugs to fight the infection. He admitted her to the local hospital. Mum was determined to do whatever it took to beat the bug. After all, her dream trip to San Francisco, celebrating the end of chemo and the resumption of normal life, was in two weeks' time.

I visited Mum every day in hospital. She was very weak from lack of food and had lost even more weight from her frail, stick-like frame. I rubbed her cold feet and gave her drinks. She asked me to read aloud chapters of this book that she had not yet heard. She insisted that she was "resting her eyes" rather than nodding off to sleep while I read. We had fits of giggles when I gave her mock exams on each chapter.

Three days after admission, the test results came back. The stomach bug turned out to be cancer cells that had multiplied aggressively since her last chemo at Christmas. Five days later, she was moved to a hospice. If ever I needed my inner core, it was now.

I went to see Mum the next day. Her cheekbones stood out from her sallow cheeks and her bright blue eyes sank back into her face. Her bony hands were all that could be seen outside the enormous bedjacket that had fitted her perfectly the year before. She lay propped up on pillows, too weak to sit up. I sat at her bedside in her line of sight.

"When are you leaving for that conference?" Mum said. "It's this weekend, isn't it?"

She knew how much I had been looking forward to attending a big writers' conference on the San Francisco Peninsula.

"I'm staying here for now," I said and squeezed her hand.

"But I can't have you missing it because of me."

She grew agitated and tried to sit up.

"Mum, I'm missing it because I want to be here," I said and rested my hand on her shoulder. "And it's not all bad news. The conference organizer emailed me today to say my book chapter had won a prize in the writing competition."

"I knew you would! I'm so proud of you." A big smile

broke out across her face and she relaxed back into the pillows. Her voice choked up to a whisper. "That's such special news for today."

We held hands in silence for nearly two minutes, Mum with her eyes closed, me watching her shallow breathing.

"I'm glad you stayed." She rallied out of her stillness. "I wanted to tell you something too." I leaned closer to hear her. "I'm too tired to fight any more. I'm ready to move on."

Stillness settled round us. I stroked her fragile hand with its paper-thin skin. Birdsong floated in through the open patio door and filled the room with peace. The long net drapes opened and closed in the soft breeze, as though parted by an invisible person.

Then Mum and I had a long, quiet, goodbye conversation. We said all the things we wanted to say. I had to let her go.

She had that same final conversation with all her family members that day. But I was astonished that she also told others of my writing competition win. She never stopped being proud of me. She slipped into a coma the next day and died three days later. She was 63 years old.

When David and I returned home after her funeral, he was my rock of support. But he could only do so much. I had an inner core of steel hiding somewhere deep inside, but I wasn't sure where. Somehow, I had to pick up the threads of my life and find a routine to shape the emptiness. Time to return physical therapy.

I trudged through my daily exercises, some days with more intensity than others. My knee showed some improvement. But mentally I had left the building. I couldn't understand why I was trying to fix my knee when life had little meaning. Even leaving the house took willpower on some days. I told myself that grief was playing tricks on me and that I would recover my vitality at some point. I just had to persevere. Jeff took my grief in his stride. He knew when to let me ride it out and when to push me to test my knee.

I also suffered from an upper back problem. When I awoke the first night after returning from England, my neck and upper back were sore. The ache continued to trouble me for three weeks. One morning, my neck was so stiff that I couldn't turn my head. Jeff spent our next session treating my back.

He also gave me clues to the problem. Around eighty percent of back problems have a psychosomatic root. I should be conscious of times when I think I am relaxed but find that my back muscles have tightened up of their own accord. I should make a deliberate effort to stretch when it happened.

Two nights later, I put the clues together. I awoke from the same dream I had had every night since Mum died. In the dream, Mum and I would plan our special trip to visit me, delighting in the details like two kids planning a birthday party. We both knew she was dying, but she had the strength for one last trip. I always awoke at the same point every night, just after she showed me the plane ticket. For those few seconds after waking, I held my breath in excitement that she was still coming out to see me. Then I would remember she was dead. That night, as the dismay of her death flooded through me, I became aware that my upper back muscles were rigid with tension. The same thing happened the next night. I had discovered my problem.

My back pain was at its most severe over the next two weeks. During the day, I felt as though I were carrying a heavy backpack strapped between my shoulders. Jeff worked on my back for the next three sessions. I had a more peaceful night's sleep on the days I saw him. But I was reminded once more about the mind-body connection.

My mind could drive my body on to do great things. But if

I refused to listen to myself, my subconscious made itself under-stood through physical signs. My mental burden had transformed into a physical burden on my shoulders. Once, when Jeff was massaging the area between my shoulder blades, I was overcome by a sensation that his fingers reached deep within and touched the inflamed, inner hurt that hid beyond my grasp. My subcon-scious wanted to let me know that it was in pain, even if I pre-ferred to ignore it with all the steely inner core stuff I fell back on to get me through each day. My shoulders shook with deep sobs that took me several minutes to control.

I recovered a little more each day after that. I gave myself permission to let grief run its course. I put my sales work on hold. No more stress of forced smiles. Instead, I wrote every day. The back pain receded. My knee improved. And I ran.

Following Jeff's instructions, I now ran thirty to forty min-utes every other day. I fell into the rhythm of breathing, emptied my mind of words, questions, half-answers, and allowed myself to just be. I ran on autopilot while my mind retreated to a quiet inner sanctum that touched on meditation, even prayer. Repeti-tive steps and regular breathing poured soothing balm on my in-flamed inner core. I connected to my inner self in a way I couldn't put into words. Maybe that was the point. I had been drowning the inner silence with words. Now I needed to be still. Running was my channel to tranquility. Finally, I understood the inner calm that Dean Ottati had described in his book *The Runner and the Path*. Running had let me into its secret.

Running continued to be central to David's life too. He reached another milestone in July when he ran his first full mara-thon in a time of 3 hours, 50 minutes, smashing his personal goal of four hours. His achievement marked one of the best days of his life. We celebrated at the finish line together.

Jeff signed me off from physical therapy in July. I continued to build my running strength over the summer and could now run for one hour. The farther I ran, the more my grief receded. I began to tackle new work and home projects. I started seeing friends again. I had a greater reservoir of energy to dip into.

In late August, Rogue Code resurfaced. This time it insisted, in the same unyielding tone it had used about the triathlon, that I was about to do a half marathon. I balked at the idea. I may have found inner peace on a sixty-minute run, but how on earth did I expect to get round 13.1 miles?

But I knew how this story would play out. Rogue Code had spoken. I drew up a training schedule to work towards the US Half Marathon in San Francisco on the first weekend in November.

Race for Life

Farthest I have ever run in my life without stopping: 10.5 miles

Half marathon distance: 13.1 miles

First Sunday in November. 6:30 a.m. Promenade of Aquatic Park. Dark, sleepy morning. Subdued runners in sweats wander to and fro in ones and twos. I stand alone by the inflatable finish line arch, illuminated by streetlights. The air is damp and still. Tranquil black water unfolds in gentle waves over the sand. So different from the stormy anger of that April day two years ago when Mike and I swam thirty-six bone-chilling minutes in freezing, hostile water.

I look up at the word "FINISH," written in bright blue letters across the dark blue arch. My half marathon will end at this spot. But when will I cross the finish line? Kevin arrives, followed two minutes later by David, back from the loo queue. The three of us will race today. Plus my close friend Nicole Lazzaro will be here at the finish. I will share the celebration of this day with people who are important to me.

6:41 a.m. I look across at the twenty-deep loo queue by the Dolphin Swimming and Rowing Club. Forget it. I'll try my luck in the queue by the start line. Bad choice. Nearly two hundred people line up for a handful of portapotties. No time to rush back to the Dolphin Club loos at the opposite end of the promenade. Will I reach the front of this queue before the race starts?

7:05 a.m. Five minutes past race start. Dawn on this gray, foggy day reveals a pack of fifteen hundred runners waiting to race. No sign of Kevin or David. They will have lined up in the pack by now. Still eighteen people ahead of me in the queue for twelve pale green portapotties. The announcer warns us that the race start can't be delayed any longer. The police have closed off both walkways of the Golden Gate Bridge so that runners will have the path to themselves. Any further delay and they'll open the bridge before the race has finished.

My turn. I head for a vacant portapotty. Once inside, the starting horn sounds. Not quite where I'd anticipated starting my first half marathon, but I didn't have a choice. I hold the door for the next person when I exit, then weave through competitors heading across the start line on my way to the gear drop-off point. I leave my carrier bag containing my sweats in the compound and join runners walking down the narrow road towards the start. Too many of us crammed together to find space to run. Large yellow numbers on the race clock display 1 minute, 22 seconds when I reach the start line. I ping my stopwatch.

The crush of competitors thins out. Pick up the pace. A river of silent, bobbing heads floods down past Fort Mason and funnels into the arrow-straight road along the Marina. I bob along, drawn forward by threads of silent energy connecting me to hundreds of runners around me. Mile one. The stillness of the day cushions the slap-slap-slap of running shoes on tarmac. I pass cheering staff and loudspeakered music outside the Sports Basement store. Mile two. Runners uncurl along the headland, ready for the climb from sea level up to the Golden Gate Bridge, towering into the fog.

My mind settles into neutral, content to be carried along by my body, allowing thoughts and feelings to freefloat. My best thinking time. This is why I run.

So much has happened over the last three years. I pick over

my checkered history with running. How much I hated it at the beginning. My struggle to run 1.8 miles and conquer Hell Hill. The knee injury that threatened to stop me running permanently.

Nowadays, I run because I cannot bear not to. I crave the challenge of humbling myself on the altar of running. I work at it relentlessly. And when I least expect it, I am rewarded with small but meaningful improvements. Conquering something that doesn't come easily makes each achievement all the sweeter. Like this half marathon.

Round the hairpin bend. Sharp ascent through ponderosa pines into the wooded, residential seclusion of the Presidio. Runners toil uphill. I've trained on steep grades. I overtake three people. Ping my stopwatch by the four-mile board. I've run the first four miles at an average pace of 11 minutes, 13 seconds. My goal is to finish in 2 hours, 30 minutes, although my secret time is 2 hours, 25.

One more turn, then the stream of runners emerges into the open space of the Golden Gate Bridge visitor car park. Famous russet-brown pinnacles of the bridge loom out of the damp mist. Adrenaline tingles through to my veins.

I glance across to the other walkway. A couple of runners fifty yards apart head back in the misty gloom. Are they the race leaders? I spot a flash of bright yellow shoes, worn by a muscular guy in black shorts and white shirt. He wears a baseball cap back to front. Something about the square-set jaw makes me take a second look. It's Kevin, pounding down the last ten yards of the bridge. He disappears out of sight.

I run under the first russet pillar of the bridge. Last year, I watched David cross the finish line in this race, convinced I would never compete here myself. Today I will run my first half marathon. And I won't forget to taste the sweetness of reward for relentless effort.

Endurance sport woke me up to my habit of bypassing celebration and remaining constantly in pursuit of the next goal. Now
I acknowledge and celebrate achievement more often, not just in
sport but across the whole spectrum of my life. Celebration gives
my life more tone and definition, a splash of vibrant color on a
smooth canvas. Not that my life was all that gray beforehand. I
just hadn't realized until I changed my attitude that life could play
out in Technicolor instead of pastels.

Second russet pillar. Not much of a view today through the
damp mist. The island of Alcatraz squats in the middle of the Bay.
A container ship edges silently towards the Port of Oakland, still
hidden in fog. Runners thin out on the bridge. I glance across. A
white shirt with royal blue stripes down the side leaps out at me
from amongst a bunch of white-topped men. David. I recognize
his running style, his hands curved inwards into fists.

"Go Dave, go!" I call out.

He can't hear me. I wave with both arms. Something
prompts him to look up at that moment. He catches sight of me.
Even from this distance, I can see his face crack into a wide smile.
He waves back with both arms. We give each other a thumbs-up
sign.

I feel connected to him, even though we are separated by
sixty yards of traffic lanes and two high fences. I am no longer an-
noyed by his grinning, but we rarely train together. He still runs
faster than I do. Yet we share a common battle with the challenge
of endurance sport. We make space in our lives for each other's
training. We are each other's support crew at races. And on a few
rare occasions, like this one, we will both cross the same finish
line.

I run past the Golden Gate visitor car park on the Marin
headland. Stewards direct me down a cinder track that leads under the bridge. Uncharted territory. This path is usually closed to

the public. But I won't panic. David warned me ahead of time about the moderate descent and sharp climb up the other side. Half a mile at most.

I squeeze past a bunch of three women chatting to each other as they run. I'm in a race, after all. I'm here to pass people. I cross under the bridge. The climb up the other side is the steepest gradient on the route so far. I slow down but continue running. I can run hills.

I slow down to a walk by the aid station at the top just long enough to drink a cup of water and discard it in the trash can. But walking disturbs my rhythm. I ignite into a run. I settle back into my familiar, mantra-like groove. My legs make an ultrafine adjustment to latch on to my mile pace of 11 minutes, 13 seconds. Not too fast, not too slow.

The fog is so thick on the bridge that mist hangs suspended in the air. I'm coated with a thin layer of water. Definitely water. Not sweat, although there will be some of that mixed in. Right now, I'm not warm enough to sweat that much in the cool air. Silence amongst runners around me. Just the slap-slap-slap of shoes. A woman in a pink tracksuit listens to her iPod. No one overtakes me. I overtake no one. We all move forward together in space and time, moving as one across this majestic, familiar span.

I round the corner at the end, past the spot where I saw Kevin. Mile nine. Ping the laptime. 11 minutes, 10 seconds. Right on track. The path leads us under the bridge and back downhill along winding, wooded Presidio roads. Round the hairpin bend, back through the flat, wide, Crissy Field recreation space. Mile ten. Still plenty of energy in reserve.

Fitness. Another payback from my triathlon quest. More energy to squeeze more into my life. More mind/body balance. I even look better in my clothes. How could I ever return to my unfit self? I love the challenge of a difficult ride, run or swim now that I have energy to cycle harder, run farther, swim faster. But there are also times where I simply take time out to admire the view, my body purring along at sixty per cent effort, the flow of endorphins warming me from my core. I feel that flow now. Endorphins spread out from my center, like a warm river of chocolate, until I brim over with confidence.

I run along the wide tarmac path. To my left, a few hardy souls play on the beach. I glance down at my red kneestrap sitting just below my right kneecap. No murmurs from my knee. Even though my knee has been strong enough not to need the kneestrap for a few weeks now, I don't trust myself to run without it. The bright red band is my comfort blanket, a reminder of the care and nurturing that my knee required to heal.

The eleven-mile board appears out of the mist fifty yards ahead, reminding me that I have now run farther without stopping than I have ever run in my life. Uncharted territory of a different kind.

The board disappears behind me. A long 2 hours, 4 minutes to reach this point. Shoulders sag. Legs grow heavy. Two final, elongated miles stretch out before me. My step shortens to a shuffle. The chocolate river has run dry.

I turn inwards. Time to dig deep, to find the reserves of determination that will push my legs home. I've been through worse than this at the San Jose Tri. Focus. Mind over body.

Just then, my running opens a channel between me and my inner core, one of those fleeting moments when I see deep inside myself. I glimpse that steely resilience, the bedrock that sustained me through my mother's death, through the bleakness of grief and through the uncertainty of knee problems. I wasn't a particularly wimpy person before I started triathlon. But I'd had a pretty easy life for a couple of years. My inner core was in danger of melting away without me noticing. Rogue Code pushed me into the triathlon to reconnect me with that inner strength. Times like this, when my legs signal their exhaustion but do not stop, reconfirm that I possess the strength to deal with adversity.

I look up. Runners scattered along the route. Endorphins return. I pick up the pace.

Back onto the arrow-straight road by the Marina where I ran the outward leg two hours before. More activity now. More cars, more passers-by out walking their dogs, groups of parents playing soccer with their kids on Marina Green. Mile twelve. 2 hours, 15 minutes. Another eleven-minute mile.

David has warned me that just before mile thirteen, the course veers off the road and over a steep hill. He had to walk this hill the first time he ran the half marathon. But I built hills into my training, just so I could deal with this one. He may run faster than me, but I'm going to run this hill without stopping. I'm determined to score one personal victory in the husband/wife race.

I run past Fort Mason on my left. Arrows divert the route through the park. The path snakes upward. I will run this hill. I will not stop.

I remember back to my first San Jose Tri. My strategy, the one I devised myself by picking and choosing the bits of training I liked and ignoring the rest, had failed me on the run. Endurance sport humbled me that day by reminding me yet again that my way is not always the best way. Since San Jose, I've recommitted to listening to advice in the rest of my life. I watch out for warning signs that tell me I am dismissing information that doesn't fit with my preferred plan of action. A signal to pause and review my rationale.

When I prepared for this race, I heeded the advice of others. I'm confident I can run this hill. I pass stranded runners reduced to a walk. I count them off on my fingers. Seven. Eight. I slow down. Tension builds in my legs. How much farther? Eleven. Twelve.

Fifty yards to the top. I will not stop.

I crest the hill. My one victory today over David. I punch the air. Legs clamor with relief. Run downhill. Less than a quarter mile to go.

Halfway down the hill I turn the corner. Aquatic Park lies before me, bursting with runners, spectators, noise from the loudspeakers and that welcoming dark blue arch. I'm on the brink of finishing my first half marathon.

Past the thirteen-mile board at the bottom of the hill. David stands to the side, a yellow-ribboned finishers' medal round his neck. A reminder that my medal is waiting for me, two hundred yards ahead.

"Do you want me to run the last stretch with you?" he calls out.

I nod and give him a thumbs-up. No spare energy to talk. I am buried too deep in my running.

We sweep round the home stetch along the promenade, David at my side. No words. Just running. I spy Kevin, a huge grin on his face, cheering and clapping from the stands on my right. I nod and smile.

The banner grows larger. Crowds cheer. Today I've run farther than I have ever run in my life. I've performed at my very best, giving everything and beating my expectations. My perfect race.

The announcer calls out my name. Nicole stands by the finish line, camera in hand. My stopwatch shows 2 hours, 25 minutes, 17 seconds. David and I cross the line together. Side by side, through this race and through life.

Once past the finish arch, I know with complete certainty that I'm ready to resume life at full pace after losing Mum. I want to step closer to the edge, to stop pottering around on the easy slopes of life and embrace new challenge farther up the mountain. Triathlon taught me that I have the strength to deal with whatever comes next. It taught me to take a risk and push the boundaries of my comfort zone. And showed me that life on the other side of triathlon could be richer, deeper and splashed with vibrant color.

Rogue Code will no doubt let me know soon enough what it next has in store for me. When it does, I'll listen. And this time, I'll be ready.

Resources

How-to and training books:

Triathlons for Women, Sally Edwards (Velopress, 2002).

A motivating read for beginner triathletes with an introduction to using heart rate monitoring in training.

The Heart Rate Monitor Guidebook to Heart Zone Training, Sally Edwards (Heart Zones Publishing, 2002). More detail on using heart zones to improve performance.

Peak Fitness for Women, Paula Newby-Fraser (Human Kinetics, 1995). The first book I bought on training. This taught me how to get the most out of my training time.

Slow Fat Triathlete, Jayne Williams (Marlowe & Co, 2004). A mix of how-to and humorous anecdote, Jayne encourages anyone of any shape to get off the couch and give it a tri.

The Courage to Start, John Bingham (Fireside/Simon & Schuster, 1999). Humorous encouragement to run from a man destined never to run a three-hour marathon.

Swim Bike Run, Wes Hobson, Clark Campbell, Mike Vickers (Human Kinetics, 2004). Detailed look at the techniques of the three sports.

The Triathlete's Training Bible, Joe Friel (Velo Press, 1998). Huge tome on everything from how to train, how to race and how to recover from a sprint distance to an Ironman.

Breakthrough Triathlon Training, Brad Kearns (McGraw-Hill, 2006). Brad proves that you can train hard, train smart and keep life in perspective.

Marathon: the Ultimate Training Guide, Hal Higdon (Rodale, 1999). My husband used this book to prepare for his first marathon. I haven't read it yet. But who knows what's in my future?

Stretching, Bob Anderson (Shelter Publications, 2000). Contains a stretch for just about every part of the body. And a reminder that stretching is essential!

Strong Women Eat Well, Miriam E. Nelson (Perigree, 2001). An easy-to-understand guide to good nutrition.

Inspirational sports writing

Once I began training, I devoured many books about great sporting achievement. Here are a few of my favorites.

The Runner and the Path, Dean Ottati (Breakaway Books, 2002). Running as the meaning of life. Finally, I got it.

Paula: My Story So Far, Paula Radcliffe (Simon & Schuster, 2004). Live and breathe the life of the women's marathon world-record holder.

To the Edge: A Man, Death Valley and the Mystery of Endurance, Kirk Johnson (Warner Books, 2001). A man who has never run a marathon runs 135 miles across Death Valley.

Ultramarathon Man: Confessions of an All-Night Runner, Dean Karnazes (Tarcher/Penguin, 2005). Find out how and why Dean runs 226 miles non-stop as a solo runner in a race meant for a ten-person relay team.

Becoming an Ironman, Kara Douglass Thom (Breakaway Books, 2001). Collection of stories about athletes competing in their first Ironman triathlon.

The Four-Minute Mile, Roger Bannister (Lyons Press, 2004). Story of a pivotal moment in athletic history which captures the true effort and significance of the achievement.

Touching the Void, Joe Simpson (Perennial, 2004). Presumed dead after a fall in the Andes, Simpson recounts his solo struggle to return to base camp with a broken leg.

It's Not About the Bike, Lance Armstrong (Berkley Books, 2001). Lance has won more Tours de France than anyone but his biggest win was against cancer.

Every Second Counts, Lance Armstrong (Broadway Books, 2003). Living life to the full as a cancer survivor, Lance takes us along on some of his biggest wins, both on and off the bike.

26 Miles to Boston, Michael Connelly (Lyons Press, 2003). A mile-by-mile account of the Boston Marathon, historical snippets and the personal journey of a first-time marathoner.

Swimming to Antarctica: Tales of a Long Distance Swimmer, Lynne Cox (Harvest Books, 2005). Lynne not only swam in waters too cold for most of us to dip a toe in, she also made history with a swim from the US to the former Soviet Union.

Websites

Starting out

www.danskin.com/triathlon

Site of the national series of women-only sprint-distance (that means short!) triathlons, designed to encourage women to take up the sport.

www.heartzones.com

One of the Danskin event sponsors, Heartzones organizes tri training camps, online coaches and more besides for women new to the sport.

www.teamintraining.org

The world's largest endurance training program, TNT trains over 30,000 people in a year while raising funds to treat Leukemia and Lymphoma. Focused on beginners.

www.ymca.net

Central site for one of the 2,594 YMCA gyms across the country. Look for a class, join a tri group or just work out.

www.swimmersguide.com

Directory of publicly-accessible, full-size, year-round swimming pools.

Triathlon

www.usatriathlon.org

Site for the national governing body of triathlon. Lists all triathlon clubs nationwide, plus news, championship info and of course, national rankings. Find a club near you and go for it!

www.slowtwitch.com

Triathlon website with product reviews, training plans, interviews, news and general gossip about triathlon. Check out the Beginners section; great articles, plus the original 21-week training program, often quoted on more mainstream sites, written by Dan Empfield, the man behind the slowtwitch site, the tri-specific wetsuit, race director and general tri guru.

www.trinewbies.com

Stacks of articles, training tips and race reports from first-timers in tri. You're not alone!

www.triathloninformer.com

A very nice site. Amy White is a former newspaper editor, current website editor and self-proclaimed "middle-of-the-pack" finisher. The articles are beautifully crafted and being a writer myself, I appreciate that.

Women-specific sites

www.tridivas.com

Site of Team TriDivas, a national women's triathlon team covering beginners to experienced.

www.trichic.com

Site of Team TriChic, a national women's triathlon team covering beginners to experienced.

www.velobella.org

Women's cycling club originating in NorCal but with branches in CO, GA, MI and MN. They also have a cool cycling strip.

www.nikewomen.com

More than a gear site—online workouts, running groups in major cities, plus details of the annual Nike Women's Marathon.

www.womenspecific.com

Broader than triathlon, this site encourages women to take up outdoor pursuits, with sections on skiing/boarding, climbing, cycling and "living adventure," a potluck of great outdoor stories.

Events

www.trifind.com

Lists just about any triathlon event in the country. Now there's no excuse that you can't find an event at your level.

www.active.com

This site lists over 100,000 events and activities in over 50 sports in 5,000 cities nationwide. Also a knowledge base for beginner and expert alike.

www.marathonguide.com

Not a site I'll need for a while but if you've set your sights on endurance running, this is for you.

www.japroductions.com

Organizers of the race that started it all for me - the San Jose Tri. Check out also other NorCal events.

www.onyourmarkevents.com

Organizer of the Salmon Duathlon, my first multisport race, plus dozens of fun runs, tri for funs and longer endurance events in Northern and Central California.

Publications

www.triathletemag.com

Training tips, articles, resource guide. Subscribe to the print version or check this online site of Triathlon Magazine.

www.insidetriathlon.com

Training tips, articles, resource guide. Subscribe to the print version or check this online site of Inside Triathlon Magazine.

www.transitiontimes.com

Training tips, articles, resource guide—an online only publication.

www.runnersworld.com

Training tips, articles, resource guide. Subscribe to the print version or check this online site of Runner's World Magazine.

For a more comprehensive and updated list, visit
www.transformedbytriathlon.com

Acknowledgments

Little did I realize when there was just me, my computer and a word count less than 5,000, that a book project could grow so big and owe its success to so many. Be prepared for a Very Long List of People Who Count.

Starting first, foremost and always with my tremendous husband David, survivor of a twenty-year-plus marriage to me. Thank you now and forever for your encouragement, support and being-there-ness. Enormous thanks to Kevin Kennedy, who not only took time, every time, out of his busy day to email calming words of advice on every last perceived training crisis, but offered ongoing business advice for this book. And special thanks to my mentor, Charlotte Cook, who challenged me in the way only she can to become a better writer.

Thanks to my editors Tom Bentley and Kathy Clay for pouring over every word. To current and former members of my critique circle the Famous Writers' Group, who read without complaint numerous iterations of each chapter: Meredith and George Angwin, Kathy Clay, David Cyrluk, Danielle Fafchamps, Melanie Heisler, Gerry Kane, Richard Waldinger, Roxana Wales, Dave Wolf and Olivia Wu. To my Wednesday-night group of Leslie Burton, Laurel Anne Hill, Lee Paulson and Tony Russo, with special thanks to Jill Hedgecock and John Randolph for reading far beyond the call of duty. To more brave souls who read the draft at various stages of its life cycle: Mike Knowles, Li Miao Lovett, Kent Price, Susanne Riehemann, Karen Tremain and Beth Weber Guarino. And thanks go to Brandi Chastain and Sally Edwards for taking time out of their busy lives to listen to a complete unknown, read the book and write the Forewords.

Thanks to my marvelous physical therapist Jeff Jaramillo, who fixed both my knee and my book title. To designer Victoria Pohlmann for her stunning cover design and typography. To Marlene Bjornsrud, Michael Connelly, Tim Fox, Paula Hendricks, Wendy Ingraham, Dean Ottati, Forge Toro, Elisabeth Watson and Jayne Williams for their contributions to making the book happen. And to my good friend Nicole Lazzaro, for persevering with the cover photo and still remaining on speaking terms.

So many people also helped me become a triathlete. Thanks to my coach, Gail DeCamp, for her advice and unfailing support. To my friend Elaine Yarranton, for encouraging me into the pool and teaching me to swim freestyle. To Cristina Sorrentino, the other member of the Running and Chatting Club. To Karen Preston, Julie Sweeney, Susan Halet, Susan Foianini and countless others of the Peninsula Family YMCA, San Mateo and Central YMCA, San Jose, for their coaching help. To the Velobella Girls for never leaving me behind on their bike rides. To my friend and neighbor Mike Popa for being on hand to swim, fix bikes and provide moral support. And to my dentist Brett Hofmann, who unwittingly launched me on my journey to becoming the Improbable Athlete.

Thank you to all these and more besides.